# SUCCESSFUL
# USER EXPERIENCE
## STRATEGIES AND ROADMAPS

# SUCCESSFUL
# USER EXPERIENCE
## STRATEGIES AND ROADMAPS

Elizabeth Rosenzweig

AMSTERDAM • BOSTON • HEIDELBERG • LONDON
NEW YORK • OXFORD • PARIS • SAN DIEGO
SAN FRANCISCO • SINGAPORE • SYDNEY • TOKYO
Morgan Kaufmann is an imprint of Elsevier

**Acquiring Editor:** Todd Green
**Editorial Project Manager:** Charlie Kent
**Project Manager:** Punithavathy Govindaradjane
**Designer:** Victoria Pearson

Morgan Kaufmann is an imprint of Elsevier
225 Wyman Street, Waltham, MA 02451, USA

ISBN: 978-0-12-800985-7

**British Library Cataloguing in Publication Data**
A catalogue record for this book is available from the British Library

**Library of Congress Cataloging-in-Publication Data**
A catalog record for this book is available from the Library of Congress

For information on all Morgan Kaufmann publications,
visit our website at www.mkp.com

Working together
to grow libraries in
developing countries

www.elsevier.com • www.bookaid.org

# Dedication

To my sons, Max, Lev and Dan, with love.

# Contents

# Foreword

It's around 10:30 a.m. and I'm sitting in a hotel restaurant sipping tea. The year is 2004. With me at the table is a bright-eyed, smiling woman named Elizabeth. We're the only people in the restaurant because the staff is closing down breakfast to prepare for lunch. But they are indulgent and let us sit undisturbed.

I'm just getting to know Elizabeth. We are both attending a conference at the hotel. We've been at some of the same conferences in the past, but we've never really sat down and talked. After running into each other yet again at the conference, we decide to set up a day and time to meet. Here we are.

We've been talking for about 20 min about our experience in the industry that we share when Elizabeth says something and suddenly I feel the tingling-up-my-spine-and-over-my-scalp sensation that I get when I am having an "intuitive hit" about something big.

I consider myself a scientist (a behavioral scientist). I have a Ph.D. in Psychology. I write books and do consulting for Fortune 1000 clients. And, yes, I have "intuitive hits." I believe we all do. I've read and studied the research on unconscious mental processing, so I actually don't think that intuition is something mystical or "other-worldly."

I often get flashes of ideas, inspiration, and vision about all sorts of things. The really strong intuitive hits are accompanied by the tingling feeling—like the one I am having this morning in the restaurant talking to Elizabeth.

She is telling me about an idea she was working on to start a "World Usability Day." I'm not entirely sure what she means at first, and, to be honest, I am distracted by thinking about the talk I am scheduled to give at the conference today. But then I get the spine and scalp tingling "hit," and I know I need to pay attention. I interrupt her. "Start from the beginning," I say, and this time I listen very carefully.

Elizabeth is thinking that there should be a special day set aside each year to promote awareness of Usability around the world. She is thinking about getting it going. "Do it"! I almost shout in that empty restaurant. I think I surprise her with my vehemence. "Do you think it will take off? Have any impact?", she asks? "Yes." I say. "It will become much bigger than you think."

That was 2004. The first World Usability Day occurred in 2005. This year, as I write, will be the 10th year. It's April of 2015 and for the November 2015 event there are already 134 events planned in 40 countries.

If you look up World Usability Day on Wikipedia or if you go to the World Usability Day Website, you won't see Elizabeth Rosenzweig's name right away. You'll have to do some searching. That's because Elizabeth is a great leader. She gets things going and then gracefully moves over, lets others step in to move it forward. She lets the idea take on its own momentum.

When we were first having that conversation in the restaurant about World Usability Day I kept thinking about how to turn the idea into a great business opportunity. I realized that Elizabeth wasn't thinking about it that way at all. I like to think that I see the big picture and the vision. But I tend to see it in terms of what the big picture means for my clients and my business. As in, "Oh, this looks like where we should all be heading. I wonder if I should offer that as a class or workshop? Or a consulting service?" Or I might think, "Will people think I'm just trying to get business if I start this movement?" And then I stop myself from moving forward with, "Oh my gosh, that would be so much work and I'm already so busy."

This is, I think, the big difference between Elizabeth and me, and is one of her best and most amazing qualities and talents—she sees the big picture, the vision, of designing for humans and designing for humanity, and she doesn't stop. She sees what needs to happen next to move the idea forward. She acts on it without getting mired in the ego of it. Maybe she does have doubts and worries about implementing big ideas. But regardless, she still plunges in and takes us all to the next level. That's what this book is; it's Elizabeth's next "big picture, let's take the world to a new place" plunge.

Thinking about the user experience is not new. Many people have been writing, teaching, and doing user experience work for decades. Sometimes the goal of user experience is to design products that are less prone to human error, and therefore to save money for the owner of the product. Sometimes the goal is to sell more stuff, or reduce the cost of development by saving the cost to redesign later. And saving or making more money is a good goal for user experience.

But along with these practical goals there is another goal. World Usability Day is an example of a worldwide trend that asks "Can we create products that fit humans better? Can we collectively—businesses, organizations, governments, designers, developers—create products that bring out the best human possible? Can we create products that are fun and a joy to use? Products that help those in need?" And the answer is Yes! It's 2015, and we know how to design these human-centered user experiences. So no more obstacles, right? We're ready to make the world a better place through great user experience design, right?

Well, we're not there yet. Anyone who purposely and intentionally sets out to design a positive user experience too often runs into a wall—often many walls. You know what to do to design the optimal experience, but the organization you are in doesn't see the value of what you are trying to do. Or they see the value but they aren't willing or able to commit the resources to make it happen. This is the current challenge. How do we remove these obstacles to creating great user experiences? How do you get organizations to commit? How do you get them to put into place a strategy for user experience so that it can achieve its potential?

Elizabeth, of course, in her usual, big picture vision—what does the world need now—point of view is plunging in again. She's written a book to move us forward—the designers, the organizations, the businesses. If you want to design and implement great products and solutions to problems, then you need to design the user experience. And if you want to design a great user experience then your business, company, organization needs to commit to the resources and strategies to make it happen. This book is your roadmap.

Thanks, Elizabeth, for once again showing us the path forward!

Susan Weinschenk, Ph.D.

Author of *100 Things Every Designer Needs To Know About People*

Edgar Wisconsin

April, 2015

# Introduction

## Who is the book for?

This book is intended for two audiences. The first are professionals or students in the field of innovation design, technology research and product development, who are looking to understand how to create successful user experiences. This book will provide specific strategies and roadmaps you can use in your work today.

The second audience is anyone who wants to understand how to build things in a humanistic way, by putting the person first.

Professionals or students who are creating products:

- Anyone who is developing a technology, product or service. You could call yourself any of the following:
- Program Manager
- Product Manager
- Software Developer
- Product Manager
- Project Manager
- UX Designer
- User Interface Developer
- Usability Engineer
- User Experience Professional
- Information Architect
- Website Designer
- Website Developer
- Natural Language Engineer
- Artificial Intelligent Scientist
- Human Factors Engineer.

Anyone who wants to understand how to make machines work better for humans:

- People who want a basic understanding of what makes a successful user experience read chapters 1–5.
- People who want to understand methodologies and put them in context read chapters 6–11.
- People who want to influence others to create better user experiences (in addition to chapters 1–4 chapter 12, 14 and 15).

## What is this book about?

- How to make products and technology work better for people;
- Why is it important to develop technology by putting people first.

## How to use this book

- Chapters 1–3 give you the big picture of design and UX including foundation theories and methods.
- Chapter 4 presents the model for UX strategy.
- Chapter 5 addresses mobiles and the evolution of UX past desktop.
- Chapters 6–11 present UX methodologies and when to use them.
- Chapter 12 explains different ways to get buy in for UX work.
- Chapter 13 explains service design and its relation to UX.
- Chapters 14 and 15 are about success and failure.
- Chapter 16 provides actionable roadmaps and checklists.
- Chapter 17 is a glossary.

# About the Author

Elizabeth Rosenzweig is a Principal Consultant at the User Experience Center. Elizabeth has worked as a consultant and employee in several major corporations for 30 years. Her experience includes design and development, ranging from websites and applications, to hardware products and technology development. Elizabeth has completed projects for many major corporations, not-for-profit organizations and academic institutions. Elizabeth holds five patents in intelligent user interface design and is Adjunct Faculty in the Bentley University, Human Factors and Information Design Master's degree program.

Elizabeth is Past President of the Usability Professionals Association and founder and Director of World Usability Day, which she started in 2004 after her term as President of UPA was completed. World Usability Day has grown to include an average of 40 countries with over 150 events. Elizabeth frequently publishes in industry journals, has written chapters in four published books and presents lectures at conferences around the world.

Elizabeth holds a Bachelor of Art in Fine Art Photography and Printing from Goddard College and a Science Masters in Visual Studies (User Interface Design and Computer Output) from the Media Lab at Massachusetts Institute of Technology.

# Acknowledgments

A book cannot be produced by one person alone and this one came about with a lot of help, support, and case studies from my family, friends, and colleagues.

First thanks to my parents, Sandy and Rosie Rosenzweig, who taught me from an early age to ask good questions, be brave, and do your part to make the world better. To my mother Rosie, who inspired me to be a writer, and gave up hours to do in depth, tireless copy editing, all while pushing me hard to be the best I can be. To my father Sandy Rosenzweig, who always encouraged me to dream big, who was sure I was on to something and always sent me great articles, quotes and books to help me think bigger and connect the dots.

A special thanks to Max, Lev, and Dan for understanding all the time I needed to take away to write this book, and for being patient and not rolling your eyes when I comment on all the unusable or incredibly well-designed parts of our world. You guys are my inspiration.

I could not have written this book without the help of my friends and colleagues who provided not only encouragement and support but also really helpful editing.

Thank you, Lena Dmitrieva, my friend, and colleague at Bentley whose countless hours of editing pages and pages (several versions of the same pages) helped me stay on track.

Diane Demarco Brown, who really inspired me and cheered me on, from the very first time I uttered the phrase, "I am thinking of writing a book" to the last review. Diane, your guidance and review of the book as it evolved helped me focus and keep it real.

Working together, off, and on for almost 20 years, Vicky Morville reviewed this book, both for little details, and larger messages, making sure it was consistent throughout.

Watching Fiona Tranquada write her book provided me with a role model and made me think that I could write a book in evenings and weekends. The pep talks and inspiration was always appreciated.

Henry Lieberman for providing honest and frank reviews, providing a big picture view that made me dig deeper with my message and for doing that for the last 30 years.

From the first time, I was encouraged to take on a leadership role at UPA to the most recent straight talk about my book, Mary Beth Rettger has always helped me push my work to be the best.

Thank you to Sandy Spector for tirelessly editing chapters, right down to the end, and digging deep to correct both grammar and content, and to Ken Bresler for carrying out helpful 11th hour editing, and asking good questions.

The many colleagues and friends at the Bentley User Experience Center and the Human Factors and Information Design Program deserve to be acknowledged for listening to my theories, reading parts of the book, provided notes on ideas or a case study, or just taking a walk with me on a sunny day. To Bill Gribbons, Bill Albert, Gail Wessell, Heather Wright-Karlson, Pete McNally, David Juhlin, and all the students that worked with me over the years at the UXC.

The book would not be what it is without all the case study authors who provided wonderful stories and examples of important work in making products and services more usable for everyone. Thank you. Your strategies and roadmaps are wonderful illustrations of the basic foundation of our work, I am honored to be in the field with all of you. In order of appearance, Chris Hass, Meena Kothandaraman, David Juhlin, Pete McNally, Rich Buttiglieri, Dorie Rosenberg, Cory Lebson, Lydia Sankey, Mandi Davis, Diana DeMarco Brown, Chris Avore, Vicky Morville, Fiona Tranquada, Silvia Zimmerman, Jason Huang, Liz Burton, Yina Li, Deb Reich, Tulsi Patel, Brian Sullivan, Bob Thomas, Janice James, and Scott Williams. The world is better because of your work.

Thank you to my sister Rebecca Rosenzweig Askinasi for teaching me all about style. And to my brother Ben Rosenzweig for patiently answering all my questions about databases and computer programming.

A special thank you to my dear friends Trudy and Les Fagen who provided a beautiful location for me to get away from it all and do a big piece of the writing in the peaceful White Mountains in New Hampshire.

# Case Studies

| Case Study Author | Chapter | Order | Title |
|---|---|---|---|
| Chris Hass | 2 | 1 | Lifting the Fog of War |
| Elizabeth Rosenzweig | 2 | 2 | Intelligent Photo Shoebox |
| Meena Kothandaraman | 3 | 3 | Personas: Getting Back to the Basics of Behavior |
| David Juhlin | 3 | 4 | Comparative Study of Information Architecture from Three Community Banks' Websites |
| Elizabeth Rosenzweig | 4 | 5 | Building Strategic Models for Medicare.gov |
| Elizabeth Rosenzweig | 5 | 6 | Responsive Design Test of Nursing Home Compare |
| Pete McNally | 5 | 7 | Mobile Usability Testing |
| Rich Buttiglieri | 6 | 8 | One Size Does Not Fit All |
| Dorie Rosenberg | 6 | 9 | Grocery Shopping Expert Review and Competitive Analysis |
| Cory Lebson | 7 | 10 | User Research for a Disaster Relief Organization |
| Amanda Davis/Lydia Sankey | 7 | 11 | User Experience across Platforms |
| Diana DeMarco Brown | 8 | 12 | Agile UX Failure |
| Elizabeth Rosenzweig | 8 | 13 | Design at Compugraphic |
| Chris Avore | 8 | 14 | Lean and Agile at Work: NASDAQ IR Mobile |
| Victoria Morville | 9 | 15 | A Site Visit at Buffalo General Hospital Researching Use of a Cardiac Workstation |

# Chapter 1

## WHAT IS USER EXPERIENCE?

This chapter discusses the field of usability and UX, its background and its history. Definitions are included. A case study on the first Kodak camera demonstrates a successful UX (and usability). Discussion of the field includes its growth through professional organizations.

# Chapter 1

Men have become tools of their tools.

**Henry David Thoreau**

## Usable Technology Can Change the World

Properly designed technology that is centered on the user experience (UX) can make a positive difference in many domains. For example, a medical device that is easy to use can save lives. Voting machines that help a citizen easily and securely vote for the candidate of their choice secures the freedoms of an entire nation. Financial systems that guide people to make appropriate choices with their money can affect a family's future. An accessible cell phone connecting a small village in a remote developing country to the Internet can change the world for its inhabitants.

Usability is a system in and of itself. A system is usable when it provides a service and is of use to a person. User-centered design produces technology that makes life better, that puts useful tools in people's hands and that helps them reach their potential through a successful UX.

UX Story: The Kodak Camera

The Kodak camera is good example of powerful system usability, because it was a product that provided an excellent UX. Kodak enabled the average person to do what only skilled artists and technicians could previously do: produce images of the world around him.

Prior to the introduction of the first Kodak camera, the idea of an unskilled person using the complicated technology of photography to capture and share pictures with family and friends was impossible. The power of capturing a photograph was left to the experts, who were the technologists comfortable with the bulky and complicated equipment of the time. A nonspecialist had no hope of ever capturing an artistically composed picture.

George Eastman, the inventor of the Kodak camera, understood the power of developing products with user satisfaction at the forefront. The evolution of photographic technology, from something only experts could fathom to snapshot photos that anyone could create, developed historically into an iterative process of incremental improvements with the user fully in control of the process. Although Eastman had probably not heard of the term UX, he used many of the relevant principles to invent the Kodak camera; he put photography within the reach of those who could spend the money to buy the product. This focus was clearly demonstrated in his marketing line "You push the button, we do the rest."

During the height of the industrial revolution, Eastman, a prolific inventor, created a series of innovations that led to the development of the Kodak camera in 1888; the product that introduced snapshot photography to the world. Until then, a photographer needed to use a large wet glass plate to capture a picture with ready access to a darkroom where he or she could coat the glass with photosensitive emulsion; when this glass plate was hit with light an image would imprint on the plate. After the image was exposed on the plate, it was developed, creating a glass negative, which in turn was used to print the picture. The camera had to be light tight. The plates were bulky (8″ × 10″) and the darkroom had to be large enough to fit them. If a photographer wanted to take landscape photographs, he or she had to take a horse and large cart with them into the field. The equipment was expensive and cumbersome and the subjects had to hold still for a long period of time.

The Kodak camera introduced a major change in the process of taking photographs through Eastman's many patents. He started by breaking down the problem into smaller steps and one by one worked to solve them. The first was to solve the problem of having to use wet plates and so he came up with dry film. Eastman worked methodically to solve further problems related to the difficult technology by next inventing flexible roll film and, subsequently, the mechanism for rolling the film through a camera. Finally he put it all together by introducing the complete Kodak camera (Figure 1.1).

The Kodak camera was sold preloaded with 100 pictures, in the form of an unexposed roll of film inside. Once the consumers had shot all the pictures, they sent the camera back to Kodak for processing. The camera was reloaded and returned to the consumer with the developed pack of pictures. The dark room, long poses, and heavy equipment became a thing of the past for the new consumer.

The effect snapshot photography had on the world was enormous. People could now see pictures of relatives they had never met, places they had never visited, and major world events like wars and natural disasters, that they had no need to witness in person. Such strong images exposed people to ideas and realities that had not been experienced before and created new kinds of thinking. For example, if people saw pictures of a war, they might reconsider their opinion of that war, or if they saw pictures of a natural disaster, they might be more inclined to donate time or money to alleviate the suffering caused by it.

After the first Kodak camera came a low-cost version: the Kodak Brownie camera. The Brownie camera introduced the idea of a snapshot, which was a picture that people could capture, almost in a snap. The Brownie was developed as a result of several inventions and evolutions in imaging technologies that, combined, created a whole that was greater than the sum of the parts, and offered a new experience to those who bought it. These incremental inventions included:

- Dry film;
- Flexible thin film and rolls of film;

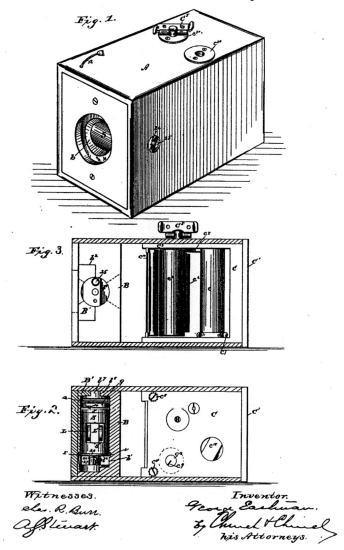

Figure 1.1 Kodak's original patent.

- A mechanism to roll film through a box camera;
- Manufacturing plant to mass produce cameras.

Kodak brought a complicated technology to a simpler level, allowing novices to use it easily. The Brownie camera made the complicated process of photography more accessible to the nontechnical user, which broke down the barrier to entry into photography. After that, anyone could use the Kodak Brownie camera, through the simple UX that Eastman provided. This, in effect, is a user-centered design process that changed the world. The Brownie camera created new ways for people to communicate and interact; laying the groundwork for the social media sharing that goes on today (Figure 1.2).

> Not everybody trusts paintings but people believe photographs.

**Ansel Adams**

### You Push the Button; We Do the Rest

Kodak's easy, simple product introduced the world to the field of snapshot photography and helped pave the way for other imaging inventions such as motion pictures and, eventually, medical imaging. A lot has happened since the invention of the Kodak camera. New technologies include digital cameras, the

Figure 1.2 Kodak Brownie camera.

Internet with email, text messaging, instant photo sharing, as well as the many applications on our mobile devices.

People now have the ability to connect with others and get information in ways never seen before now. People often interact with their devices more then with other people. It is not enough any longer to develop products and services that demonstrate amazing technical feats and functions. With these new inventions, UX has acquired new meaning. Product and system developers need to develop strategies that include the direction new products and services will take, and use them to make the world closer and shore up connections with other people. Some products and services declare that their goal is to connect people; while it is obvious that with profit as a bottom line the priority is not on personal human needs.

UX strategy could be the key to unlock technology's potential to improve the world, but only if it truly can put the person at the center.

## Usability and User Experience

Usability refers to the ease-of-use of a human-made object, digital or physical, or a combination of both. It is a part of the UX and is really the extent to which a person can use the object. A general definition of usability can be found in the Merriam Webster online dictionary:

**"Usable:**
1. Capable of being used
2. Convenient and practicable for use"

Usability is often seen as a subset of the UX. In many ways, that is true, since a key factor in a positive and successful UX is that the system is usable. However, the field has evolved in such a way that usability has also come to include the holistic experience of the user. These are intertwined and should be thought of together. Usability inspection methods are tools for the practitioner to evaluate the usability of a system. Usability itself is the all-inclusive environment and experience within which the user lives.

UX is a person's involvement with any technology, product, or service. The object or system can be software, mobile device, appliance, dashboard on a car, a smart phone, a medical device, a voting machine or any other human-made object. UX is the overall experience, including many touch points over different devices and platforms. UX and usability include all types of interactions:

- Physical (with any of the five senses: sight, hearing, taste, touch, and smell);
- Mental (such as problem solving);
- Mechanical (such as operation of machinery).

UX includes not just the person's interaction with the product or service or technology itself, but with all the touch points of the brand, such as the Web site, the store, operating instructions, customer service, and online help. A good UX is not just about the graphics and gizmos on our gadgets and computer screens. UX means looking at all the touch points at which a person interacts with a product, service, or technology and building the experience around the person, helping them to solve problems and reach their potential.

## Usability

The field of usability can be defined simply as creating systems, services, and technologies that are usable, convenient, and practical.

Initial efforts to formalize the field started in 1998 when the International Standards Organization (ISO), which is based in Geneva, produced [ISO 9241-11:1998] *Ergonomic Requirements for Office Work with Visual Display Terminals (VDTs)—Part 11: Guidance on Usability*. This standard has been revised by: ISO 9241-210:2010.

In 1999 the ISO defined usability with its ISO 13407:1999, which standardized requirements for interactive system as follows:

"Human-centered design is characterized by: the active involvement of users and a clear understanding of user and task requirements; an appropriate allocation of function between users and technology; the iteration of design solutions; multi-disciplinary design."

This development enhanced the legitimacy of the field of usability and caused its methodology to proliferate. ISO's definition of usability refers to the "extent to which a system can be used by specified users to achieve specified goals with effectiveness, efficiency and satisfaction in a specified context of use."

User experience touch points (UXTs) are all the places a human being interacts with a machine. In the example of the automobile, a user's touch points would be the car dealer, the experience of sitting and driving in the car, filling it with gas, maintaining it, adding features and sharing it with others. These UXTs are important to note and track, since these indicate where the design of that experience will be the most important.

As was demonstrated earlier with the invention of the Kodak camera, the total UX did not begin and end with the user's interaction of the camera. The touch points started with the message conveyed in the line, "You push the button, and we do the rest." This meant that the complicated technology of photography has been transformed and was now easy to use for people who were not experts in the field.

Technology and customer experience are all wrapped up in one value proposition. The customer is the user of the camera, and the touch points begin with the advertising of an easy-to-use tool. Touch points continue to the act of taking the picture by pointing and pressing a button. Wind the film and the customer/user can take 100 pictures without reloading. That act alone was uncharted territory, because a novice user had never before taken so many pictures at one time.

A simple way to understand the concept of touch points is to consider the UX of an automobile. As a user of an automobile you interact with it on many levels—how does it feel when you are seated? Can a person see over the dashboard, above the steering wheel? Does it fit family or friends? The gas mileage is part of that experience as well—it determines how many times you have to refill and how much that costs you. The servicing includes a person's interaction with the mechanic and garage and is also part of the experience. The user's interaction with the Web site, online help and telephone customer support all work together to create an overall UX. When done right, all the user touch points are coordinated.

## UX is an Evolving Field

Why is UX important? There are many different interpretations as the field is still evolving. In 2004, Peter Morville created the User Experience Honeycomb, which defined a meaningful and valuable UX as one with information that was:

- Useful;
- Usable;
- Desirable;
- Findable;
- Accessible;
- Credible;
- Valuable.

The humanistic side of UX incorporates the belief that people are the center of the experience and therefore need to be considered when designing systems. This means that human error is really a misnomer. We know that people themselves are each a system, with many components operating simultaneously and coming together so that the whole is greater than the sum of the parts. Our minds are analyzing data while our heart and lungs are keeping us alive. Our emotions and cognition work together to create a set of internal rules we use to make decisions every day.

The limitations of human beings are affected by the following factors:

- Cognitive load limitations;
- Potential visual and audio limitations;
- Potential for making mistakes is high while under stress.

Since we know that even the smartest, most physically fit people have human limitations, innovation and development of technologies must take these limitations into consideration. For example, it is now known that the person driving an automobile can be distracted by numerous factors including technologies such as texting. However, newer vehicles now include hardware to integrate more interactive technologies without taking into account the driver's cognitive load. Overloading the driver's cognition can cause the driver to be distracted resulting in accidents, which must be taken into account when developing these new technologies.

## The History, Necessity, and Growing Influence of UX

Designing systems and services by putting the person at the center does not seem like a novel idea, and yet, this work has only been formalized since the late 1990s when the term UX was introduced by Don Norman.

The field of UX has some origins in human factors and ergonomics (HFE), as well as computer-human interactions (CHI).

UX has evolved quickly since the first conference organized by the CHI special interest group of the Association for Computing Machinery (ACM) in 1982. Prior to that, the field of human factors was concerned primarily with the interaction of humans and machines, from the physical or ergonomic point of view. Now, the field has grown to include all industries. UX is having an effect in life-and-death domains such as healthcare, medical devices, and emergency-response systems. Equally important is the impact the UX is having on civic life, from voting machines to understanding legislation and regulations. Transportation is greatly impacted by UX, as it includes safety standards for automobiles, airplanes, boats, and many other forms of transport. However, the usual focus is on the physical human factors and not the intellectual interactions. Education has changed dramatically, as courses are now offered online, educational systems must be intuitive and allow for easy of learning.

Many predecessors to the field of UX include the pioneers in Industrial Design Human Factors and Ergonomics. It makes sense to think of these fields as evolving simultaneously, one informing the other. Industrial design was one of the first fields to look at the ergonomics of a machine.

The International Ergonomics Association defines ergonomics as follows:

"Ergonomics (or human factors) is the scientific discipline concerned with the understanding of interactions among humans and other elements of a system, and the profession that applies theory, principles, data and methods to design in order to optimize human well-being and overall system performance."

The term "industrial design" was first used around 1919 at the widely known design school—the Bauhaus. This school focused on crafts and fine arts, and embraced modern technology: its basic tenet was that form follows function and that design must include an awareness of how the object is being used. In essence, this approach to design was the first step in building the foundations that have evolved into UX. The Bauhaus was established in Germany and flourished until the Nazis encouraged the school's administration to close it down in 1933. However, the impact had already been made; the influence of the Bauhaus can still be found in Modernist architecture, art, graphic design, typography, industrial design, and interior design.

Human factors as a field became solidified during World War II (WWII), when machines and weapons became more complex. Prior to this, the focus of any design had been on training the operators to fit the machines. However, during WWII it became clear that machinery had become too complex for the operator to figure out; this caused "operator" errors. Researcher Alphonse Chapanis found that certain controls in the airplane cockpit could be easily confused, with fatal results. This finding broke new ground in the design of instrumentation, and resulted in establishing the goal of reducing human errors.

The term human-computer interaction (HCI) became popular after Stuart K. Card, Thomas P. Moran, and Allen Newell published their seminal book, *The Psychology of Human-Computer Interaction*, in 1983. HCI as a field produced many methodologies and techniques for designing the user interfaces to machines. New interaction technologies as well as predictive models and theories of interaction continue to come from this area of study.

The field of UX design started to grow during the early 1990s when the Internet exponentially created millions of computer users who could not always understand and interact with the machine language that was shown on their screens.

## UX History Through Growth of Professional Organizations

The term UX was first used by Don Norman, the director of the Design Lab at University of California San Diego, and an advocate of user-centered design, at the **Special Interest Group on Computer-Human Interaction** (SIGCHI) conference in 1995. SIGCHI describes itself as "the premier international society for professionals, academics and students who are interested in human-technology and human-computer interaction (HCI)."

The Human Factors and Ergonomics Society (HFES) was formed in 1957 and mainly focused on hardware and ergonomic issues. It was important to understand the interaction of humans with systems, such as computers, planes, and automobiles, but primarily to insure that there was a good physical fit between the user, their equipment and the environment. Safety was also a major concern.

HCI as a field came into being in the early 1980s, first as a specialty area in computer science, combining cognitive psychology, design and human factors.

The field grew and professional associations were organized. In 1982 the ACM created the organization of a Special Interest for Computer Human Interaction (ACM-SIGCHI). It ran its first conference that year and grew to become the world's leading organization in HCI. ACM-SIGCHI is often credited with creating the field of HCI.

In 1991 with a core membership of 50, the Usability Professionals Association (UPA) was formed and grew to having nearly 2400 members worldwide, providing conferences and professional opportunities for a more practical approach to the computer UX. In 2005, it began the annual World Usability Day as a global event, including 35 countries with 115 events, and it has grown exponentially since.

Sometime around 2010, UX became a central factor in design and in 2013 the UPA became the User Experience Professionals Association (UXPA).

Why Does it Matter?

The usability of our systems affects our daily lives in many ways, big and small. Unusable mechanisms can hurt our lives physically and emotionally. Our day-to-day living can be improved by designing things that contribute holistically not only to our personal experience, but also to our societal experience (Figure 1.3).

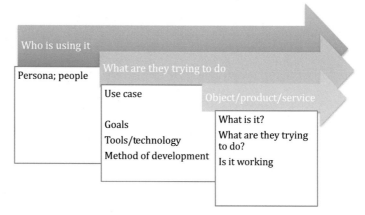

Figure 1.3 UX process.

# REFERENCES

ISO 13407, 1999. Human-Centred Design Processes for Interactive. www.iso.org/cate/d21197.html.

ISO 9241-11, 1998. Ergonomic Requirements for Office Work with Visual Display Terminals (VDTs)—Part 11: Guidance on Usability. https://www.iso.org/obp/ui/#iso:std:16883:en.

# BIBLIOGRAPHY

Albert, B., Tullis, T., 2013. Measuring the User Experience: Collecting, Analyzing, and Presenting Usability Metrics. Morgan Kaufmann, Waltham, MA.

Bogner, M.S. (Ed.), 1994. Human Error in Medicine. Lawrence Erlbaum Associates, Inc., Hillsdale, NJ, England, p. 411.

Card, S.K., Moran, T.P., Newell, A., 1980. The keystroke-level model for user performance time with interactive systems. Commun. ACM 23 (7), 396–410. http://dx.doi.org/10.1145/358886.358895.

Card, S.K., Moran, T.P., Newell, A., 1983. The Psychology of Human-Computer Interaction. Lawrence Erlbaum Associates, Inc., Hillsdale, NJ.

Dawson, J.W., 2006. A Holistic Usability Framework for Distributed Simulation Systems. Doctoral Dissertation, University of Central Florida, Orlando, FL. ISBN: 978-0-542-86761-3.

Fleming, J.H., Asplund, J., 2007. Human Sigma. Gallup Press, New York.

Kodak No. 1. http://camerapedia.wikia.com/wiki/Kodak_No._1.

Kogan, M.J., 2000. Human factors viewed as key to reducing medical errors. Will Health Care Partner with Social Scientists to Tackle Medical Errors? Mon Psychol. 31 (11), 29.

Myers, B.A., 1996. A Brief History of Human Computer Interaction Technology. Human Computer Interaction Institute, School of Computer Science, Carnegie Mellon University, CMU-CS-96-163, CMU-HCII-96-103.

Sauro, J., Kindlund, E., 2005. A method to standardize usability metrics into a single score. In: Proceedings of the SIGCHI conference on Human Factors in Computing Systems. dl.acm.org.

Spengler, C., Wirth, W., 2009. 360° Touch Point Analysis: Maximising the Impact of Marketing and Sales Activities. In: IO New Management (Ed. ETH Zurich/Axel Springer Switzerland), no. 3/2009. Online: http://www.accelerom.com/en/wp-content/uploads/2012/10/2009_io-new-management_Maximising-the-impact-of-marketing-and-sales-activities.pdf.

Usability Body of Knowledge. http://www.usabilitybok.org/what-is-usability.

Usability. usability.gov.

4-o-Forbes. http://www.forbes.com/sites/johnkotter/2012/05/02/barriers-to-change-the-real-reason-behind-the-kodak-downfall/.

# Chapter 2

## DESIGN THINKING

This chapter shows the importance of design thinking and putting the person at the center of the design process. It discusses the effect of design on people as well as how creativity and innovation can integrate UX. Case studies describe design thinking in both processes and product.

# Chapter 2

Simplicity is the ultimate sophistication.

**Leonardo da Vinci**

## Design

Many organizations and companies use the term design to mean many things. It is a plan, an organization or structure of elements that make up a work of art, a building, an object, or a piece of software. Good design is invisible, because, when something works well, people don't necessarily notice. For example, people rarely think about whether a doorknob is designed well, because it opens the door without a problem.

### Elements of Design

One of the easier to understand domains of design is graphic or visual. Elements of design are clearly defined in terms of an easily viewed visual grammar. This means that the images work together to communicate a message, just as words do. Language has grammar and understanding how to use images to communicate clearly is visual grammar. This design structure is made up of elements such as:

- Point;
- Line;
- Form, shape, space;
- Movement, direction;
- Color, value;
- Pattern;
- Texture;
- Size.

Elements of a well-designed object can be unpacked in other sectors. Design of large objects and open spaces combine the elements of visual design with object design. Environmental design uses the same principles of design to create a successful user experience (UX) in the physical domain. This can be on large and small scales, such as a well-designed small garden or an urban landscape that provides places for people to live and work comfortably.

Form follows function is a principle that came out of industrial design and is correctly applied to software and system design. Accordingly, the shape of an object should be based on its function or purpose. Form follows function means that the technology's look and feel must match its intended use. Form follows function is a rule for usability.

Designers ask questions like:

- How do we solve this problem?
- What does the person need?
- How can we make it beautiful and enjoyable?

Design practices are also applied to computer science and software development. When a software programmer writes codes for an object, it is first designed and broken down into functional elements. Another example can be found in object-oriented design (OOD), which is the planning and organizing of a system of software objects. The process of OOD separates the objects into elements for easier interaction, trying to balance simple design with complex systems. Each element becomes a separate building block that contains operations that can be combined to perform complex operations. OOD is realized in the software world as best of class software design. This can be evolved to create complex systems that provide enough flexibility to allow users with different levels of expertise to easily interact with it.

Design can be applied to all aspects of life; designing a comfortable living space, a fast and sleek car, a good meal, and a good story. Good design answers the question of what do we need now by focusing on the problem and having a vision for the goal. Any great invention came from design thinking. The Kodak camera, the light bulb, the doorknob, and the car dashboard started with ideas, a bit of research and experimentation, and, ultimately, iteration, trial, and error.

## Design Thinking

Design thinking is often referred to as the cognitive skills a designer uses in conceiving a new approach, or creative problem solving through breaking down an object into its smaller elements to find new ways of looking at things. Design thinking combines the understanding of the context of the problem and taps into empathy for the user to access the tools that are appropriate to a successful solution. Concisely defined, design thinking implements creative disruptive to introduce a new market disrupting and improving the previous technology in its innovative wake. For example, the car, once mass-produced, disrupted the market for the horse-drawn carriage or cart. This can also be called discontinuous innovation, which creates a product that is new to the world; one that has never been known before. This new product causes a paradigm shift in consumer thinking by eradicating previous approaches in an industry or science with previously unheard of inventions.

Well-designed products and technology take into account the micro and macro levels of functionality. These products keep the users' larger goals as the focus, while balancing the limitations of technology with people's many different modality preferences for interaction. A good example is the ATM for people's interactions with their banking institution. The ATM has evolved over time to provide a simple interface on a freestanding system to the more recent connection with mobile applications and the Internet. Now that people have so many touch points with their banks, the complex functionality must be consistent and easy to use, no matter with which touch point a person is interacting. The ATM and the mobile banking application are the micro interactions with the larger macro system of banking. The micro interactions such as deposits and withdrawals require touch points that interact with physical objects such as checks and money. The macro system of the banking institution can allow people to also hold credit cards, and connect all their accounts, so that people can track their money at all the touch points.

The process of creation should also reflect the effective design of the final product. During this process the needs of the user must be the guiding principle. It will then follow that the product will reflect this and that the UX will be excellent as well.

Many well-meaning design teams have trouble being productive because of numerous process issues. For example:

- The group's internal systems become flawed;
- Individual contributors can be overworked;
- Little administrative support can cripple the outcome;
- Individuals sometimes focus on their own deliverables;
- They can fail to prioritize UX;
- They can misjudge and conclude that other goals are more important than the needs of the users;
- Revenue targets can become a hard master so that the product teams put all their energies into making a profit.

When a development team has conflicting agendas it can hurt the product. The time spent on dealing with internal conflict takes away from time spent creating innovative results in the UX. Development teams that can integrate design thinking into the innovation and development of products and services that create a successful UX becomes a high priority. When something is well designed,

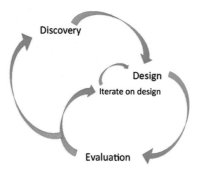

Figure 2.1 Design thinking process.

people might not notice. For example a light switch that has a form that matches the function, flip up for on, down for off, is a good design. It simply works and people don't think much about the design of the switch. When something is well designed, the design might seem invisible to the untrained eye.

Design thinking inserts the principles of design into all areas of the process. The next case study is an important and amusing example of how important it is to remember there is a person using the product or technology. Once the person is forgotten and conflicting roads are taken, the focus is lost and design deteriorates (Figure 2.1).

## Lifting the Fog of War

Chris Hass

"Things are getting pretty dire," the potential client said to me. "We've been working on this medical device interface for nearly eighteen months and have nothing to show for it. Nothing. We're burnt out, angry with our previous UX consultants, and we have only two weeks left before we have to send specs to our manufacturer in China to begin production. We need fresh eyes and someone who can help us define and execute a vision. In under two weeks."

If memory serves, at this point in the call there was a lengthy pause while I gathered my thoughts. Seriously, who in their right mind would step into this bear trap?

Clearly: me. As an optimist and a consultant, the answer is always "yes," which frequently leads me into professional territory my colleagues describe as "where Angels fear to tread." But, on the other hand, such incaution has led to defining career moments, happy clients, unique solutions, and, you know, getting paid.

So against all reason a colleague and I donned our UX capes and set out for the airport: client bound. I was careful to describe the project in detail to my colleague only *after* the plane was in flight. (Turned out to be a good idea.)

We arrived at the clients' headquarters a few hours later. A top-tier medical device manufacturer nestled into a corner of the United States, as snowbound as it was, we would discover it was also creativity locked. After a warm (and somewhat wary) introduction to the team we entered their war-room for an impromptu but very thorough and cogent two-day Boot Camp designed to bring us up to speed on the client, their product line, the current interface boggle, and anything else that might help us get them unjammed. The team was polite, fiercely intelligent, and, as we would also learn, very good at their jobs. Yet as they laid this cornucopia of information before us, we began to see some familiar patterns. What were missing were the requisite (to us): user needs research, task flow and workflow documents, and journey narratives.

We grew quickly to respect the company's team, thought leadership, and the institutional values that led them to envision how this product might enhance healthcare providers' capabilities. Yet something still bothered me. Even after all this discussion, introduction, and overview, I still wasn't "getting" what exactly the product WAS. Subtle differences between how each contributing member of our war council viewed the product and its use, even its overarching purpose, would flicker through our conversations.

On day 3 we charted out the next, vital 2 weeks. We discussed the need to triage some of our usual approaches and move quickly toward a solution. We leapt through task analysis, and began to circle in on sketching out the underpinnings of the interface. We spent a productive day roughing out screens and yet I couldn't shake the nagging feeling that I still wasn't seeing the product's purpose clearly. I felt naïve, as if I'd missed something obvious, especially in light of the confidence radiating from the client's team. I lacked clarity. The end of the statement: "This product is for _____" was still foggy for me. "Keep moving," I thought, "you'll catch up." That evening my colleague admitted privately that he too was still a little foggy on the guiding concept for the product.

By midway through day four we stalled out. The interface concepts just weren't jelling as we would have expected, given the intellectual capital and experience levels of the contributors. Finally, I felt compelled to draw things to a halt, suggesting that we take a step "backwards." "I'm sorry," I said, moving to an easel. "I'm still not 100% clear on what we're making here. Let's draw a conceptual model."

As I sketched a large circle on a post-it pad, I could feel the tension throughout the room. "If you don't mind, I'm just not seeing the product's purpose clearly. Can you help me?" Tense, but willing, the group began to throw out suggestions in a reverse-pictionary process drawing a conceptual model entails. I asked the usual questions: "This big circle is the product. What does it contain? Who uses each part? How are these sub-bits organized?" Interestingly, the subtle viewpoint differences my colleague and I had been sensing turned into palpable fractures as members of different teams leapt up saying "No, it would look like THIS," and drew over the "bubble" diagram to make different connections, different organizational schemes. I added additional colors to reflect different viewpoints.

Our diagram grew muddled visually, but conceptually, suddenly, lightning struck. Hard.

"OMG" (Oh My God!) the client lead said, growing a bit pale. "We've been seeing the entrance to the product as *here*," indicating the top of the diagram, "when the secondary audience would see it as the exact opposite." He drew an arrow pointing to the bottom of the diagram. "We're mixing oil and water and we didn't even know it."

And there it was. Two differing underlying assumptions so subtle they remained invisible until we drew them out in circles and lines. You could see it on the faces around the room in widened eyes, held breath: Eighteen months of hard work, brilliant prospective engineering and design that had all come to naught—the fog enveloping the team evaporated in an instant. The tension: gone. These tiny differences in assumptions had insidiously warped every structure they had tried to build until it couldn't stand. And there it was, clear as day on a post-it pad.

You could hear a pin drop. You could hear minds opening. You could feel near-instant relief that we had discovered the thorn in the project's paw and pulled it without even knowing it for what it was. We took a breath. Reoriented our thinking, and dove back in.

Having pulled the thorn, the rest was easy. And I should have known. User-centered design offers strategic and systematic techniques from which we cavalierly pick and choose as time, budgets, and capabilities allow. But embedded in our processes are the checks and balances that enable us to see what we're envisioning, and ourselves, clearly. It's not about intelligence, or money, or fancy equipment. At the heart of user-centered design is seeing the fog for what it is, and parting it breath by breath until it is gone.

Within our allotted two weeks the final design was off to China. I asked for, and was given permission to keep the conceptual model we had drawn. It's proprietary, so I can't display it, but I wanted a physical keepsake of that crystalline moment where assumptions and confusions melted away. To remember the power of a simple set of hand-drawn circles. And a rousing success.

A designer is an emerging synthesis of artist, inventor, mechanic, objective economist and evolutionary strategist.

**R. Buckminster Fuller**

# How Does Design Affect a Person?

Since every person is different, we can conclude that not every person will interact with systems and products in the same way. People are not all the same. This is true in ways large and small. This understanding builds on work done in the field of education and learning styles. It is clear the people learn in different ways, making use of different modalities (Pashler et al., 2009). It stands to reason, then, that people digest information in different ways. Some people find linear information the easiest to understand in the form of words or numbers. Others find pictures and graphs more informative, while still others benefit from kinesthetic or tactile learning, whereby they learn from doing.

Some individuals may have a physical disability that requires the technology to accommodate those physical challenges. For example, someone who is visually challenged and cannot see the monitor may need to use a screen reader to interact with a computer. The design will need to incorporate that person's need in order to be successful. People don't interact with technology in the same way. One user may simply interact with technology in a linear mode, working through each small step one at a time. Other users may be more holistic in their approach, and tie the larger elements together immediately prior to any examination of the microelements. It is important to understand the primary users of the design, so that it works best for the intended person.

## Persona

In order to better understand the user, a Persona needs to be developed. User Personas take different forms, ranging from specifications and description of specific users to a fictional character that represents a group of users for a product or systems. Each Persona describes a group of users that include details such as:

- Specific demographics:
  - Age range,
  - Gender,
  - Education level.
- Goals: What are they trying to accomplish?

- Limitations: What gets in their way?
- Motivations: What are the driving forces?
- Environment including context of use, which defines the conditions within which the product or service will be used. These conditions are defined in terms of both the environment and user.

There are many fields that involve the study of how people work: what physical, emotional, and cognitive issues they face in day-to-day life. Good design is multidisciplinary and integrates the following fields of study:

- *Cognitive science* looks at the mind including what and how it processes information. This is important to consider when designing something a person will use; it takes into account human limitations and potential.
- *Human factors* studies the overall effect of an individual's limitations by combining psychology, engineering, industrial design, biomechanics, and cognitive abilities.
- *Human memory* acts as a processor of current and past events, storing and retrieving them upon request. Human memory has limits connected with cognitive load, emotional and physical state, as well as past experiences. In terms of design, it is helpful to keep in mind that a person can only hold seven, plus or minus items at one time. It is important not to overload individuals with more than they can remember.
- *Human perception* includes information translated through the five senses as well the individual's emotional and physical state; this influences perception.
- *Accessibility/disabilities:*
  - Physical limitations can affect whether a person can use tools like computers and mobile devices:
    - Physical disability: if a person can't move their hands and click a mouse or type on a keyboard it is harder for them to take full advantage of a computing device. The person has to make use of adaptive devices and these are not always easy to use.
    - Visual disability: reading a computer screen is a key to using a computing device. If a person can't see, then they can't digest the information on the screen. There are several types of adaptive technologies that help blind people interact with computers, the most popular being screen readers. These tools read aloud the text on the screen.
  - Learning styles: differing learning styles create challenges when designing products and systems that are complicated with lot of information for people to learn. The more flexible the UX becomes, the more easily the system will be able to accommodate differing learning styles.

Live the questions now. Perhaps then, someday far in the future, you will gradually, without even noticing it, live your way into the answer.

**Rainer Maria Rilke**

# Creativity and Innovation

Creativity and innovation are key elements in understanding designer thinking innovation comes from creativity and, therefore, innovation is a creative process.

## Creativity

As the root of innovation, the creative process is the foundation for all design and innovation. It includes:

- A vision of the project's direction;
- The ability to focus on the task at hand without distraction;
- Enjoyment, satisfaction, and sometimes loss of self-consciousness;
- An open mind to immediately feedback (to determine success and failure).

## Innovation

- Combines many disciplines, often in new or improved ways;
- Needs a vision and a goal;
- Precludes a questioning approach:
  - What problem is it solving?
  - What opportunity is it providing people?

In order to be creative and produce innovative solutions to users' problems, UX professionals need to think differently: out of the box. The process is moved along when designers can generalize from the specific problem to related projects or technologies. Perhaps you will find solutions to a different problem that you can apply to the project you are working on. This creative approach to problem solving that includes combining methodologies from other fields can be seen in various methods of human-computer interaction (HCI) whereby Information Architecture is a good example. The terms Information and Architecture had not been combined until the mid-1970s when Richard Saul Werman, author and founder of the TED conference series, put the terms together to describe a conceptual structure mapped with functional behavior using methods from the field of architecture to create easier-to-use computer interfaces.

## Where Do You Start?

- After locating a problem that needs to be solved, write it down including all the barriers to success. Correlate the barriers with the Personas identified with the problem. Any problem that exists has a solution. Define the problem thoroughly now step back and envision the future with the solution. Brainstorm without judgment in the beginning, don't hold back and build out a list of possibilities. Have fun with it. Play around with ideas. No idea is a bad idea in the beginning. Focus and refine the idea until it feels complete. The key is not to rush the answer.

### Iterate

- Research the solution, experiment, learn from your mistakes;
- Live with some questions;
- Test the results;
  - Evolve the idea!
  - Live the questions!

The following case study illustrates how successful design thinking led to a patent award for an innovative intelligent software application. It illustrates how the design of a computer interface evolved into such excellence that it became invisible.

# Intelligent Photo Shoebox

Elizabeth Rosenzweig

While I was working at Eastman Kodak Company, I spent several years involved with teams at the Kodak Research Lab on several projects focused on solving what was called the Shoebox Problem. Kodak had been working to find a digital solution to the age-old "Shoebox Problem" where people collect so many photographs in shoeboxes that they often have trouble locating the pictures they want. The Shoebox Problem could become so frustrating it sometimes resulting the abandonment of the search for a specific picture. The Shoebox Problem can also result in a positive experience, because browsing for one picture can sometimes produce pleasure when finding others that also have significance (Figure 2.2).

While the Shoebox Problem was a big one in the physical world of traditional photography, because people actually did have many actual shoeboxes full of pictures, it grew 10-fold after the introduction of digital photography. With the ease of use of the new technology, people took hundreds of digital pictures, and put them all onto their computer hard drive without editing them. Subsequently, each picture appeared as an image name on the computer file system. However, the file names were not helpful since they usually defaulted to numbers and letters without reference to the actual contents of the picture file. There was still the problem of how to find the desired pictures. It became tedious to flip through hundreds of digital pictures, opening and viewing each one, and this required patience.

An early project emerged called The Electronic Shoebox Browser; try to make searching, browsing, and retrieving digital images easy and fun. With individual

Figure 2.2 Shoebox of pictures.

or family image collections accumulating thousands of images, which included cross-references from one family member to the other, sharing was increasingly difficult. Designers of The Electronic Shoebox Browser created a three-dimensional interface that graphically showed the number and the type of each image, which were each classified according to four axes. The axes are listed below:

- Who: Are the people in their lives?
- When: Special dates like birthday and anniversaries;
- What: Places or things that were important to the people;
- Where: Places that they live, travel or otherwise have a connection to.

This allowed the user to customize the interface with their own data, adding tags and keywords to images to help further categorize them. The inventors at the Kodak Research Labs used it in their daily lives.

I spent numerous vacations with my family photographing them with numerous and varied devices. For example, Kodak had previously invented a digital capture system that automatically connected to a GPS and collected this geographical information about the images. This helped to sort and tag the images along the four axes listed above. Additionally calendar data could collect time and date tags. Facial recognition was in its early iterations to tag the name of each individual in the image.

Many searchable photo databases existed, but technology had not yet progressed to include a system with some sort of image understanding: this was not feasible until recently. Without this component image search, systems had to rely on the keywords often entered manually by the users. These were stored as metadata in the image database, and were not very helpful because the user had to remember the exact keyword to initiate the search. For example, it became difficult to find my picture from the family Colorado trip because I had to recall numerous details to recall the keyword. The process of typing in keywords is disconnected from the purpose of the search, which is, to tell a story.

Designing an interface involves a scenario of steps driven by the questions like: What is essential? Which steps are necessary and meaningful to the end users? Which steps are just bureaucratic: steps that the mechanisms need to complete the job, but which are uninteresting to the user? These must be automated into the invisible design.

After several years of internal research, Kodak took the decision to include research from experts outside of the company. Until then Kodak had not funded research in the computer science field of artificial intelligence (AI), this was a field I had studied and done research in while I was a graduate student at the MIT Media. There the Software Agents group was directed by Henry Lieberman, a world class AI expert. Lieberman's work explores the intersection between AI and HCI. Kodak Research Labs funded a project to help solve the digital Shoebox Problem. During subsequent meetings outlining the questions and issues of the Shoebox Problem, we brainstormed at the Media Lab and our design thinking emerged as the underlying methodology to find innovative solutions to the Shoebox Problem.

Lieberman and I worked together first creating user Personas and then various user scenarios. Soon, it became clear that the primary use for browsing photographs in the shoebox was to tell stories about people, including trips, events, and lifecycle milestones. People want to record events in their lives and then share them with family and friends. In the past using paper photographs this was done face to face, but now this communication was increasingly taking place online. People share pictures instantaneously, creating new modes of connection in real time. In the past people had to be face to face, physically in the same location to communicate and connect. Now, people can be face to face online, in real time and share more information and media than ever before. This has created a paradigm shift in communication that is still evolving as people individualize their communication and connect to people who are not in their physical location.

## Our Design Thinking Process

We brainstormed and came up with several different scenarios listed below describing various Personas and their needs.

**Capturing Images:**

- "I am on a family vacation with many members of my family. We want to save the best pictures and be able to find them again based on who is in the pictures."

- "My friends and I meet for a getaway, and we take pictures to share with each other to remember the fun."

- "My family is having an event and since we will all be dressed up nicely, I want to make sure I take group pictures of everyone."

**Retrieving Images:**

- "We are having a large party for my father who has an upcoming milestone birthday. I want to create a collage that will show the various stages of his life, what he was doing and with whom. I have so many pictures to go through and am concerned I will miss something."

After we elaborated on the various scenarios, we brainstormed to select the most workable approach. These questions arose to direct our design thinking:

- "Could we get the tags into metadata for the pictures without manually tagging them each time?"

- "Is there another way to sort images, another type of metadata besides keywords?"

- "Could we take information from calendars, GPS or other sources?"

Choosing a wedding scenario as our example, we processed each step of this whole scenario, and completed the process with an email to share the pictures with our friends. The email was written in the manner of a live conversation with natural language. For example, in talking about a recently attended wedding, one might say: "Last weekend, I went to Ken and Mary's wedding." This descriptor is valuable information about the significance of the associated pictures. However, the computer program was ignoring it!

Conventional systems had directed the user to a separate interface and to type keywords. In this case, the system used natural language processing to find the obvious key words from the above example. These keywords might include "wedding," "Ken," "Mary." The conventional system would have only been able to use keywords that the user would have to remember to type in and tag a picture. From the user point of view, it was easier to get keywords automatically from the email since the keywords words were already there!

In other words, if while typing a story, the user's natural inclination is to search for a relevant picture. However, the text of the story also provides the search keywords, so why switch applications and retype them?

Since the text of the story might not be *exactly* the right keywords, so AI techniques were introduced to parse the sentences, and to even generate implicit keywords. Also AI dealt with commonsense matches that were semantically related like connecting "bride" with "wedding."

MIT scientist Henry Lieberman designed the automatic AI keyword tagging component by having the image browser automatically tagging images with previously tagged keywords as shown in Figure 2.3. It was named an Annotation Retrieval Image agent (ARIA).

The left side of the above window is an email and web page editor, while the right side of the above window illustrates a scrolling list of keyword-tagged pictures. As the user types an email on the left, the right side immediately and continuously updates with the most relevant pictures. When choosing a picture and dragging it into the text, keywords computed from the surrounding text are automatically attached as tags to the picture.

As soon as "Ken and Mary's wedding" is typed, the right side is updated with a list of photos in order of their relevance. These are the photos most likely to be chosen for insertion. The top photo (with keywords "Ken," "Mary," "wedding") is selected by the user and inserted. The photo depicts

Figure 2.3 ARIA photo agent.

the Golden Gate Bridge, and opening a text to describe the event results in the keywords "golden gate" to be automatically added. This produces a seamless experience.

To streamline interfaces all inessential steps should be automated away. The computer can make common sense assumptions about the user's intent as a result. Lieberman had previously implemented one of the first Web browser agents called Letizia; this browser looked ahead at clickable links on the page, filtering them through a user profile and recommending relevant ones. One of the principles that led to the development of Annotation Retrieval Image agent (ARIA) to make the Web more accessible to those with disabilities, was an attempt to understand and anticipate how the user's actions could be applied to the photo-sharing scenario. It also

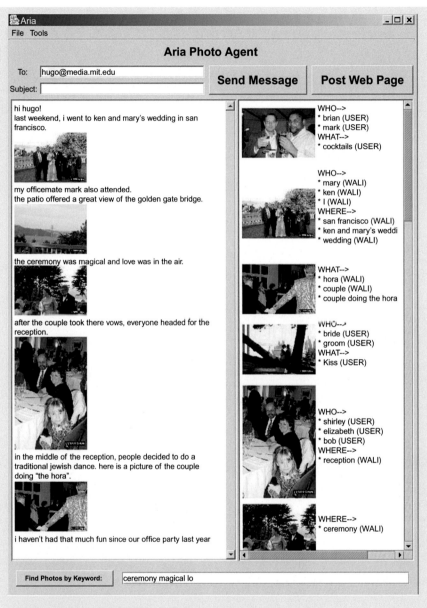

Figure 2.4 ARIA and natural language processor.

automated other associated tasks, such as routinely downloading pictures from a connected camera. This broke the boundaries of so-called "applications" and "commands," which were dedicated interfaces for a particular task (Figure 2.4).

The collaborative, user-centered design process produced a smart and innovative solution to a complex problem, finding images that are stored within a large database (Lieberman et al., 2001).

Kodak subsequently patented the idea. The success of automatic tagging had created simplicity out of a complex system, and no one understood how complex that system was. The good design was invisible.

Apple Inc. had been working on iPhoto when they had a demo of ARIA. Many of the features of auto tagging later appeared in Apple's iPhoto.

## Key Concluding Recommendations

- Know your audience. If an innovation works so well that its complexity is not apparent to the user, make sure you find a way to explain it to them. Presentations that gloss over these details will result in the audience misunderstanding the key points. Unpack the steps and present each one in smaller, more understandable pieces.
- Clearly describe the end user and the context of use for each product or service. These details should be included as part of the overview and "the big picture." If the design is hard to understand, then build an additional set of use cases that demonstrate what the LACK of the innovation would look like.
- Never give up; innovations need to come at the right time with the right explanations to be accepted.

# REFERENCES

Lieberman, H., Singh, P., Rosenzweig, E., 2001. ARIA: An Agent for Annotating and Retrieving Images. IEEE Computer, pp. 57-61.

Pashler, H., McDaniel, M., Rohrer, D., Bjork, R., 2009. Learning styles: concepts and evidence. Psychol. Sci. Public Interest 9 (3), 105–119. http://dx.doi.org/10.1111/j.1539-6053.2009.01038.x, ISSN 1539-605.

# BIBLIOGRAPHY

BenZion(Westreich), G., 1999. An Analysis of Kinesthetic Learners' Responses: Teaching Mathematics Through Dance. Doctoral Dissertation, American University, Washington, DC.

Cooper, A., 1991. The Inmates are Running the Asylum, Why High-Tech Products Drive us Crazy and Hot to Restore the Sanity. SAMS Publishing, Carmel, IN.

Fry, C., Lieberman, H., 2013. Decision-making should be more like programming. In: Int'l Symposium on End-User Development, Copenhagen, Denmark.

Hilliges, O., Terrenghi, L., Boring, S., Kim, D., Richter, H., Butz, A., 2007. Designing for collaborative creative problem solving. In: Proceedings of the 6th ACM SIGCHI conference on Creativity\& cognition (C\&C '07). ACM, New York, pp. 137 146. http://dx.doi.org/10.1145/1254960.1254980.

James, W., Gardner, D., 1995. Learning styles: implications for distance learning. New Dir. Adult and Contin. Educ. 67, 19–32.

Leborg, C., 2004. Visual Grammar. Princeton Architecture Press, New York.

Lieberman, H., Rosenzweig, E., Fry, C., 2014. Steptorials: mixed-initiative learning of high functionality applications. In: ACM Conference on Intelligent User Interfaces (IUI-14), Haifa, Israel.

Liu, H., Lieberman, H., 2005. Metafor: visualizing stories as code. In: ACM Conference on Intelligent User Interfaces (IUI-2005), San Diego, CA.

Muller, M.J., 1991. PICTIVE—an exploration in participatory design. In: CHI '91: Proceedings of the SIGCHI Conference on Human Factors in Computing Systems.

Norman, D.A., 1999. Affordance, conventions and design. Interactions 6 (3), 38–43.

Ruston, L., Muller, M.J., Cebulka, K.D., 1991. Designing software for use by humans, not machines. In: ICSE '91 Proceedings of the 13th International Conference on Software Engineering. IEEE Computer Society Press, Los Alamitos, CA, pp. 104–113.

# Chapter 3

## UX THINKING

This chapter explains how to apply design thinking to UX. It describes the importance of good user interface and graphic design breaking down the steps by looking at personas, use cases, and information architecture. The examples of use cases are from real-world situations from two different domains.

# Chapter 3

Any sufficiently advanced technology is indistinguishable from magic.

**Arthur C. Clarke**

## Applying Design Thinking to UX

Good design is invisible; when something works well, many people will not notice. Products, or any object that works well, are often ubiquitous. Think about a common light switch or doorknob. You know how to operate it, it is consistent and simple, it does the job and we don't think about it.

User experience (UX) design thinking produces products and services that people will use because they work. UX design thinking takes the best of both UX and design thinking principals and puts them together.

User Interface and Interaction Design

The physical and graphical layer between a person and the technology for computing is the user interface, which includes modalities of interaction that make us the interaction design. It is the design of these elements that creates the overall UX.

Graphical user interface (GUI) is composed of elements:

- Graphics (see Figure 3.1):
    - *Windows*: an element of the user interface that contains some of the information of the system. The Window is a metaphor for a view, and is part of a larger information system.
    - *Icons*: a graphical representation of an idea. For example, an image of an arrow pointing down is an icon for the function—download.
    - *Labels*: name or title of a software function or file.

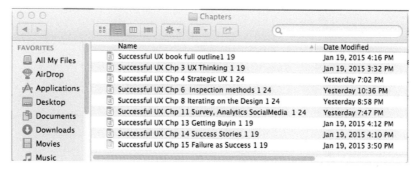

Figure 3.1 Windows, icons, labels.

- *Dialog box*: a window that is usually displayed over other graphical elements in a screen. The dialog box provides immediate information to the user and requires some form of interaction to close it, for example buttons such as "OK" or "Cancel" are often part of the dialog box.

- *Menus*: an element of the user interface that lists commands or functions for a computer application or system (Figure 3.2).

- Interactive graphical affordances:

  - Buttons used for selecting items and initiating actions;

  - Checkboxes used for selecting items;

  - Sliders used for navigating through windows (Figures 3.3 and 3.4).

- User interactions include modalities such as gesture, voice, audio, and other sensory interactions:

  - Gestures include:

    - Point and click**;

    - Drag and drop;

    - Swipe.

Figure 3.2 Menus on a computer.

Figure 3.3 Buttons and checkbox.

Figure 3.4 Scroll bars.

- Biometrics include:
  - Eye-tracking and eye-gaze used for input;
  - Voice and natural language processing;
  - Galvanic skin response technologies for tracking and adjusting interfaces based on user's state of stimulation.

Another key element in a good UX is the information architecture (IA). IA can be defined as the organization of information within the system or product this includes the labels and menu structure as well. On a Web site the IA encompasses the menu structure and labels as well as the navigation from one page to another.

## Participatory Design

Participatory design is a process that includes the stakeholders in the early stages of design. This involvement of stakeholders and end users together allows the design process to be more open to considering the UX. Participatory design lends itself to user-centered design innovation since it nurtures a more creative development atmosphere. This can be seen in methodologies such as PICTIVE, developed by Michael Muller in 1991 PICTIVE provides a shared design environment for users and developers. This is one methodology that demonstrates how important it is to create collaborative approaches to innovation that bring the human into the center of the technical development process:

- Brainstorm;
- CoCreate;
- User: Job/Task Scenario;
- Developers: System Components.

Many approaches have been developed and some work well with a less formal approach. Often a developer and a UX designer can brainstorm and then walk through several options to find the one that works best for the user.

## Prototype and Wireframes

In order to test designs, prototypes must be created. These can take many forms, and in the early stages of design, low-fidelity prototypes are often best. The benefit of low-fidelity wireframes and prototypes are the ability to evaluate a product before it is fully built out, saving time and resources early on in the development process. Another benefit to testing wireframes is the data produced; because the prototype does not appear to be fully functional, the user can focus on the interactions and not get distracted by design. Figure 3.5 illustrates a generic low-fidelity wireframe that can be used to get feedback from users early in the development process.

# UX Design Thinking

Holistically, think about how things fit together: the person, their environment, task, capabilities, restrictions, and available technology. The result is the best possible UX given the above.

## Principles of UX Design

- Easy to use: not too many clicks, functions are easy to find;
- Easy to understand: the user does not have to get help to do the tasks;

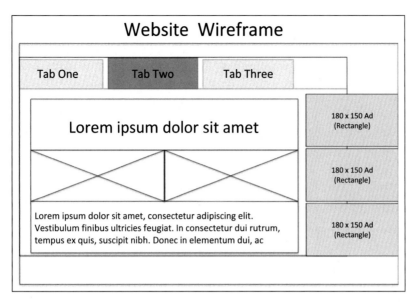

Figure 3.5 Low-fidelity wireframe.

- Visual focus: the call to action;
- Clarity: information is easy to understand, directions are clear;
- Effective: the users can perform their task efficiently and correctly;
- Works for the user.

# Methods to Kickstart UX Design Thinking

## Competitive Analysis

Sometimes, we can use competitive analysis as a way to brainstorm, to help us to see what has already been done, and as a benchmark to make a better product. Sometimes, this work can make us look at a problem in a new way. How did others solve it? Were they trying to solve the same problem we are? Is there something that can be used or combined with something else to create a new thing?

This includes environmental scans and literature searches, both of which can help start the creative juices flowing. Perhaps you will find a pattern, or a solution to a problem you are working on—if you put together some technologies that have not been combined before.

Literature Review

Literature Review

While this is similar to competitive analysis, it is a bit more high level, since literature can also include ideas that have not yet made it to product. The literature review produces information on current knowledge and advancements in the domain and can be used to build a foundation for UX design.

# Persona and Use Cases

One of the fundamental rules for achieving good design is to understand the person who is going to be using the object. A common tool for accomplishing this is the persona and use case, which is the foundation of success according to Alan Cooper, who first introduced the notion of personas in 1999 in his seminal book *The Inmates are Running the Asylum*. The idea was to develop empathy and to understand the person who would be using the product or service. The persona has evolved quite a bit since its inception and is now a common tool for understanding users.

Persona

UX personas define the person who is using the product and includes the following:

- Demographics including age, income, and education level;
- Goals: What are they trying to do?
- Motivations: Why are they trying to do it?
- Frustrations: What gets in the way?
- Behaviors and tasks: How do they act, what do they do?
- Constraints/limitations: What limits their actions?

Figures 3.6–3.8 illustrate a simple persona set for a family of digital photography users.

# Daughter / Mom Marla

Age 40-55

Key Tasks
- Capture moments, take pictures
- Share pictures with family and friends via social media and email
- View pictures that are shared by family and friends
- Occasionally print pictures and put them on display at home or office

| Motivations | Frustrations | Opportunities |
|---|---|---|
| Remember meaningful event<br>Relive events<br>Evoke warm memories | Can't find pictures when I want to<br>Too many pictures, no organization | Create organization of pictures as a by product of everyday events |

Figure 3.6 Persona example 1: digital photography.

# Teenager Theo

Age 14-18

Key Tasks
- Capture moments, take pictures
- Post pictures on high school web magazine
- View pictures that are shared by family and friends
- Post pictures on social media as a means of communication with friends

| Motivations | Frustrations | Opportunities |
|---|---|---|
| Stay connected with friends<br>Communicate with peer group<br>Stay connected with family | Quality of pictures not consistent<br>Too many pictures, no organization | Create organization of pictures as a by product of everyday events |

Figure 3.7 Persona example 2: digital photography.

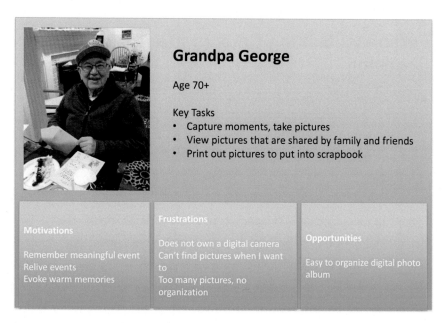

Figure 3.8 Persona example 3: digital photography.

## Use Case

Personas are the most useful when paired with use cases which discuss in detail the process and steps of the task the user is carrying out using the object or the use case includes:

- Goals;
- User touch points with product, system, or technology;
- Environment;
- Actionable steps in order of execution;
- User flow or journey;
- Formulaic "In order to do this, [persona] must first do this."

The following case study demonstrates the value of personas and use cases by focusing on the person and their behavior (Figure 3.9).

# Personas: Getting Back to the Basics of Behavior

Meena Kothandaraman

Vice President, Motivate Design

## The Problem

A major news distributor was faced with questions regarding the design of their (free) news website. The website was considered a prominent part of daily life in a major US city, yet the news organization was receiving mixed feedback about its current design. After considerable discussion, the organization decided to create a completely new version. Given this decision, there was one important question that needed to be answered first: "Where should the new design start? A news organization has to satisfy the needs of everyone." Given the various methods of accessing the news, how could the new design address the needs of a diverse population? Furthermore, how would the design be manifested on a desktop/laptop, tablet, or mobile device? How did technology access play into the design presentation?

Using existing information and quantitative data to establish a direction for personas, a survey was employed to then refine and further define reader behaviors for consuming the news.

## Identify the Basic Behavior

The news organization had quantitative data and outdated personas that served as a good starting place. Upon further analysis of the existing data and discussions with key client leads, the problem that really needed solving emerged: going deeper to determine how consumers were reading and taking in the news. How has two parts: access and why. Delivery devices such as laptops/desktops, tablets, and mobile web allow access, yet at this point in discussing the new design, access became somewhat unimportant. What really required further clarification and study was the "why": basically, determining user reasons and motivations for reading the news. The organization needed to answer "Why do people read the news?" and "What motivates users to read the news from this organization?"

Identifying motivations for news consumption would also lead to uncovering gaps within the experience. If the reader intentions could be accurately defined and the gaps adequately identified, then opportunities to improve the experience could be addressed through design. Thus far, the news organization had focused on market demographics and segments to identify their readers. The first step in this design process would be the discovery of reader motivations, which could clearly be documented by a set of personas.

Personas 101

Personas are a common method used to describe motivations and behaviors of customers. They offer helpful insight into the world of design by focusing on motivations for consumption. If the current motivations and goal of consuming the news could be discovered, as well as barriers or frustrations that the consumers experienced along the way, then the logical approach would be to understand the barriers, measure the "size" of the gaps, and then present design solutions that would address the gaps. This way consumers would be served up news in a way that satisfied not only their basic needs for reading the news but their underlying expectations for the experience of reading the news.

The existing personas in the news organization were recognized as being outdated. There was also interest in giving attention to social media interplay and usage. Other studies conducted by the news organization cited that readers were changing their consumption of news from major organizations due to the meta-level of news that social media offers. Considerable discussion occurred about when social media is a trusted news source and when traditional media outlets are a trusted news source. The new personas needed to reflect the dimensions of source and trust.

## Keep It Quick and Iterative: Learn About the Masses

The time frame to identify reader motivations was short. Quantitative data was studied in order to understand what readers were doing with the news. Specific behaviors were identified due to the large amounts of data. Some readers came to graze, some truly absorbed the news, and some were visibly vocal in sharing their opinion on certain columns.

Using the behaviors studied, defining statements were created for what seemed to be a representative set of personas. The defining statements represented behavior that exemplified why people read the news. By employing a survey, the defining statements could be posed to readers who could then indicate which persona they felt most like—and more importantly—how they might differ from the persona they felt they resembled. Ultimately, it was the best chance to obtain the information required to clarify the personas without having to meet and interview each reader.

The survey took the form of a self-selection set of questions:

We are interested in finding out more about how you consume the news. Are you like any one of these people? Tell us who you are most like:

- I want to follow articles or information, but I also want to contribute comments on a topic. I like being a part of the conversation with other readers
- I look for information that will help me with everyday life. When looking for a job, a car, restaurant recommendations, or fashion tips, I am likely to check the news
- I regularly look for updates throughout the day to see if there is any breaking news. I look at the headlines to get a quick snapshot of what has happened since I last read the news. I don't need depth, I need a good summary
- I want to follow issues, stories, features and really understand all the viewpoints. I read the news content to thoroughly digest the facts and opinions presented
- I read the news just to fill a few minutes of time, while taking a break or waiting for something. I scan, enjoy the pictures and snippets about different stories. It gives me a little break

An additional question was asked at the end of the survey: "How are you different from the person you chose?"

Key goals were established for the survey: it needed to be short and take under one minute to complete. Readers would identify which statement best described them. They were also offered the option to share any additional information that could further inform us of their reading behaviors.

The survey was first executed with a small sample size (50 users) to ensure that the defining statements made sense. Over time, the survey was opened up to a larger reader population, resulting in approximately 700 responses. In subsequent rounds of surveys, different populations were constantly approached in order to get fresh data and trends on what drove readers to consume the news the way they did. The survey served its purpose: quickly iterate on statements that define motivation for reading the news, and identify additional behavior that could give insight into the larger personas being created.

## Persona Definitions

The self-selected responses came out with resounding clarity. Readers resonated with the defining statements and were able to clarify some of the statement details. In addition to the persona information, other information was divulged through statement details.

- Headliners wanted to be aware and in the know. They want to understand what is going on and get a sense for the general topics that were being discussed on a given day. Their goal was to gain breadth and not depth of the news. They picked at the news just to stay aware.

- Deep divers were interested in getting all the details to the news. They were interested in being a repository of information on a topic, truly digesting all the facts presented to them in an article.

- Engagers took pleasure in not only digesting the news article, but also responding back and providing their view point. They wanted to "play the journalist" a bit and have their opinion heard in the mix. (This persona addressed the social media aspect and incorporated active responders to articles).

- Pleasure seekers were interested in simply passing time by scanning pictures or snippets of information. The information was often pictorial, or quick in nature for them to enjoy, and not necessarily long-lasting for them to keep.

- Info users were interested in key pieces of data that were presented throughout the news. They looked for easy access or recall of information so that data could be used or stored.

Once the personas were further fine-tuned, the defining statements were issued in a survey for each section. Additional questions were then raised: how did the personas relate to the different sections or content of the news (headlines, sports, health, technology, real estate, obituaries, etc.)? How did technology affect the personas?

This personas inquiry defined the way readers consumed the news at a high level. The defining statements were then sent out with an additional question, which related reading behavior to each section. This information would prove incredibly meaningful for the design since it would show which sections readers consumed in a particular way. If the majority of readers were "headliners" who wanted breadth and not depth, then the design could be adjusted to suit these people needs. Additionally, this information helped determine macro and micro design decisions as well as dictated how some of the information would be supported by different devices.

## Recommendations

The persona approach paved the way for the design team to create multiple, competing solutions for evaluation. A few thoughts left with the design team based on the persona data were:

- Focus on ways to encourage the behaviors of the different personas
  - If someone was a headliner, enable them to quickly scan to read. Offer a good summary of the news and the story (Ex: bullet points in a summary box, or a timeline that could indicate the key points gathered about the news story)
- Identify how readers consumed the different sections/content within the paper. Which personas read which content? Design the content to suit the majority persona.

## Key Takeaways

There were many benefits to doing this kind of research in an iterative fashion. Some of the benefits were:

1. The personas research was started on an outdated set that helped to quickly define and clarify some characteristics of users.
2. The analytics team was able to inform more aspects of current user behavior, studying what people were doing with articles in different sections and collecting data on how much time users were spending on content.
3. The iterative nature of the surveys allowed for quick feedback from participants. Response rate was incredibly high because the entire survey was really a selection among five personas and how the consumption differed. This simple, quick format earned the trust of readers. They were comfortable in responding because participation was voluntary and required less than 1 minute of their time.
4. The personas created were a strong start, but needed to be revisited each time readers were approached, for accuracy and possible change.

An example of a final persona created is included on a separate page.

# HEADLINER (FIRST)

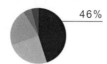

46%

*"I check [newscompany.com] pretty regularly throughout the day to see if there are any breaking updates.
I look at the headlines to get a quick snapshot of what's happened since I last visited the site. I don't need
depth, I need a good summary. I need to be 'in the know'."*

## MOTIVATIONS

- Maintain awareness of latest information and current events (never feel left out)
- Avoid spending too much time digging for details

## BARRIERS

- Cannot obtain quick snippets of information, and good summary of latest content
- No obvious location for what content is new, what content is old – how do I know what I read and didn't read?

## OPPORTUNITIES

- One-stop information delivery with exclusive summaries
- Customization of headlines to select topics of interest
- Visual update of what has and hasn't been read

### LEVEL OF ENGAGEMENT

▽
|———————————————————|
SCAN      ABSORB      ENGAGE

### AGE RANGE

|—— 35-64 ——|

| 16-24 | 25-34 | 25-44 | 45-54 | 55-64 | 64+ |

### GENDER

MOSTLY MALE

### CONTENT

BUSINESS  //  LOCAL  //  HEALTH
TECHNOLOGY  //  OBITUARIES

### LOYALTY

VISITS MULTIPLE TIMES A DAY

MOTIVATE ∞ D E S I G N

// PERSONAS, BY MEENA KOTHANDARAMAN

Figure 3.9 Persona.

# Information Architecture

IA is the system for organizing and labeling Web sites, softwares, and systems. It was used originally by Richard Saul Werman who said "used in the words architect of foreign policy. I mean architect as in the creating of systemic, structural, and orderly principles to make something work—the thoughtful making of either artifact, or idea, or policy that informs because it is clear."

IA provides a navigational system and a structure for the user to understand the Web site, software, or system gestalt. The structure of the information must match the user's mental model or there will be a disconnection and it will become unusable. The most complex the system, the more important it is to get the IA correctly aligned with the user.

The labels are important, not only because they provide the user with a way to find what they need, it also provides keywords for searching.

Why is it important?

This next case study demonstrates the important of IA in important functions on financial Web sites.

## Comparative Study of Information Architecture from Three Community Bank Web Sites

David Juhlin

Goals

The goal of this research was to gain insight into how bank Web sites' IA can be improved, as well as to showcase a more advanced tree testing method.

We were also able to show the benefits of combining parallel and iterative design/research.

## Background

Jakob Nielsen concluded in 2009 that "10% of task attempts fail due to problems with the information architecture."[1] In other words, 10% of your visitors can't complete their tasks due to issues with the IA. This statement was made five years ago now, and we may hope that things have since improved—but truth be told, it has not improved that much.

Many clients hire us to test their design, and over and over again I notice issues with the IA. There are many different research methods that can be used early in the design process to ensure a well-functioning IA, and that would eliminate late (and expensive) changes to the design. Since our client work is confidential and I am not able to share it, I decided to create an academic research case to share.

## Process

The three banks evaluated were: Blue Hills Bank, Cambridge Trust, and Rockland Trust. The reasons we picked these financial institutions were varied, but the primary reason was that we wanted to show the value of IA studies to smaller financial institutions—not just larger ones. Another reason was that these particular financial institutions had fairly simple navigation, which was easy to reverse-engineer. The final reason was that these financial institutions

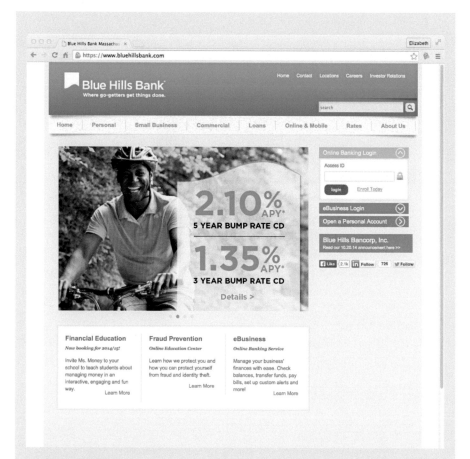

Figure 3.10 Blue Hills Bank.

were located in the New England area; thus, they could potentially utilize our expertise and become clients. Something to keep in mind is that we only evaluated the IA of their public sites, since we did not have access to their secure sites (section requiring login and where you can see your balance, transfer money, etc.) (Figures 3.10–3.12).

Figure 3.11 Cambridge Trust.

Before launching the tree test,[2] we conducted a survey collecting data about what information is most important to users when they are looking for a new bank or switching banks. The outcome of the survey provided us with a prioritized list of the most important information, which we could use to create the tasks for the tree test. This ranked list was also used as a weighting formula when the data were analyzed (information users find that more important information should be easier to find than less important information).

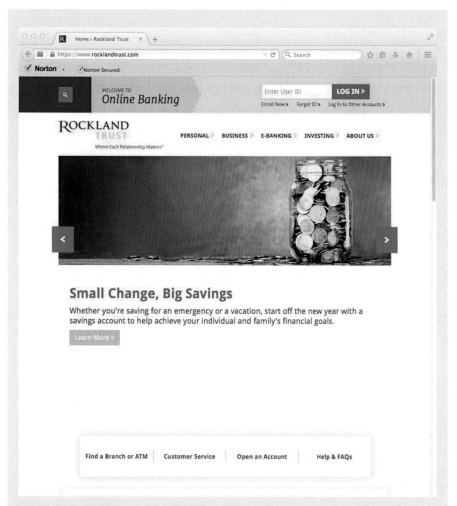

Figure 3.12 Rockland Trust.

The comparative study is a type of parallel research design and provides a broad insight. By identifying strengths and weaknesses in the different IAs, we were able to iterate on the IA by creating our own (Bentley User Experience Center IA). As a final step, we tested this new IA to make sure it was an improvement.

# Weighted Score

Imagine you have two tasks (T1 and T2). I will allow you to choose between two IAs. The first IA has a 90% success rate for T1 and a 10% success rate for T2. This means your average success rate is 50%. The second alternative IA has a 10% success score for T1 and a 70% success score for T2, resulting in an average success score of 40%. With only these data provided, most would prefer alternative 1 since the average is higher. But what happens if only 10% of your users preform T1 and 100% of your users preform T2? Do you still prefer alternative 1?

If you create a weighted score for the tasks (success rate x percentage of users who want to perform the task), alternative 1 would have a score of 9% (90% × 10%) for T1 and 10% (100% × 10%) for T2, resulting in an average of 9.5%. Alternative 2, on the other hand, would get a score of 1% (10% × 10%) for T1 and 70% (70% × 100%) for T2, resulting in an average score of 35.5%. Would you still select alternative 1?[3]

This weighting calculation can be made even more complex by taking into account the business side (for example, if T1 and T2 were to represent products, and the profit margin on T1 were 20 times more than the profit margin on T2). The point I want to make is that only looking at pure task success alone is not enough; other aspects also need to be taken into account when deciding which IA to pick.

Lastly, if T1 is doing better in one alternative and T2 is doing better in the other alternative, and if it is possible to combine those two options into a third IA, this is obviously the way to go.

## Recruiting and Participants

The range of people searching for new banks is broad and most likely skewed towards a younger audience. With this type of target group it is ideal to use guerilla recruiting. We used a combination of different methods: a post on our LinkedIn group, Craig's list, email lists, and Amazons Mechanical Turk. By eliminating a recruiting service, we were able to hold the cost down—though it did result in more work in the cleanup process of the data. This increased cleanup was anticipated, so we had included a control question to make it easier to weed out unserious respondents.

In our research, we did not find any significant differences with regards to the source of the participants (mechanical Turk vs. Craig's list, etc.). The slight difference we noticed was for participants above the age of 65, who had a slightly lower success rate, and participants with a higher income, who may have a slightly higher success rate.

## Result

When analyzing the average success rate for the three banks, Cambridge Trust had the highest with 71%. Blue Hill and Rockland Trust had approximately the same success rate (57% and 59%, respectively). The UXC IA (iterated version) had an average success rate of 88%, demonstrating the importance of iteration.

With the adjusted weighted score, Cambridge Trust received a 78%, Blue Hills 68%, and Rockland Trust 59%. This demonstrates how both Cambridge Trust and Blue Hills has been better at supporting the tasks most important to users, while Rockland Trust has been equally successful with both important and unimportant tasks. The UXC IA received an adjusted weighted score of 89%, demonstrating a slight improvement compared to the average. With a high success rate across all tasks, it's hard to improve on the adjusted score. This once again demonstrates the value of combining insights from the three earlier designs to achieve high performance for all tasks. At points where we had to make compromises in the IA, we looked at the task importance and allowed that to guide us.

## Takeaways

Our main takeaway is that smaller financial institutions can improve their IA significantly. However, there were many other interesting takeaways as well. The first is that it is of tremendous value to combine parallel and iterative design/research methods. The second takeaway is that companies with fairly small IAs also can benefit from using appropriate design methods; it's not only for larger companies.

If you design the IA for a financial institution, there are some key things to keep in mind. For one, there is a range of user mental models. In one case, for example, approximately half of our participants went to Investing → Personal in order to find personal retirement information, while the other half tried to find it under Personal Banking → Investing. In these cases, it can be good to support both mental models—but always make sure they are not interfering with one another.

Another thing to keep in mind is how terms are being perceived. "Account Services," for example, is too vague and can make it very hard for the user to know what they will find here. Even some labels you may think are pretty straightforward may not be so. For example, the term "Rates": it may seem straightforward at first, but it can actually be perceived in two ways (rates as in "interest rates," or rates as in "fees").

The final key point I want to highlight is the concept and discussion about the number of levels you should use. Jakob Nielsen has an interesting article about depth and leans more toward shallow IA.[4] However, our research found that it was more beneficial to add another level and thereby chunk the content; this yielded higher success rates. The main takeaway with regards to this is that it depends on the situation. In some cases, the shallower IA will outperform the deeper; in other cases, the opposite will be true. If you are unsure about what approach you should use, the best answer you'll ever get is by performing a test with users.

---

[1] http://www.nngroup.com/articles/ia-task-failures-remain-costly/.

[2] An example of a tree test is available on Optimal Workshop's Web site, www.optimalworkshop.com. They have named their tool Tree Jack.

[3] The observant reader may notice this manipulation of the formula will by default decrease all average success rates since it is a multiplication of percentage. It is possible to use another formula to scale it back, but I have left it out since the main point I wanted to make is that tasks should have different importance levels.

[4] http://www.nngroup.com/articles/flat-vs-deep-hierarchy/.

## Putting It All Together

Personas, use cases and good IA are the foundation of a good UX. There are many methods for evaluating the designs presented in the following chapters. All these methods will be successful if there are clear personas and use cases, however if that is not possible, there are still opportunities to improve the UX. You can use the methodologies for evaluation to collect more information about the personas and use cases, and then iterate that data back into your design.

# REFERENCE

Muller, Michael J., 1991. PICTIVE- an exploration in participatory design, In: Proceeding CHI '91 Proceedings of the SIGCHI Conference on Human Factors in Computing Systems. ACM, New York. ISBN 0-89791-383-3, pp. 225–231.

# BIBLIOGRAPHY

Bittner, K., Spence, I., 2002. Use Case Modeling. Addison-Wesley Longman Publishing Co., Boston, MA.

Carroll, J.M., 2000. Making Use: Scenario-Based Design of Human-Computer Interactions. MIT Press, Cambridge, MA. ISBN: 0-262-03279-1.

Cockburn, A., 2001. Writing Effective Use Cases. Addison-Wesley Longman Publishing Co., Inc., Boston, MA.

Cockburn, A., 2002. Use Cases, Ten Years Later. Alistair.cockburn.us.

Constantine, L., Lockwood, L., 1999. Software for Use: A Practical Guide to the Essential Models and Methods of Usage-Centered Design. ACM Press/Addison-Wesley Publishing Co., New York.

Cooper, A., 1999. The Inmates are Running the Asylum. Macmillan Publishing Co., Inc., Indianapolis, IN. ISBN: 0-672-31649-8.

Dillon, A., 2002. Information architecture in JASIST: just where did we come from? J. Am. Soc. Inf. Sci. Technol. 53 (10), 821–823.

Grudin, J., Pruitt, J., 2002. Personas, participatory design and product development: an infrastructure for engagement. Paper Presented at Participatory Design Conference 2002, Malmo, Sweden.

Jacobson, I., Spence, I., Bittner, K., 2011. Use Case 2.0: The Guide to Succeeding with Use Cases. Technical report, Ivar Jacobson International, Sweden.

Miller, G.A., 1956. The magic number seven plus or minus two: some limits on our capacity to process information. Psychol. Rev. 63 (2), 81–97.

Pruitt, J., Adlin, T., 2006. The Persona Lifecycle: Keeping People in Mind Throughout Product Design. Morgan Kaufmann, San Fracisco, CA. ISBN: 0-12-566251-3.

Rosenfeld, L., Morville, P., 1998. Information Architecture for the World Wide Web, first ed. O'Reilly & Associates, Sebastopol, CA. ISBN: 0-596-52734-9.

Wurman, R.S., 2000. Information Anxiety, 2nd edition. Que, Indiana. ISBN 0789724103.

Wurman, R.S., 1997. Information Architects, first ed. Graphis Inc., New York. ISBN: 1-888-00138-0.

# Chapter 4

## THE STRATEGIC MODEL

This chapter explains the user experience (UX) strategic model through goal setting and alignment with UX best practice. The example is a case study for UX strategy on Medicare.gov.

# Chapter 4

However beautiful the strategy, you should occasionally look at the results.

**Winston Churchill**

## The Strategic Model

The success of any project depends on developing a good strategy, which is an overall master game plan for a project. It includes defining high-level goals and then mapping out the smaller steps that help get the project to its goal.

Defining a successful path is not easy, some companies just want to put one foot in front of the other, and others need a 5-year plan. Add the big picture first, and then create actionable steps, to focus on the task. Big and little steps together can help build one strategic model. The strategy only works if there are tactics, with specific roadmaps to help get you there. Even in the best situations, design and development get sidetracked and stalled by unforeseen events. If the project has a clear model of strategy and tactics, then the team can more quickly recover from problems and distractions and keep focused on the goals.

Projects often have several goals and conditions of uncertainty, and a strategic model helps the project moving in a forward direction.

User experience (UX) design projects are notorious for having many conditions of uncertainty including:

- Unclear or conflicting goals;
- Team members with different agendas;
- Different ways of measuring success;
- Different team members' understanding of the role of UX.

In order to resolve conflicting goals it is helpful to think ahead and be strategic about solving the problems that are contentious.

One way to think ahead, and align goals is to develop a strategy that is inclusive of all goals, to the extent possible. It is useful to look at how the goals might fit together, or come into conflict. Developing a matrix of dependencies between the goals can create strategic models that prioritize the specific tactics for the best outcome. The motivation to create a strategic model is to ensure the product, technology, or service is:

- Meeting the needs of all users;
- Creating confidence in the information presented on the Web site/product and in the social media channels;
- Encouraging product developers/marketing teams and consumers to utilize the information to improve the process, product, service, or technology.

The field of UX has evolved several methodologies and processes for innovation and development. To implement a relevant strategy, it is necessary to build a model that includes goals, strategies, and specific tactics to achieve those goals.

## Technology Driven vs. Market Driven

Product development can take several different paths, depending on the organization that is developing the product. Some companies are driven by what they can invent, while others are driven by what they can sell. The value of UX is not a primary driver in either of these approaches. However, there are parts of each that can be incorporated into successful UX practices.

Technology Driven

Many innovative products are "technology driven." The term "technology driven" can be defined as "Management philosophy that pushes for development of new goods or services based on firm's technical abilities instead of proven demand: to make keys first and then look for locks to open. Practically every breakthrough innovation is based on a technology driven orientation" (Businessdictionary.com).

A company can be a technology company—one that sells products and services that involve technology. However, this does not necessarily mean that the company is technology driven, especially if it focuses on the UX. A company, such as Apple, could be selling technology, but still put the user or customer at the heart of the product, thus creating a strong UX. This makes Apple a UX-driven company.

At first glance in the early 1900s, Eastman Kodak Company was a technology company. Their focus was selling new technology, packaged and put together so that the average consumer could use it. However, the focus was on the person, the human who would use the technology. Therefore, the company was not technology driven, so much as being user centric. George Eastman focused on what the UX was—how could users take snapshots, and use sophisticated technology—even though they were not experts in the field of photography.

## Market Driven

Many good business strategies come from focusing on what products can be sold to the market. Many successful companies use market-driven strategies, which can be defined as strategies focusing on creating products their consumers will buy, basing its product development on market forces.

Market-driven technology means that what and how much people want to buy control the product development. In essence, the market is driving the technology development. The downside of this kind of process is one called Market Creation, whereby the products that are produced drive the market. A good example of that is mobile phone service. The market incorporates planned obsolescence, following a product lifecycle that creates a need for a new device, with new features, every few years. The positive side is the production of products that provide life-saving and life-changing services. An example of that is the communication provided by mobile phones, allowing for more connection between people than ever before, making the world smaller.

Sometimes this means that the company focuses on their customer, but often with the point of view of selling. This means that when the market research is done, the company looks at what products and features customers want.

The approach becomes, "What can we sell?" Sometimes that means the company looks to help solve customer problems, and innovate with the customer needs at the forefront. More often, the focus of product development in the market-driven company looks to answer the question, "What kinds of delight can we create?"

This approach differs from user-centered design because it measures results mainly by market share, not customer satisfaction.

Sound strategy starts with having the right goal.

**Michael Porter**

## UX Strategy for the Long Haul

This model and this book apply to all products/services/technologies, not just Web sites. Certainly, there are specific issues to be addressed for certain platforms. Even though web-based systems are a bit different than mobile devices, medical devices, and other hardware-based technologies, they can all benefit from the same UX strategy and its emphasis on iteration (Figure 4.1):

1. Ideate: come up with the design;
2. Collect data: find out what works and what does not;

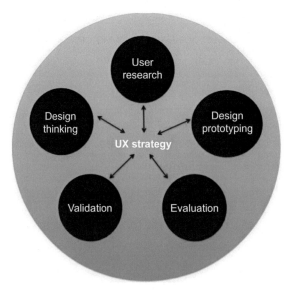

Figure 4.1 UX strategy.

3. Assess, evaluate, analyze;
4. Re-idea: integrate the data and findings to make the design better.

The plan for building a strategic model is both simple and complex. It appears simple, since it looks like a straightforward mapping of goals to tactics. The complexity comes into play when this model integrates business goals with user and product goals. The model creates a matrix that represents best practices. This does introduce some complexity, because the relationship between goals and tactics works on many levels.

## Building the Model

To ensure success, a project, person or team, must set clear goals with explicit metrics to measure completion. Without measurement there is no way to recognize success. Conditions often surface with numerous conflicting issues: for example one team member's goal may be to achieve record sales for the product, or to produce numerous patents, while the UX professional's goal is primarily to serve the users. Each one will measure success differently: the developer could be measured by the number of patents secured; the marketing person could be measured by how much product they sell; and the UX professional may be measured by a reduction in calls to customer support. These goals could certainly conflict. A developer, who is only concerned with patents, will spend most of their time looking to invent new and interesting things, regardless of how useful these things may be to the user. The marketing person could think that as long as they sell product, they don't have to worry about whether people can use it right away.

UX projects are no different than other projects, except that the goals are often more complicated. It is not just one person or even one team, which needs to be considered. In the case of UX projects, success is defined when others are successful.

Are the developers able to code and build a good UX? If they can, users will be more productive and satisfied. If users are happier, then they will probably recommend the product to others and will buy more of the product. This, of course, will make the marketing folks happier, which makes everyone happy. Each member of the team needs to works hand-in-hand with the other members.

**Setting Goals**

Identifying different types of goal helps to sort the priorities and determine the best tactics and tools to reach those goals. There are three types of goals in building UX strategic models: product goals, business goals, and user goals. For each category, there are long-term, short-term, and even intermediate goals. While this might sound complex, it does provide a taxonomy, whose classification keeps the project defined and on target, insures that the right issues are constantly addressed, and keeps the focus in the right place.

Below are some examples of goals.

**Product Goals**
- Empower users to make decisions;
- Provide relevant information to users when they need it.

**Business Goals**
- High profit margin for the company;
- High market share for the product;
- Create smaller wins, such as pleasing customers, hand holding to solve their problems.

**UX Goals**
- Provide consumers with information they need, when they need it;
- Deliver important information no more than two clicks away.

In order for a strategy to be effective it must achieve the goals of the various stakeholders. Business goals are often part of a value proposition. Product goals are often features or functions of the product.

## Aligning Goals

Creating personas and use cases sets UX goals. A Persona will describe a user in terms of their specific characteristics, needs and goals. A use case will describe the functions and processes needed to accomplish persona goals. The use case will also define how the system interacts with the user. The use case helps connect product goals to UX goals.

One of the most important steps is the creation of these agreed upon assumptions about the product or project as the basis for the strategic plan development. This can be accomplished by writing out the clearly stated and agreed upon goals so that anyone can access them. This includes aligning goals with outcomes, for example:

- Information provided in our product will help many people live healthier lives.

In order to achieve the goals for the product or service, the strategic plan incorporates two different areas for evaluating and iteration. Using a general Web site as an example, we can set the following basic strategy:

1. Awareness Strategy:
   - Creating knowledge of the Web site online and offline;
2. Usability Strategy:
   - Ensuring the Web site meets the needs of users.

Goals can then be broken down into long term and short term. This helps create a roadmap. The first step is to define the long-term goals. What is the product or service trying to achieve. Then define the Intermediate Goals, the steps and milestones that tell the team whether they are achieving the long-term goals. This is illustrated in Figure 4.2.

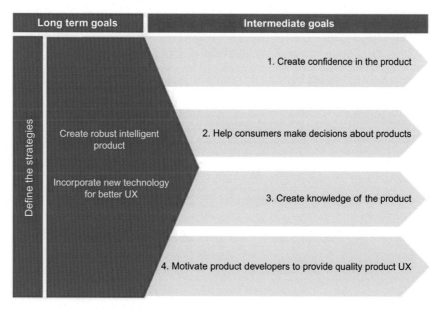

Figure 4.2 Strategic model.

## Meeting Goals

Once the goals are set, the next step is to identify the tools and methodology that the strategic model will incorporate. These are the specific tactics that help achieve the long-term goals. The tactics can be specified more clearly by first creating personas and use cases for the product or service. This next step in the strategic model building creates a matrix to map the persona and the intermediate goals.

Use cases, combined with persona development provide a narrative for the product/service, which fill in the gaps in the matrix (Figure 4.3).

This narrative creates the "who, what, when, and where" that become the milepost of the product lifecycle. The model that is developed from this narrative creates roadmaps. The who is the persona, the what, when, and where are specified in the use case.

---

### EXAMPLE Intermediate goals by user group/audience

In order to meet the high level strategic goal of improving the overall quality of nursing homes, the following intermediate goals need to be met based on the target user group/audience:

| User groups and intermediate strategic golas | | | |
|---|---|---|---|
| **Goal** | **Consumers** | **Advocacy groups** | **Marketplace** |
| 1. Create confidence in the product | ✓ | ✓ | ✓ |
| 2. Help consumers make decisions using the our rating system | ✓ | ✓ | |
| 3. Create knowledge of the rating system among consumers | | ✓ | ✓ |
| 4. Motivate product developers to provide quality product UX | | ✓ | ✓ |

---

Figure 4.3 Intermediate goals.

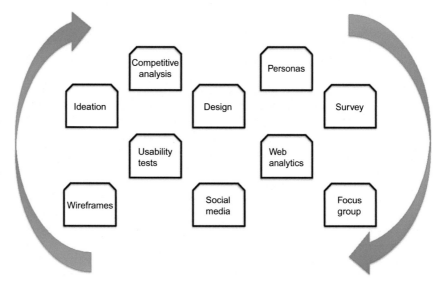

Figure 4.4 Iterative UX tools.

In order to meet the high level strategic goal of improving the overall quality of the Web site, the following intermediate goals need to be met, based on the specific user group/audience.

- When do we use what—or does it matter?
  - Product lifecycles: why it matters;
  - Understanding the process of product development;
  - Living with constraints: understanding what can be done when the resources are limited;
  - Matching goals to metrics;
  - Measuring success (Figure 4.4).

# Using Available Tools and Methodologies

## Benchmarks and Deliverables

In order to build a comprehensive roadmap, specific tools, benchmarks, and deliverables are identified. This includes a comprehensive review of the goals and

**EXAMPLE** Intermediate goals by tools

| Tools and intermediate strategic goals | | | | | | | |
|---|---|---|---|---|---|---|---|
| Competitive analysis | Expert review | Focus groups | Usability testing | Surveys | Web analytics | Social media | Personas |
| **1. Create confidence in the product** | | ✓ | ✓ | ✓ | ✓ | ✓ | ✓ |
| **2. Help consumers make decisions using the our rating system** | | ✓ | ✓ | ✓ | | ✓ | ✓ |
| **3. Create knowledge of the rating system among consumers** | ✓ | | ✓ | ✓ | ✓ | | ✓ | ✓ |
| **4. Motivate product developers to provide quality product UX** | ✓ | | ✓ | ✓ | ✓ | | ✓ | ✓ |

Figure 4.5 Intermediate goals by tools matrix.

metrics for measuring success. A more detailed goal matrix is then built by mapping the tools and methodologies to the intermediate goals. This will provide information about the gaps, and point to areas where there are more data needed to make informed UX design recommendations (Figure 4.5).

# Building Strategic Models for Medicare.gov by Elizabeth Rosenzweig

The government of the United States of America, through the Center for Medicare and Medicaid Services (CMS) maintains a Web site that is a central portal for Medicare services and information at Medicare.gov. On this site there are several tools for people to use to find and compare healthcare providers, hospitals, nursing homes, and more. The case study focuses on the project to redesign the Nursing Home Compare (NHC) tool.

Bentley Universities User Experience Center (UXC) worked with the CMS and other vendors as part of the development of the NHC tool. The tool is a simple one. It allows users find and compare nursing homes in any geographical region in the United States.

In order to better understand NHC, let's start with CMS. The United States Department of Health and Human Services runs CMS. The CMS.gov Web site provides online services, as well as information and links to other important health-related Web sites. In addition to providing services, CMS has been tasked with improving the quality of care helping to bring down the costs of healthcare. This means that CMS also focuses on program integrity, innovations in healthcare as well as the establishment of Affordable Insurance Marketplaces.

CMS have four primary goals:

- Goal 1: Better Care and Lower Costs;
- Goal 2: Prevention and Population Health;
- Goal 3: Expanded Health Care Coverage;
- Goal 4: Enterprise Excellence.

CMS runs Medicare.gov, the Web site that is the focus of this case study. The UX work on Medicare.gov focused on the CMS Strategic Objective, correlated with Goal 1: Better Care and Lower Costs:

- Reduces harm, improve mortality rates;
- Promotes best practices;
- Focuses on individual and families, employees, and government.

Medicare.gov has several tools to find and compare doctors, hospitals, nursing homes, and more. The NHC tool was a model for the other tools, so that improvements made to NHC could be applied to the other tools on the Web site.

The quality ratings are calculated in a 5-star rating system that culled data collected by nursing home inspectors. The measures include specifics like overall quality, inspection results (including a full report), complaints, and staffing ratio, as well as recent penalties. This is displayed in a tabbed screen system that has become easier to read as we iterated through our design and test cycles. This 5-star rating system, the most important piece of the tool, was not even used because the users were unable to arrive at the final search list.

During 2011, Abt Associates with CMS contacted Bentley Design and Usability Center (now User Experience Center—UXC) to do a simple Expert Review on the NHC tool on Medicare.gov. A standard usability test evolved, to include high-level strategic models, competitive analysis, Expert Reviews. Usability tests, focus groups, interviews for persona development online surveys, Web analytics and social media coordination.

What started as a simple Expert Review evolved, through the building of a strategic model, into ongoing work that is reviewed at least once a year. The factors for the Expert Review included: competitive analysis, user field studies, use case and persona development, usability testing (desktop and mobile device), focus groups, online surveys, environmental scans, Web analytics, and social media.

## Expert Review

The use case story starts with an Expert Review on the original version of NHC, which was considered a legacy compare tool for Medicare.gov. The tool is called NHC and is a model for all the compare tools on Medicare.gov. The legacy system included a 7-click process to get a basic list of nursing homes.

The Expert Review team from Bentley UXC walked through basic tasks on NHC, such as finding and comparing nursing homes and used UX best practices to determine whether NHC was providing the best experience for the intended user.

The Expert Review seemed easy; it took the user too many clicks to find a single nursing home. When the user did find a suitable nursing home, it was too hard to get to the real information about it. NHC searches a database that is created by CMS; the resultant list displays the nursing homes and their related quality data.

The Expert Review included simple recommendations such as "put the call to action front and center on the tool's homepage, and reduce the number of click for displaying the search results." A prototype was developed, based on the recommendations from the Expert Review.

Usability Test

The next step for the prototype was to test it with actual users. A usability test was planned, putting nine users in front of the tool, and having them perform the same tasks, finding and comparing nursing homes. This usability test was run on the new prototype, with nine participants for 90 min using the walkthrough tasks for finding a nursing home, and choosing three from the search results display to compare.

## Competitive Analysis

After the results of the Expert Review were delivered, the team immediately acted on the recommendations and produced a new prototype of the NHC tool.

While CMS was redesigning the NHC based on the results of the Expert Review, the Bentley team did a simple Web search to find other Web sites that were using the 5-star rating system for nursing homes. The motivation for competitive analysis was to discover whether other Web sites were using the data from the 5-star rating system. At the outset, the expectation from all team members was that there was a low occurrence of other Web sites using the 5-star rating system. The research showed that in fact, several sites were using it, sometimes crediting CMS and sometimes not. This was important information for CMS because the integrity of their data was the foremost concern; if the data were being used incorrectly, it could harm the data integrity. The result of the competitive analysis was the impetus to create a more detailed strategic model with specific roadmaps.

## User Field Studies, Use Case, and Persona Development

Field studies were administered in various modes, to better understand how users might want to access the 5-star rating system data, as well as other information about nursing homes, such as location. This work included field interviews, use case, and persona development.

The UXC team ran several interviews with professionals who either advised clients on choosing a nursing home, helped choose a nursing home for someone else, or provided services. The result was seven personas, listed below which were used in the strategic model to help correlate goals to methodologies:

- Primary Care Giver;
- Secondary Care Givers;
- Self;
- Nursing Home Provider;
- Eldercare Attorney;
- Geriatric Care Manager;
- Healthcare Researcher.

This deliverable provided important information to CMS in planning the focus of the compare tools. Understanding the nuanced difference between primary and secondary caregiver was important since they need similar, but not exactly the same information.

## Focus Groups

As part of the field studies, UXC team members ran focus groups at a conference for providers. While this supplied important data to help build the foundation for the strategic model, it also became difficult to recruit as less people showed up than were confirmed. Even so, this difficulty helped make the case for more field studies; these were integrated into the strategic mode.

## Usability Test on Responsive Design

The project worked on several levels simultaneously. While one team of UX professionals was running focus groups, the other was building the strategic model. At the same time, the CMS development team was building a responsive Web site for NHC. When the development team recommended a test for the new design, the UXC team designed a 9-subject usability test for the new prototype. Since the new site had to be responsive, the usability test was performed on two platforms—a desktop computer and an iPhone.

At this point the strategic model included the persona and use case development. These findings showed that some users would possibly access NHC on their smart phone, either at a doctor's office or hospital; they would urgently need to find a facility for their family member. While the hospital might have some caseworkers to help some patients with moving the family member to the new facility, it often fell to a family member. As a result, many used a smart phone to make these arrangements. This information was integrated into the test protocol for the responsive usability test.

Many other important issues were addressed and were included in the next iteration of the design.

## Online Survey

CMS runs a regular survey to users on Medicare.gov. Since the strategic model for NHC included online surveys, the UXC team worked directly with CMS to include the UX questions in the next round of the survey. These data were helpful both for validation that the functionality was working and was usable; it also provided new insights into the users' expectations and unmet needs.

## Environmental Scan

This scan is used in several business strategic models. It is similar to, but not exactly the same as, competitive analysis, which often measures marketing, issues like the product's uniqueness and its comparison to existing products in the marketplace. Environmental scans look at the bigger picture, either the entire industry or a single piece of technology; it takes into account political, social, economic, and micro environmental data to assess the influence of a product, technology, or service.

## Web Analytics

A review of data from Google analytics showed that the user visits were more efficient—with more users visiting, spending more time per page, and hitting fewer pages; this indicator measured if the information retrieval required fewer or more clicks for each finding.

## Social Media

After performing the environmental scan and the Web analytics, the team decided to include any data available on social media channels. Although CMS did have staff responsible for the messaging on social media, there were inadequate resources to closely monitor what was written on social media about their different programs. The UXC team recorded what Twitter, Facebook, LinkedIn, YouTube, and Google + messages referred to nursing home in relation to CMS. The most surprising discovery was a YouTube video series by a single consultant. This professional had posted several videos describing the improvements that were made in the most recent revision of the NHC tool. Several other professionals and consulting groups also started posting videos, tweets, and information on LinkedIn about the success of the NHC tool. This e data reported to CMS resulted in continued support for the UX strategic model.

Setting Goals

In order to create a successful UX strategic model for NHC, it was important to understand the goals that Health and Human Services (HHS) set for CMS. The business goals for CMS were how HHS measured success. Therefore, matching goals for NHC to Medicare.gov, which mapped to CMS.gov. All these government Web sites are connected and the strategy had to include a basic understand of the context in which NHC functionality was placed. It turns out that the UX strategic model work became integral piece of work that pulled together everyone's priorities, in a simple actionable model (Figures 4.6–4.10).

**Intermediate goals by user group/ audience**

In order to meet the high level strategic goal of improving the overall quality of nursing homes, the following intermediate goals need to be met based on the target user group/audience:

| User groups and intermediate strategic goals | | | | |
|---|---|---|---|---|
| Goal | Consumers | Advocacy groups | Providers | Marketplace |
| 1. Create confidence in the 5-star quality rating system | ✓ | ✓ | ✓ | ✓ |
| 2. Help consumers make decision using the 5-star quality rating system | ✓ | ✓ | | |
| 3. Communicate the impact of the 5-star quality rating system | | ✓ | ✓ | ✓ |
| 4. Create knowledge of the rating system among nursing home providers | | ✓ | ✓ | |

Figure 4.6 Intermediate goals grouped by persona.

| Goal | Consumers | Advocacy groups | Providers | Marketplace |
|---|---|---|---|---|
| 5. Motivate nursing homes to provide better care to residents | | ✓ | ✓ | ✓ |
| 6. Encourage the market to use the 5-star quality rating system | | ✓ | | ✓ |
| 7. Assist consumers in finding nursing home information | ✓ | ✓ | | ✓ |
| 8. Help consumers find and compare nursing homes | ✓ | ✓ | | ✓ |

Figure 4.7 Intermediate goals groups by persona 2.

### Tools

The following tools were used to collect information about NHC and the 5-star quality rating system; the information collected provides the foundation for the strategic plan.

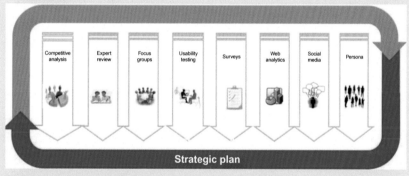

Figure 4.8 Strategic plan tools.

## Evolution of the Strategic Model

This evolution included direct links to CMS Strategy, which connected to the HHS strategic plan. The Bentley team revised the plan continually. UXC team reviewed the goals set by CMS and that alignment was ultimately reviewed by US GAO—Us Government Accountability Office—who in turn used this as a model for the CMS Web site.

## Intermediate goals by tools

| | Tools and intermediate strategic goals | | | | | | | |
|---|---|---|---|---|---|---|---|---|
| | Competitive analysis | Expert review | Focus groups | Usability testing | Surveys | Web analytics | Social media | Personas |
| 1. Create confidence in the 5-star quality rating system | | ✓ | ✓ | ✓ | | | | ✓ |
| 2. Help consumers make decisions using the 5-star quality rating system | | | ✓ | ✓ | ✓ | | ✓ | ✓ |
| 3. Communicate the impact of the 5-star quality rating system | | ✓ | ✓ | ✓ | | | ✓ | ✓ |
| 4. Create knowledge of the rating system among nursing home providers | | ✓ | ✓ | ✓ | | | | ✓ |

Figure 4.9 Intermediate goals and tools.

Success

The CMS and NHC strategic model are closely linked. Other compare tools, such as Hospital Compare, are being modeled after NHC. The strategic plan of CMS matches the UX strategic model for NHC. The work has support from several levels of the government.

Lesson Learned

Clear discussion and presentation of data are key, especially with a government project. Patience is necessary when dealing with administrative paperwork and processes. This could take a long time to administer but once complete, the process often runs smoother than lean projects. Lean projects are great for teams that have limited time and budget. NHC did not

**Intermediate goals by tools, contd.**

| Tools and intermediate strategic goals | | | | | | | |
|---|---|---|---|---|---|---|---|
| Competitive analysis | Expert review | Focus groups | usability testing | Surveys | Web analytics | Social media | Personas |
| 5. Motivate nursing homes to provide better care to residents | | ✓ | ✓ | ✓ | | | ✓ |
| 6. Encourage the market to use the 5-star quality rating system | | ✓ | ✓ | ✓ | ✓ | ✓ | ✓ |
| 7. Assist consumers in finding nursing home information | ✓ | ✓ | ✓ | ✓ | ✓ | ✓ | ✓ | ✓ |
| 8. Help consumers find and compare nursing homes | ✓ | ✓ | ✓ | ✓ | ✓ | ✓ | ✓ | ✓ |

Figure 4.10 Intermediate goals and tools 2.

need to run in a lean fashion, since they had time and enough resources to run usability tests and produce reports, whose findings and recommendations were reviewed by teams from other compare tools on Medicare.gov. In this case, UX reports, such as usability tests, competitive analysis and focus groups, provided a body of information for many teams from Medicare.gov to incorporate into their projects.

Takeaway

Although the first screen is simple, overall, NHC is a complicated tool, only because it lives on Medicare.gov and is part of the strategic plan for Medicare and, therefore, must link to many other sites, as well as manage and display lots of data. NHC is a model for all the other compare tools on Medicare.gov.

As a result, the UX work becomes central to the process and success, not only for NHC, but also for Medicare.gov. This case study shows that long-range thinking and perseverance pays off. Thinking through the larger picture from the outset helps with every small step and always leads to a better process. The UX strategic model included specific roadmaps that helped both the development team and the larger organization (CMS) bring a better experience to the users. The results are better quality of care and better quality of life for the patient. This brings peace of mind the NHC users, who are most often the patients' family members. UX is making the world a better place.

# BIBLIOGRAPHY

Baker, M.J., Hart, S.J., 2007. Product Strategy and Management, illustrated ed. FT Prentice Hall, Upper Saddle River, NJ. ISBN: 978-0273694502.

Day, G.S., 1994. The Capabilities of Market-Driven Organizations. J. Mark. 58 (4), 37–52.

Lockwood, T., 2009. Design Thinking: Integrating Innovation, Customer Experience and Brand Value, third ed. Skyhorse Publishing, New York. ISBN: 1581156685.

# Chapter 5

## BEYOND MOBILE, DEVICE AGNOSTIC UX

This chapter describes UX as being independent from any specific device, and reviews what is common and important from device to device, including responsive web design. Mobile UX issues are discussed including two real-world examples of mobile UX research.

# Chapter 5

Never trust a computer you can't throw out a window.

**Steve Wozniak**

## Device Agnostic UX

Ivan Sutherland's Sketchpad, which came out in 1963, introduced the first graphical user interface (GUI), which allowed people to interact with computing devices. The GUI made it possible for a person and computer to communicate with code, through graphics on the screen. This was done with input from a hardware-pointing device in combination with a keyboard (Figure 5.1).

The first GUI and pointing devices laid the groundwork for the more natural interfaces such as gesture and speech that we see on products and systems today. While these interaction modalities still have not evolved to their full potential, many products and services are now employing them to create a more successful user experience (UX). As computing power has evolved into smaller more powerful devices, these natural interaction modalities need to be evolved to create the most successful UX.

### Beyond WIMP

The Window Icons, Menu, Pointing device (WIMP) system has been around since the Sutherland's Sketchpad; it evolved to the next level in the early 1980s, when the term was used as a feature for the XEROX Alto that was produced for research at Xerox PARC. Today, the WIMP interface is seen on most computing devices (Hinckley, 1996). Desktop computers still employ the traditional WIMP interfaces, while mobile touch screen devices use fingers as the pointer.

Figure 5.1 Ivan Sutherland and Sketchpad.

Mobile devices such as smart phones and tablets combine all the functionality of a desktop computer, but with a smaller touch screen. This new technology has prompted the innovation of new interaction technologies that allow people to use modes that are more similar to human-to-human than human-to-computer interaction. Examples of these modes of interaction are voice and face recognition as well as natural language processing (NLP). These modalities are still at an early stage in development, and success will be achieved through paying proper attention to the user when developing the products and systems, thus creating interfaces that will more closely resemble human-to-human communication. If these new interaction modalities are successful they will create a more ubiquitous and easier-to-use computing environment.

Even the most powerful computer can only process interactions as fast as its input allows. In other words, the means and modality of interaction create both the ability to interact and constraints. Therefore, not all interactive modalities will work for everyone. One of the reasons for this is that people process information differently; some digest information visually, so graphics are helpful, while other can digest information in a more linear fashion, so words and numbers work better.

Combine this human complexity with computers that still don't understand the nuances of spoken words, tones of voice or subtle gestures, and it is easy to create a less then optimal system. The solution to getting beyond WIMP and creating a more natural interface will be through user-centered design evolution. Improving the natural gestures allowed to communicate with the device will make computing devices more flexible, thus providing better and more natural modalities for people.

Technology push will create powerful computing. Market push will create nicer looking products, with better form factor. User-centered design will lead the way for both, to enable the technology and market to bring their strengths together in innovation. The whole will be greater than the sum of the parts.

## Form Factors

The word "Form" has different meanings depending on the context. Form as part of a UX refers to the physical dimension and components of the object. Form factors are pieces that make up the experience in relation to how it feels when a person uses it. For example, the size and shape of a smart phone has a huge impact on how it is used. If it is too big and/or too heavy, a person's hand, neck, ear, or shoulder might be tired after talking for only a few minutes. The physical features need to allow the phone to be comfortable to hold while it is in use, as well as being easy and comfortable to use when taking a picture or a video.

Now that computers have become smaller, and hand-held devices can communicate, take pictures and video, and share them in real time, the form factor becomes a critical aspect to creating a good experience for the user.

The key to success is to mimic the human-to-human interaction. If a device can make a person think the interaction is natural, then it will be more successful than if a person is always struggling. That might seem obvious to the reader, but many developers and marketing professionals do not consider this as part of their own strategy.

> The best way to predict the future is to invent it.
>
> **Alan Kay**

# Successful UX for Mobile

UX design methodologies have evolved to include and often prioritize the UX of mobile devices over desktop environments. Mobile devices are becoming ubiquitous and developers often innovate by starting with the mobile experience. While there is merit in designing first for the smaller screens and more common use cases, there is also a risk of creating designs that become too narrow. Sometimes this creates a dumbing down of a device, so that functions become hidden and the user journey becomes long and choppy. The key is to keep the functionality and create a good UX for the person, on whatever device that they happen to be using at that time.

Responsive web design (RWD) is another approach to designing Web sites for both the desktop and mobile device. The design essentially responds to the screen of the device it is on, or if it is on a desktop, it will respond to the size of the window in which it is being displayed. RWD has a lot of advantages and helps users feel familiar with Web sites that they visit on both their desktop and on a mobile device.

Mobile First is a strategy that many companies are using now. This has come to mean that they design their software first for the mobile device and then for the desktop. While that has merits for the mobile users, it also runs the risk of hiding more complex operations and information under nicely designed visual layers.

Mobile applications can create their own separate UX, but the person can start to lose track of their key goals if there are too many interfaces for them to remember.

At what point will the smart mobile device contain too many separate apps to be useful? Research needs to be done to create an intelligent system to integrate the applications so that they could be personalized to provide more easy access for the user to the apps they use the most. A good development team, putting the user at the center with good UX methods and processes, could solve those problems, but it is more likely that technology and market drivers will shape the direction of mobile device development.

Design for mobile needs to incorporate the use cases from the desktop's WIMP interface into the real world, using the technologies like natural language processors and voice recognition, and gestures.

The balance still must be maintained between natural interactions and using all the functions we have available.

## Context of Use

Where the device gets used—not just how, but in what context—can inform how the device should interact with the senses.

### Modes of Interaction

People digest information and are comfortable interacting in many different ways. It is helpful to understand this when developing successful UX. A good way to accommodate the use of different modalities of interaction is to incorporate interactions with a combination of senses. Of the following senses, interaction with only the first four is currently available through technology, while the final two would be interesting to develop:

- Vision: uses the visual stimulus of people, places, and things;
- Hearing: provides information and stimulates our senses with sounds, voices, and music;
- Touch: allows command and control of the world with our fingers;

- Kinesthetic: provides information through the sense of movement;
- Smell: is used in products, although not generally in technology;
- Taste: is the least used modality for technology or products other than food.

The most commonly used sense is vision. The visual interfaces include words, images, moving pictures, and graphics, all of which are used to provide information and entertainment, and enable interaction with technologies.

Mobile devices have brought gesture interface to the forefront, while creating a multimodal experience that includes touch, vision, speech, and sound.

## Testing Mobile

The following case studies are two examples of device agnostic interfaces.

The first is part of the UX Strategic Model that was developed for the US Center for Medicare and Medicaid's Nursing Home Compare (NHC) tool on Medicare.gov.

## Responsive Design test of Nursing Home Compare

Elizabeth Rosenzweig

During December 2012, Medicare.gov had been working on a RWD for the Web site (Figure 5.2).

As part of their UX Strategic Model, the Medicare.gov team planned a usability test on the responsive design prototype at the Bentley User Experience Center.

The UX Strategic Model had included extensive work on user persona and use cases. This work showed that people often needed to use the NHC tool on a mobile device when they were with a relative either at a doctor's office or a hospital, and had to find nursing care immediately. The original Web site

Figure 5.2 Medicare.gov.

design was almost impossible to use on a mobile device, so a responsive design was a logical next step (Figure 5.3).

The usability test, therefore, examined several issues including whether:

- a user could find the information they needed on both the desktop and a smart phone;
- responsive design on the smart phone was organized correctly;

Figure 5.3  Medicare.gov NHC responsive design desktop.

- the user could navigate the mobile interface and find that needed information;
- the user understood the content on the Web site;
- the responsive design actually did have any effect on the user's ability to find the content they needed on the Web site accessed via the mobile device.

The test was run at the usability labs with nine participants in a standard lab setting using the think aloud protocol. Users were asked to do the following tasks first on the desktop and then on the mobile prototype. The reason this order was chosen, and not a randomized one, was the assumption that the desktop search would yield the information the user was seeking more easily and clearly, therefore making it possible for the user to know what they were actually looking for on the (at this point) more difficult mobile device's interface. The tasks they were asked to follow are listed below:

- Find a nursing home by location;
- Examine or view the list of results;
- View a map of the results;
- Select and compare nursing homes;
- Learn about a specific nursing home.

Despite the considerations that were put into the Moderator's Guide, the participants still experienced some confusion about the information presented on both the desktop and the mobile platforms (Figure 5.4).

With regard to the navigation, it was straightforward on the desktop platforms as expected (it had been designed, tested, and redesigned several times already), but there was some confusion on the mobile platform. The user could not always navigate to the relevant information on the mobile platform since it was hard to find within the long detailed lists.

Some specific issues on the smaller screens were:

- Lists with details were very long and required the user to scroll vertically for quite some time before they were able to find the information they were looking for.
- Phone numbers that were included in the long list were hard to read and capture.

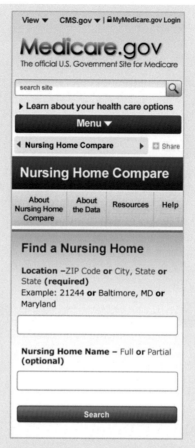

Figure 5.4 Medicare.gov NHC responsive design mobile platform.

- Sometimes there was so much information on the mobile screen that the user had to scroll horizontally, too, to see everything
- Comparing information in columns is hard to do on a mobile device.

## Outcome

The good news was the development team was interested in iterating the responsive design and making the site better for the user. The recommendations were integrated into the next release of the site design.

## Takeaway

Recommendations for responsive design Web sites that have large amounts of mission critical information can be applied to most responsive Web sites:

- *Make all phone number on Web site auto-dial on click.* This will save time for the person who is already under stress. By creating a more direct flow from task to task, the UX will become more seamless.
- *Make use of tools tips and contextual help.* Put information about labels and buttons into tool tips for all functions on the user interface.
- *Reduce number of choices for functions at the deeper menu levels.* If the design must drop down several levels in the menu structure, consider restructuring the information architecture or add clear simple action buttons on all menu levels.
- *Automatically update information on search results list.* This will reduce confusion during complex searches.
- *Don't overload columns.* If there is a lot of information that needs to be listed together in columns, break it down into chunks that can be more easily read.

This next case study describes a study of a device agnostic prototype, run on three devices.

# Mobile Usability Testing

Pete McNally

Abstract

This case study will highlight a usability test conducted in order to get feedback on a prototype of a retirement planning Web site. The client wanted to test the prototype on a three devices: desktop, smart phone, and tablet. The case study will focus on what was unique for the mobile aspects of the usability testing including planning, lab set up, recruiting, task selection, and issues identified. I will discuss what to consider when conducting mobile usability testing.

## Background

The client came to the User Experience Center at Bentley University in 2013 looking to gather feedback on a high-fidelity prototype of a Web site related to retirement planning. The prototype was developed using responsive design in order to work on a desktop PC, tablet, or smart phone. The client wanted to identify major issues across all three platforms and across two different user groups. We tested 15 participants over 3 days in our usability lab. Each session lasted 60 min (Figure 5.5).

## Overall Goals and Planning

We started out with a kick-off meeting to define usability testing goals, the project schedule, and the general approach for recruiting. We had a chance

Figure 5.5 Bentley user experience test lab: observation room monitors showing mobile device.

to view an early version of the prototype to be tested. The project duration from kick-off meeting to final report presentation took about 5 weeks. In general, this is our standard approach to usability testing, regardless of if a mobile is in the mix or not. However, participant recruiting took on more importance since we needed to understand how their experience with mobile devices would impact on recruitment.

## Recruiting

As part of the project scoping we agreed to test 15 participants over 3 days. However, we left the rest of the testing details to be worked out as we kicked-off the project. Since we needed to test the prototype on three different devices (desktop, tablet, and smart phone) we needed to determine if each participant would test on only one device or multiple during the 60 min session. Based on the number of tasks we decided to test each participant on only one device. The following table shows how we divided up the devices across the two user groups. Each device was tested with five participants (Figure 5.6).

Although the number of participants differed between profiles as well as across devices, we felt we had a good mix to get representative feedback. However, since we had an odd number of total participants, each user profile tested a bit differently across the devices however we felt this was a good mix to get representative feedback.

| 15 study participants | | | | |
|---|---|---|---|---|
| User profile | # Total participants | Desktop | Tablet | Phone |
| User profile 1 | 8 | 3 | 2 | 3 |
| User profile 2 | 7 | 2 | 3 | 2 |
| Total | 15 | 5 | 5 | 5 |

Figure 5.6 Study participants.

As is typical for the User Experience Center, we employed an external recruiter for finding and scheduling the participants. Working with our client, we developed a recruiting screener outlining the key criteria, e.g., age, income, occupation, domain experience, etc., and, in particular, if the participants had the appropriate experience using mobile devices. We tested with an iPhone and iPad. However, for the recruit, we did not restrict ourselves to only participants that had experience on Apple (iOS) devices. We felt since the interaction of the prototype to be tested was similar across mobile operating systems (i.e., iOS and Android), smart phone users could have experience with either an iPhone or Android phone. Tablet users could have experience with either an iPad or Android tablet.

In order for a participant to be a good fit for testing on a specific device, we required them to perform three or more tasks, on their own device, that were similar to what we would be testing.

To make sure we had participants that actually used their mobile devices to conduct similar tasks to what we would be testing, we added the following question to the recruiting screener as shown in Figure 5.7.

In order for a participant to be a good fit for testing on a device we required them to perform at least two of these listed tasks on that device. Most participants conducted more than two tasks on multiple devices. This was helpful as it gave the recruiter more flexibility in scheduling participants.

## Tasks

As with any kind of usability testing task, selection and wording of the task are critical for understanding the usability of the system. Working with our client we developed a moderator's guide with key scenario-based tasks. A question we discussed with the client was, *do the tasks apply to all devices or are their*

*Which of the following tasks do you currently perform on the internet? (**Read list**)*
*Note:  Ensure the recruit performs more than 2 tasks on a device (desktop/laptop, smart phone or tablet) for device scheduling.*

|  | Desktop/ laptop | Smart phone | Tablet |
|---|---|---|---|
| Use social media (Facebook, Twitter, etc.) |  |  |  |
| Pay bills |  |  |  |
| Check my investment values |  |  |  |
| Use online banking |  |  |  |
| Research online for large purchases (car, appliance, etc.) |  |  |  |
| Read newspaper online |  |  |  |
| Research mutual funds / stock investments, etc. |  |  |  |
| Make online purchases |  |  |  |

Figure 5.7 Participants device usage table.

*specific tasks that are more geared to the mobile devices?* We determined that all tasks in this case applied equally well across all devices.

However, this is a question to keep in mind in planning and moderating other systems to be tested, especially if the tasks for those systems require a lot of reading, data entry, or mental processing by the participant. For some scenarios, some participants may prefer to conduct a task on the desktop, even if they can successfully use the mobile device. On the other hand, other tasks may lend themselves more to a mobile device, such as getting directions to an office or store, etc. Ask participants in the session debrief if there might be specific instances in which they could see themselves using a mobile device even if their general preference might be in using a desktop.

## Lab Setup

We used our three-room-suite usability lab (http://www.bentley.edu/centers/ user-experience-center/facilities-and-technology/usability-labs) for the test.

The main part of the lab setup did not differ from a desktop-only usability test. The moderator sat with the participant in the participant room as they went through the tasks. A second team member sat in the control room and took notes and managed the recording equipment. Several client staff sat in the observation room and watched the sessions. We also streamed all sessions so additional client staff could observe remotely. In order to capture the screen of the mobile devices, we used Reflector software from Squirrels (http://www.airsquirrels.com/reflector/). Reflector allowed us to mirror the mobile device (iPhone and iPad) on a PC. We then used our standard recording process, i.e., Morae, to capture the mobile screen as we would a PC screen. Using software such as Recorder worked well; however, it did not indicate where the participant tapped or swiped on the screen. There are other methods to consider, for example, using overhead cameras or a Web camera mounted on a sled, which allows recording of tapping/swiping.

## Analysis and Report

After running the usability testing sessions we took several days to review our notes and analyze the data. As we always do regardless of devices tested, we were looking for trends and patterns within each user group and global findings across all user groups. We applied this same approach as we considered the three devices tested. We looked for issues that were present across all three devices and issues specific to each device. The majority (80%) of the issues were conceptual or related to content, and, therefore, seen on all devices. The remaining 20% of the issues were specific to mobile devices, mainly due to the smaller screen size (especially on the iPhone). Issues we encountered in this study, and other common mobile usability issues we have seen in other studies, will be discussed in "Key Takeaway" section. We produced a report in PowerPoint format.

## Key Takeaways When Testing with Mobile Devices

For UX professionals who are used to testing only on the desktop, mobile provides a few extra challenges, but overall the process is not much different. As you prepare for the next mobile usability test, keep the following in mind:

### Planning

- Given the popularity of responsive design, test on both mobile and desktop platforms. This ensures that you don't make recommendation that benefits the mobile user, but inadvertently penalizes the desktop user.
- Consider if each participant should only test on one device or each participant uses multiple devices. The goals of the usability test, number of tasks and duration of the test will impact this decision. If you have each participant test on multiple devices, counterbalance the order so as not to bias the results.
- Make sure you practice the transition between desktop/mobile, as this may introduce challenges to the lab set up, such as recording.

### Recruiting

- Make sure participants have the appropriate experience with mobile devices given the testing goals.
- Determine if you need to recruit for a specific mobile OS of device (iPhone vs. Android) or experience with any kind of mobile device is sufficient. The similarity or differences in interaction between different devices should guide you with this question.

### Lab Setup/Recording

- Consider which recording option works best for you. Both mirroring software and using cameras to capture the mobile screen are good choices, but each option has pros and cons such as showing finger movements.
- Test out the set-up beforehand thoroughly, especially if you are transitioning between devices during the same participant session.

## Tasks

- Consider which tasks are appropriate given the mobile context. If testing on both desktop and mobile, consider if it is best to test all tasks on (or "across") all platforms and devices.

- Be aware of tasks that require a lot of reading (scrolling) or data entry. If these are considered core tasks, test these on mobile devices. Even if most users may prefer to use the desktop for these tasks it is important to get feedback from users on mobile devices. Some users may find it necessary to perform these on their mobile device given the scenario.

- Make sure participants have to complete key data entry forms so the virtual keyboard is displayed.

- The virtual keyboard may hide important content and make it difficult to complete a form.

- If completion of tasks requires a very different interaction on a mobile device from a desktop, such as navigation, those tasks should be tested on mobile devices.

- If any content has to be truncated, e.g., menu names or not provided (e.g., definitions), on the mobile but are complete and available on the desktop, make sure the mobile experience is tested.

- Ask participants if there are tasks that they would prefer to conduct on one device over another. Are there tasks they would never or always conduct on one device over another in real life?

- Pay attention to how content displays in landscape vs. portrait mode. Let participants hold the device, such as a tablet, whichever way they want. Rather than handing them the device, place it on the table and let them pick it up and get orientated to it.

## Analysis and Report

- Determine if issues are specific to mobile, or common across all devices.

- If testing is done only on a mobile device, consider how your recommendations impact the desktop and tablet.

- Consider the following issues. These have been seen as particularly problematic for mobile:

  - Pay attention to long pages that require a lot of vertical scrolling. Are key pieces of information or links at the bottom of the page missed? Do participants even realize there is additional content all the way at the bottom of the page?

- Horizontal scrolling can be an issue. For example, consider any tables that are cut off and/or if the user must scroll to the right to see the information. Are there affordances to indicate there is more information available?

- Make sure menu interaction is fully tested on mobile devices as the information architecture may be displayed differently (e.g., more compactly using the "hamburger" menu) than on the desktop. Experienced mobile users should have no issue with "hamburger" menus (they look like an outline of a hamburger), however novices may not be familiar with it and not even realize it is there.

- Are affordances for tapping and swiping clear? In some cases, elements that designers think should be recognizable are not.

- Are buttons and other elements large enough? Elements copied directly from the desktop may be too small for the touch interaction.

- Are elements far enough apart? Selecting one element may negatively impact another if they are too close together.

- Is the default text too small? Is there a way for the user to enlarge the text size or zoom in?

# Where Is This Going?

Many computer scientists have predictions about the future and we all like to imagine the direction technology is going. In 1965, Gordon Moore, Intel Co-Founder, predicted that the number of transistors per square inch in integrated circuits would double every two years. This has come to be known as "Moore's Law" and is often interpreted to mean the power of computing is increasing at an extremely rapid rate. Now that the industry has evolved past transistors to semiconductors, the acceleration seen in the changes in hardware in terms of interactive capabilities is increasing even more quickly.

The speed of the evolution of computing is noteworthy; powerful mobile computing devices can now sit in our pockets, on our glasses, in our automobiles, and in our clothing. Speech and gesture interactions are replacing windows, icon, menus, and pointing devices. The real potential and power of computing will be reached when users can interact directly with their devices in a mode that feels natural.

Initial efforts are being made with wearable computing, such as Google Glass and Apple Watch. These technologies still need to evolve a bit more before they will become usable, and that is only a matter of time. The most successful computing devices will be agnostic; if the user interaction is natural, it won't matter if the screens are big and small, handheld or worn, success will be determined by the user's interaction with that device.

## REFERENCE

Hinckley, K., 1996. Haptic issues for virtual manipulation. Microsoft. The Windows-Icons-Menus-Pointer (WIMP) Interface Paradigm Dominates Modern Computing Systems (Retrieved December 14, 2011).

## BIBLIOGRAPHY

Hansmann, U., 2003. Pervasive Computing: The Mobile World. Springer, Germany. ISBN: 3-540-00218-9.

Hinckley, K., 2008. Input technologies and techniques. In: Sears, A., Jacko, J.A. (Eds.), Microsoft Research, Handbook of Human-Computer Interaction. Lawrence Erlbaum & Associates, New York, pp. 161–176.

Marcus, A., July + August 2013. The history of the future: Sci-Fi movies and HCI. Interactions 20, 64–67.

Markoff, J., February 16, 2009. The cellphone, navigating our lives. New York Times. http://www.nytimes.com/2009/02/17/science/17map.html?_r=0.

Moore, G.E., 1965. Cramming more components onto integrated circuits (PDF). Electron. Mag. 38, 4 (Retrieved November 11, 2006).

Robert, J.K., Jacob, A.G., Hirshfield, L.M., Horn, M.S., Shaer, O., Treacy Solovey, E., Zigelbaum, J., 2008. Reality-based interaction: a framework for post-WIMP interfaces. In: CHI '08: Proceedings of the SIGCHI Conference on Human Factors in Computing Systems.

Shedroff, N., Noessel, C., 2012. Make It So: Interaction Design Lessons from Science Fiction. Rosenfeld Media, Brooklyn, NY.

van Dam, A., 1997. Post-WIMP user interfaces. Commun. ACM 40 (2), 63–67.

Wroblewski, L., 2011. Mobile First Paperback. Inagram, Nashville, TN. ISBN: 1937557022.

# Chapter 6

## USABILITY INSPECTION METHODS

This chapter explains the different methods for usability evaluations, as well as the difference between empirical and straight inspection methods. Two case studies show real-world examples of two different types of expert reviews.

# Chapter 6

Computers are useless. They can only give you answers.

**Pablo Picasso**

## Usability Evaluations

Usability, as defined in Chapter 1, as the overall usefulness of an object/product. Can a person actually use it for something that they want?

Usability evaluations refer to any one of a set of methods allowing a user experience (UX) expert to evaluate the usability of a product or system in varying levels of detail.

Usability evaluations are often confused with usability, the holistic view in designing and evaluating systems for people overall. As described in earlier chapters, the terms usability, UX, and interaction are confused; given that the field is still evolving, this is not a surprise. Testing usability is the methodology, and not to be confused with the outcome of usable and useful objects. Evaluating usability and creating usable objects are all part of the development of a successful UX. In that way, usability and UX are the same, despite the confusion expressed in the current literature.

## What Can Be Evaluated?

Anything and everything can and should be evaluated, at least once before it comes into contact with a human being. There is no better way to create empathy with a user than watching them use the product. This brief list gives examples of the many items, which should be evaluated:

- Hardware;
- Software;

- Systems, applications, Web sites, Web applications;
- Documentation, quick reference guides, installation manuals, online help, tutorials, training materials, forms;
- Physical stores and venues;
- Packaging, "out of the box" experience;
- Final product or some sort of prototype;
- End-to-end customer experience and service design;
- Anything that you can walk through, read, or otherwise interact with.

With all these items to evaluate it might be hard to figure out which method is right for which situation. Usability evaluation methods fall in two broad categories: empirical and inspection:

- Empirical methods collect data by having a person use the product or service in various ways. This provides direct-use data collection.
- Inspection methods collect data by having an expert evaluate a product or service.

Inspection methods can be used early in the development process, perhaps before it is ready to be used by real users. One might use an empirical method when the system/product is functional and you have access to real users. Unmoderated testing and surveys are another way of collecting empirical data.

# Empirical Method

*Usability testing* (described in detail in Chapter 7). Usability testing produces data on how well a person understands and is able to use the product and how well the product matches the user's mental model of it. Evaluation is conducted by asking a user to interact with a product as they would intend to use it, and to provide feedback.

Usability testing usually involves the following:

- One-on-one moderated session;
- Tasks focused on real-world activities which strive to achieve real-world goals;

- The Think Aloud Protocol that involves the participant verbalizing their thoughts and literally saying everything that comes into their head while they are interacting with the technology.
- Remote testing is a modality that can be used to employ any of these methods. This provides a means to run a test when the session can take place online.

# Inspection Methods

*Expert reviews*. An expert evaluates the product; the user does not. This is the key difference from usability testing. Using their experience and training in the field, the expert searches for problems, stumbling blocks, and areas that will lead to confusion., In other words, anything that would frustrate the user and prevent them from accomplishing the goals that the expert assumes they require or expect the product to help them achieve.

The following are some of the methods the expert uses:

- Heuristic reviews: a holistic approach that looks at a system or product's components and measures them against usability best practice to produce ratings and recommendations.
- Cognitive walkthroughs: task-specific evaluations that start with specific case studies that break tasks down into specific steps. The evaluations walkthrough the steps, collecting data through task analysis.
- Pluralistic walkthroughs are often done as a group activity to evaluate and innovate. This is done with a group of people, either together for the first time or after each has had a chance to walkthrough the product individually.
- Some methods that are in this category are:
    - Participatory Design, which is done through collaboration of key project stakeholders, including end users to ensure that the end result meets the needs all. This method focuses on the process of interaction between a user and a system.
    - Storyboarding, which produces drawings and sketches of a user's journey through a system. These provide details about the user and the system.
    - Computer Supported Collaborative Work.

# Expert Reviews

*Expert reviews* involve evaluating designs against the established rules of design interaction, cognitive science, and human factors. This method has the benefit of uncovering basic problems. The risk with this method is that some product teams don't give this kind of feedback much value, since it does not come directly from a customer.

Here are some examples of sets of rules that consider both the overall design and each component of the object:

- Consistency;
- Clarity of design and layout;
- Clear call to action: user knows what they need to do;
- Effectiveness;
- Appropriate feedback to the user.

For a Web site, the heuristics against which the components might be measured include:

- Fonts, colors, and objects that are pleasing to the eye and do not distract or interfere with comprehension and/or accomplishing the goal;
- Easy to understand;
- Easy to use: information is in logical locations;
- Clear navigation through good information architecture.

The following case study describes how using UX heuristics can provide a solid methodology for evaluating an infotainment system in an automobile. It is important to note that the system is quite complex and had some UX requirements that could not be measured by standard heuristics. This case study illustrates how unique heuristic characteristics can be created to meet new types of user requirements.

# One Size Does Not Fit All

Rich Buttiglieri

Over the years I have conducted many heuristic reviews of products ranging from desktop software, to Web sites, Web applications, and consumer electronics. Heuristic reviews are a fast way to identify the basic design flaws and potential issues to be studied further in a usability test. We sometimes followed a heuristic review with a usability test to have greater focus on just the anticipated problem areas. This combination of conducting a heuristic review plus usability test can be an efficient way to identify design issues and their root causes while avoiding wasted time covering features and designs that aren't problematic. Other times we used heuristic reviews alone due to time or budget constraints that prevent us from running usability tests.

For some heuristic reviews, I would assemble a small team of non-stakeholders that had domain knowledge of the product, and ask each to systematically inspect every menu and every screen in order to catalog where the user interface violated Neilsen's design heuristics. When I didn't have access to subject-matter experts, but had detailed knowledge of the target end user, I used a different approach. In this situation, I assembled a team of user-experience researchers to emulate the target end user and attempted to conduct typical tasks with the product as they cataloged where the user interface violated Neilsen's design heuristics. In either case, we leveraged the general design heuristics as originally defined by Jacob Neilsen and Rolf Molich back in 1990:

- Esthetic and minimalist design;
- Consistency and standards;
- Error prevention;

- Help for users to recognize, diagnose, and recover from errors;
- Help and documentation;
- Flexibility and efficiency of use;
- Recognition rather than recall;
- Match between system and real world;
- User control and freedom;
- Visibility of system status.

These heuristics have stood the test of time, with minor tweaks and interpretations for the Web and mobile devices.

In 2007, portable GPS devices were very popular, but not well integrated into the vehicle's sound system. If your radio was loud, you didn't hear the voice command telling you to turn. Further, if your mobile phone rang, your radio and portable GPS were still at full volume. In the summer of 2007, a consumer electronics manufacturer asked me for a heuristic review of their in-vehicle infotainment system. I eagerly accepted the challenge and got to work assembling a team of user-experience researchers. We then met with the client to learn about the target user and their typical tasks as well as the features of this new infotainment system.

We learned that the target users were affluent males in their mid 50s, since this system was to be offered exclusively in high-end luxury sports cars. We also learned about the features of the system. It had the typical AM/FM/XM radio tuner, MP3 player adapter, and internal hard drive for music storage, Bluetooth phone connection, and a navigation system. It also had a TV tuner (only viewable while traveling less than 5 mph), a "panic" button that would switch a phone call from using the car's speakers (public) to the cell phone (private), and a motion sensor that would affect the display as the user reached for the dial to make adjustments. When the user's hand got close to the dial, the onscreen display would show extra details about the source (music, TV, phone, or navigation) as well as increase the font size. It gave the illusion that the head unit was anticipating your adjustments and adapting itself for optimal viewing.

With the stage set, we began our review, but quickly discovered that we needed to invent specific heuristics for this unique context of driving a car. Neilsen's design heuristics didn't cover design principles for situations when the user should not take their eyes off the road for too long or they would risk having an accident. For this situation, we invented the "Glance-ability" heuristic—a measure of how easy one can quickly interpret on screen status in a quick glance, day or night.

Also, the navigation system's turn-by-turn voice guidance must be properly timed so the driver doesn't pass the road before hearing the instruction to turn. So we invented another heuristic called "Timely instructions and natural voice cadence"—a heuristic describing that a system should be aware of its own functional limitations, such as the speed at which it can provide information to users and thereby prioritize messages. We discussed whether "error prevention" could be used to flag a driver's missed turn due to poor timing of the voice guidance, but we felt the spirit of that heuristic would catalog errors in commission ("I clicked the wrong thing"), and we needed to catalog errors in omission ("I didn't make the turn the system wanted me to").

Armed with these new custom design principles we were able to identify potential UX issues such as on-screen information overload for tasks that require a quick glance and slow turn-by-turn speech cadence allowing for missed turns. This approach has served me well to customize design heuristics to fit unique product contexts of use. Not everything fits into the Web or desktop software design context. For that reason, the research method to evaluate the UX of a product's design must be individually tailored to suit the needs of both the product team and the end user's context. If the product team is inaccessible then I make adjustments to the method to minimize dependence on their participation. If the product's context has unique characteristics, such as driving a car where distractions are a safety concern, then the best approach is to customize the method.

## Competitive Analysis Expert Review

Expert reviews can be used in many ways as part of a competitive assessment. Using expert reviews to evaluated competitive products provides rich data about their strong and weak aspects that should be considered in design.

The following case study is an expert review that is combined with a competitive analysis. It works well since it balances the goal of uncovering usability problems in the UX while also providing information about how the product measures up to its competitors.

## Grocery Shopping Expert Review and Competitive Analysis

Dorie Rosenberg

A Fortune 500 retailer approached AnswerLab to conduct a competitive analysis of its end-to-end online grocery buying experience. The client's grocery shopping experience was in its beta phase, and the organization was interested in understanding how they performed compared to competitors in categories of awareness, consideration, purchase, and delivery. The experience had been successfully rolled out in Europe and questions remained as to whether the American experience would face the same wins and areas for opportunity as its European counterparts.

## Research Objectives and Methodology

To understand how the retailer's grocery experience stacked up in the market, AnswerLab designed a task-based research study that included a review of the desktop sites of each of the competitors as well as delivery of grocery items. The items were delivered to an address in San Francisco, California in order to simulate as realistic an experience as possible. This approach taken by the UX people provided a holistic understanding of the purchase funnel and how customers' living environments impacted their grocery-shopping experience.

An expert review would:

- meet the client's tight timeline and budget;
- provide the client team direction with which to make iterative changes before their next round of UX testing;
- replicate customer routines in order to identify any issues that they may experience in real-life situations;
- reveal major usability issues.

The client was focused on four key steps in the customer journey (Figure 6.1):

1. Awareness:
   a. How does the Web site presentation encourage exploration of categories?
   b. Does the site present innovative features or tools that support the discovery process?

Figure 6.1 Customer journey.

2. Consideration:

    a. How easy is it for users to evaluate tradeoffs between products?

    b. Does the site navigation and search easily support product selection?

    c. Are the ratings and reviews provided helpful in evaluating products?

3. Purchase:

    a. Is the checkout process quick and efficient?

    b. Are total fees clear and presented early in the process?

    c. Are shipping timelines clear and understood?

4. Delivery:

    a. Did the consumer receive an order confirmation?

    b. Were the groceries received in the expected delivery time period?

    c. What was the condition of the groceries?

## How the Methodology was Implemented

### Online Methodology

Data collection took place over the course of two weeks in which the following scenario was completed one competitor's site at a time:

You are looking to buy dry stovetop stuffing, apples, and ground beef for your house.

Rather than locating items comparatively across sites (adding apples to the cart of one site and then the next), it was important to complete the scenario one competitor at a time to gain insights into the entirety of the Web experience. The one issue with this approach is that I found myself returning to previously reviewed sites in order to determine whether or not functionality existed across competitors but the frequency at which this occurred was minimal.

I viewed locating and selecting each grocery item as a separate task because it was clear that users' expectations for dry goods, produce, and meat varied. Specifically, item number, weight, and nutrition labels were important for different items.

Search was not tested as information architecture was of greater importance. In particular, the categorization of menu items, the nesting of secondary and tertiary menus, and filter options were viewed carefully as they had the greatest impact on Web site navigation.

Notes were taken in a spreadsheet and categorically organized based on the steps in the customer journey. Particular attention was paid to how well the online experience mirrored the in-person grocery shopping experience at a bricks and mortar store.

## Delivery Methodology

All groceries were scheduled for delivery within 48 h of when the order was placed online in order to provide a realistic timeframe by which groceries would be ordered and delivered. AnswerLab spent no more than $50 per merchant. This maximum was in accordance to the minimum grocery purchase amount required by some competitors.

Groceries were delivered to a city address at which there was no place to leave groceries and the doorbell was broken requiring special delivery instructions. Though the goal was to have a city resident receive the groceries, the particular nuances of each of their living situation ended up being a strong barometer by which to measure the success of the delivery experience.

## What Worked Well/What Didn't

There was one main component to our study that proved crucial in capturing the level of detail and richness we needed to meet the research objectives:

## Task-Based Approach

Using tasks as parameters for the expert review ensured that the study stayed focused on the experience of the purchase funnel. Additionally, it ensured that there was consistency across the brands. As experts in the field, it is easy to get bogged down in the details of less important criteria (e.g., layout, typography, color scheme). Though all of those affect the overall brand experience, none were enough of a pain point to produce task abandonment.

Therefore, I strongly recommend a task-based approach focused on typical user interactions with the product or service for competitive expert reviews.

There were two challenges that we grappled with during the research:

1. Online grocery market being young/not fully developed
   Of the three competitors examined, only one was established in the grocery space. Both our client and the other competitor were still in beta phases, with much of their functionality not built out. In particular, one competitor's search functionality returned irrelevant results and another's product descriptions were inconsistently presented throughout the site.
2. There was not a 1:1 match in product offerings
   It was not discovered until we were too deeply into the research phase that one of the chosen competitors had limited grocery offerings that did not offer items from the chosen task. This problem was not difficult to overcome, as other items were ordered, but I believe the research would have been more successful had another competitor been chosen that was more of a match with the client.

## Learnings

One of the more interesting findings from the expert review was how the client didn't utilize its value proposition of offering competitive pricing rather than just grocery delivery as part of its service. The other competitors researched did not have as diverse offerings and it was a true missed opportunity.

Images were important tools that replicated a sensory aspect of the in-store experience. In particular, when used in list and cart views it reduced the cognitive load of having to read through a number of items.

Product descriptions were lacking across all competitors as none offered information that was identically available on the product itself. Additionally, item comparison functionality was not offered.

The Web site menu categorization and hierarchy often mirrored the aisles of a supermarket, matching the mental model of where to find specific items.

Unfortunately, the filter options were not as granular as they were needed to be and at times they were not easily discoverable.

## Key Takeaways

Expert reviews are an excellent method to be used as part of a multi-phase iterative study. Providing clients with feedback on easily identifiable usability roadblocks prior to usability testing will help your client to get to the root of their research needs because participants won't be distracted by these more obvious usability issues in later sessions.

Expert reviews are an important methodology to have in your UX toolkit. It is a great research technique to provide to clients, where time and cost are of utmost concern. However, though an expert review can deliver helpful insights, it is not a replacement for usability testing with a target population.

It is important to understand your client's goal when it comes to expert reviews, as often clients are interested in getting feedback on every usability issue you can find. If this is the case, prioritization is of utmost importance and it provides the client team with direction as to what changes to make first. However, if you have a client that is interested in a competitive expert review, there is a great need to produce consistency. Using common user-focused tasks by which to compare various sites is a great way to provide insights to your client.

# BIBLIOGRAPHY

Divitini, M., Farshchian, B.A., 1999. Using email and WWW in a distributed participatory design project. SIGGROUP Bull. 20 (1), 10–15.

Ehn, P., Kyng, M., 1991. Cardboard computers: mocking-it-up or hands-on the future. In: Greenbaum, J., Kyng, M. (Eds.), Design at Work. Laurence Erlbaum Associates, Hillsdale, NJ, pp. 169–196.

Grudin, J., Poltrock, S., 2013. Computer supported cooperative work. In: Soegaard, M., Dam, R. (Eds.), The Encyclopedia of Human-Computer Interaction, second ed. The Interaction Design Foundation, Aarhus, Denmark. Available online at: https://www.interactiondesign.org/encyclopedia/cscw_computer_supported_cooperative_work.html.

Kensing, F., Blomberg, J., 1998. Participatory design: issues and concerns. Comput. Supported Coop. Work 7, 167–185.

Nielsen, J., 1994. Usability Inspection Methods. John Wiley and Sons, New York.

Straub, K., 2004. Cleaning Up for the Housekeeper or Why It Makes Sense to Do Both Expert Review and Usability Testing (Ph.D.). http://www.upassoc.org/upa_publications/upa_voice/volumes/2004/nov/cleaning_up.html.

# Chapter 7

## USABILITY TESTING

This chapter describes the various types of usability evaluation methodologies. Two case studies are presented; one is from the domain of emergency management systems and the other combines qualitative research with biometrics.

# Chapter 7

People's minds are changed through observation and not through argument.

**Will Rogers**

## Usability Evaluations

Usability tests are sometimes referred to as user tests (Neilsen, 1994). The basic idea is to evaluate a product, service, or system by having a real person interact with it and, as such, test it. The usability judged on various factors such as is effectiveness, efficiency, and overall satisfaction of the users during their experience. Usability tests look to evaluate many user experience dimensions of a product, service, or tochnology to understand those dimensions. Test methodology looks to evaluate several factors including:

- *Design*: how well the functionality fits into the users' mental model of the system?
- *Learnability*: how quickly a new user can learn to use the system? How easy is to remember how to use it in the future?
- *Efficiency*: how fast a user can accomplish tasks?
- *User satisfaction*: self-report of how the user views the system.
- *Errors*: how severe and frequently does a user make a mistake?

## Empirical Methods

As described in the previous chapter usability evaluations collect data through a controlled protocol, which is often task oriented, through moderated sessions with a user.

There are several forms of usability evaluations carried out when using these empirical methods.

## A/B Testing

Usability evaluation methods, as well as business and market research A/B tests are used to compare two designs. Occasionally this method is used for more than two designs or products. In any event, the evaluation method uses the same protocol for both A and B; the only variable is the different design.

A/B evaluations are well suited for comparing elements of design such as:

- Colors;
- Layouts;
- Components, such as buttons, banners, and other affordances.

A/B evaluations are done in both qualitative and quantitative studies.

### Moderated Tests

Usability evaluations that are run with a person moderating and following a script are among the most common approaches to usability testing. These are done with one person moderating, interacting with a participant to walk through a script, to conduct tasks and collect information about the central usability of the product or technology. The advantages of using a moderator include:

- Setting the participant at ease, usually through talking and body language, and by paying attention to the participant's emotional state and ensuring they are comfortable.
- Keeping the test session on time. An experienced moderator will have a script, with tasks that have allowances for specific amounts of time to spend on each task.
- The moderator can make sure the technology is working
- The moderator can ask probing and clarifying questions to get the participant to share more information about what they are experiencing during the test sessions.

## Qualitative vs. Quantitative

There are two general types of usability evaluations: qualitative and quantitative or formative and summative. Qualitative is often done in the earlier stages of

| Qualitative | Quantitative |
|---|---|
| Formative | Summative |
| Early in lifecycle | Later in lifecycle |
| >10 users | >10 participants |

Figure 7.1 Qualitative and quantitative.

development or prior to a new release; quantitative research is done later in the lifecycle, and generally collects larger amount of data. Quantitative data can be used for statistical analysis, qualitative data are used to characterize findings, and describe properties and behaviors (Figure 7.1).

Successful usability tests take planning and practice. The planning has to include a kickoff meeting with stakeholders to plan the test, which comprises: a test plan, recruiting screener and recruiting plan, moderator's guide, user satisfaction scales, data analysis, and final recommendations.

# How Many Users to Test

## Qualitative

Although there is some discrepancy among the experts, the generally accepted number of users to test is 8, with a qualifier that they are from a single user persona. Jakob Nielsen published a study in 1993 and then again in 2012 on his Web site and suggested that 5 users is enough to find most of the usability problems that you would find with much higher numbers.

If there is more than 1 user persona, the minimum of 5 participants is acceptable. Furthermore, when testing several different tasks, make sure a minimum of 5 users run through each task. The reason that these numbers have held up over time is that the field has seen clearly the most frequent and serious problems will come up within the first 5 users. I found have this to be true sometimes even through the first 3 users. However, even in this instance, it is important to run at least 5 and even up to 8.

## Quantitative

In order to get statistically significant results, the quantitative study must include a minimum of 20 users, as long as the evaluation protocol remains consistent among the user persona groups. Generally, these studies are done online and often take the participants from a large pool of users, so getting a larger number of respondents is not as difficult as it might seem. Quantitative studies can be done in person but might be more time consuming because of the larger number of participants.

The best practice for running a usability testing is described below:

1. *Kickoff meeting*: Start usability test project with a team kickoff, make sure all stakeholders and team members are present. Meeting produces agreed upon project schedule with specific benchmarks and deliverables. The team agrees on the test design, e.g., task based or open ended, how many participants and how long the test will run.
2. *Planning period*: Recruiting plan begins, tasks are tested on product or prototypes, and the moderator's guide is written and approved.
3. *Test period*: Starts with a pilot test to do a trial run of the moderator's guide, tasks, and test system. Tests are run until the goal number of tests is complete.
4. *Data analysis*: Data are analyzed, findings are written and recommendations made.
5. *Final presentation of project*: This takes many forms. They range from a findings and design meeting discussing results to a formal report and presentation.

Many of the skills required to run a good usability test are transferable and crossover from other methodologies. For example, a UX professional that is good at a field interviews and can engage participants so that they discuss the real issues being examined, can also use those same skills to moderate a usability test, to put the participant at ease and to help them provide clear feedback.

## Task-Based Usability Testing

In order to simulate a use case, the usability test often includes specific tasks for the participant to follow. The test is to determine whether the product, service, or technology is usable in real-life situations and tasks provide a structure for the user to walk through and simulate a real-world situation.

For example, if one wanted to test a financial institutions mobile application, a good way to do that is to simulate the actual tasks a user would carry out using application. The test might include tasks such as depositing checks, transferring money from one online account to another and paying bills online. Asking participants to think aloud about their experience will provide data for the researchers to help them better understand the UX. They can see if a participant has trouble depositing a check, because they might not be able to take a clear picture of the check in the specific layout the application provides on the device.

## Open Ended Usability Testing

In many cases, there are too few or too many tasks to test all at once or perhaps the stakeholders want to test the overall concepts. In these cases it is helpful to let a user explore a bit. This is important for a couple of reasons:

- People don't all process information in the same way (linear, visual, kinesthetic).
- People don't all learn in the same way (linear, visual, kinesthetic).

## Contextual-Based Usability Testing

Software developers have used context-driven testing as a way to evaluate a software system in terms of the context in which the person will be using the software. This process is similar to Agile testing since it applies many of the same principles of quick cycle times, however in this case the context is a key element in understanding the UX.

## Think Aloud Protocol

The value of putting a product, service, or technology in front of a user, cannot be over stated. Observing a person interact with an object illustrates, as no other way can, how usable the object is. Whether the person is given a task, a scenario to follow or simply asked to think aloud, and share their feedback about the object, usability testing brings the problems in the user experience to the forefront.

For example, if a person is trying to set the time on an alarm clock and they can't find the button to change the time, they might turn the clock over, look at all the affordances and still not be able to set the time.

Sometimes the usability of a system will have a huge impact on people's lives, such as in the case of emergency management systems and other technologies for first responders to emergencies. The following case study is a good example of such a case. In emergency situations, people often feel stressed and their cognitive load is impaired, as a result, do not always operate at their best. During these times, it is of the utmost importance that the system's usability is seamless and that the users can find information and perform their tasks immediately when they need to. Developing tools for emergency situations is hard to test, since it is not in the best interest of people who are affected by an emergency to evaluate them while the emergency is happening. The following case study shows how a UX team was able to conduct important research and still respect the needs of the people who were using the system.

# User Research for a Disaster Relief Organization

Cory Lebson

For the past 20 years, I have had an ongoing personal interest in emergency management and response. While still in college, I trained as an emergency medical technician and firefighter, and volunteered on the ambulance with the local fire department. More recently, I joined the Community Emergency Response Team (CERT) for my local area. When I was presented with the opportunity to provide UX support to a disaster relief organization in 2008, it was a perfect match of my professional user experience and user research background with my personal interest in emergency response. Not only did I have a base level of field knowledge, but I also came to the effort with a personal desire to help improve the experiences of those involved in a disaster.

For the years immediately prior to my arrival on the project, there had been minimal user research of any kind and I was only able to find a record of one research study that had been done in the field. I had a lot of support for my initial efforts, however, and I found the enthusiasm of the organization's staff to help me slowly gain traction for a robust user research program. By 2009, I had gained enough of a UX foothold to support a user research program. From that point onward, I had the opportunity to do user research of Web and mobile resources with survivors of disasters in Galveston, Atlanta, Nashville, Chicago, Raleigh, Tampa, and New York City; with emergency managers at four emergency management conferences; and with members of the general public.

The goal of all of this research was to improve the organization's regular Web sites as well as mobile-optimized Web sites and mobile apps for iOS, Android, and Blackberry devices. The research focused on the usability of the organization's disaster preparedness and response resources; specifically, the aim was to make sure that these resources were as easy to use as possible before, during, and after a disaster. The research examined the most critical tasks and activities for each of these three audience groups and measured whether they were able to accomplish those tasks as expected. Ease of use was critical here for safety and survival—being able to properly prepare for a future disaster and being able to gain the information necessary to survive after a disaster.

## Participants and Recruitment

Since much of the organization's Web and mobile content is geared for the general public, the goal of all of the research was that those resources be easy to understand by everyone. In order to simulate the use case of the field, it was critical to get an authentic task experience by involving people who had recently been through a disaster. This would help assure that their unique experiences were properly understood and their critical needs were met through the available Web content and functionality.

To find recent disaster survivors to participate in the research, I first had to identify a location where a disaster had occurred within the past few months, and where, to whatever extent possible, the type of disaster and response was relatively typical of common American disasters. Flexibility was, therefore, important, and for each research study, the research location and recruitment process was determined approximately two to three weeks before the study dates. Once we agreed on a location, the organization identified disaster survivor participants from among those who had already indicated, after they applied for disaster assistance, that they would be willing to be contacted for a follow-up about their experience.

**Considerations**: I generally was not permitted to engage with very recent and large disasters while they were still in the news. There were two reasons for this. First, the organization staff members were very busy at the outset of a disaster, and it wouldn't be appropriate, and would perhaps even be harmful, for me to distract them from their primary pursuit of survivor safety. Doing no harm is a critical ethical principal of research both of the User Experience Professionals Association and of the American Psychological Association. Second, given the amount of media attention that disasters often stimulate, neither the organization nor I had any interest in my research becoming part of a news story.

The other key audience group, the emergency managers, was recruited in coordination with emergency-management conference organizers. This was also done with consideration to the conference schedule and with the understanding that no sessions would be scheduled during key conference events.

Finally, we used an external recruiting firm to find people in the general public who at least had some basic inclination toward preparedness. Among the organization's three main audience groups, usability testing with disaster survivors turned out to be the most unique experience.

## What to Test? Developing the Script

Once the location was identified and the recruitment process was initiated, I began to develop the script. Since the research was run over the course of 5 years, the Web content, features and functionality that I tested varied from study to study. From my involvement with the Web team, I usually knew of a set of issues, and Web or mobile content, that was particularly important given what was currently being developed during each study time period. Once I drafted tasks for those items, I then assessed how much of the one-hour block of time I'd have available for each participant. I'd then find out from stakeholders the issues that were not absolutely critical to deal with immediately, but that would likely be on the table in the next few months, and I added these items as tasks to follow the more urgently relevant items. If I wasn't positive that I'd have time, I added these as optional tasks to deal with if time permitted.

## Session Setup at Disaster Locations

The test environment was typically a small hotel conference room that was easy to access within the designated disaster area and for the participants. There were always two of us who traveled to do the research, and in order to stay within the budget, since we only rented one conference room, both the logger and the moderator were in the same room.

**Field considerations**: Since we were not in a formal testing facility, hotel staff would generally do no more than point people in the direction of our conference room. Therefore, having two researchers at the testing location to deal with surprises such as technical issues or participants arriving while a session was still in progress, help keep things running smoothly.

Many years ago, we used to lug around a "Lab-in-a-Box," which was a huge box with all sorts of analog recording and analog to digital conversion equipment. With that in mind, I appreciated how easy it is to set up shop today. We'd bring three laptops—a participant laptop (with external mouse and keyboard), a moderator laptop (which mirrored what the participant was seeing) and a logger laptop where the logger could take notes. We had two Webcams. One Webcam focused on the participant, and the other was available to record a participant's mobile device. The test administrator could toggle the cameras to always have picture-in-picture, including both the screen (large) and participant (small bottom right) or the mobile device (large) and again the participant (small bottom right) (Figure 7.2).

## Running Test Sessions with Disaster Survivors

While some participants had used the electronic resources presented prior to the test, enough time had passed that they could approach it afresh. In some cases, survivors reported being in a panic when they applied for disaster assistance online or looked at the organization content and that they couldn't remember it very clearly. In this instance we tried to balance the authenticity of the actual experience with an avoidance of bias from a prior experience: this was not to the detriment to our research. We also recorded comments from time to time where survivors would reflect on some block of content and say things like "when I was in that freaking out state" and then go on to tell us that the text was too dense or too hard for them to absorb.

Figure 7.2 Testing setup.

When participants would arrive, we would start out by qualitatively discussing
their disaster survival experiences, letting them express to us what happened
to get a context of any extra difficulties they may have had using the
organization's Web resources (for example, loss of internet service, need to
evacuate so no access to their usual computer, etc.). We then presented a
series of tasks where as much as possible we tried to mirror participant's
actual experiences of using the organization's electronic resources after a
disaster. As a group, disaster survivors veered off topic from our tasks more
than most user groups. They were generally experiencing strong emotions
caused by the stresses and experiences of surviving a disaster that they
wanted to express, and our probing regarding their experiences of the

disaster Web resources sometimes opened the flood gates. We did gain some valuable background information from these detours, but it was an extra challenge to keep them on task to complete the assessments we needed to make. Determining when to let a participant vent and when to steer them back on task was not always easy.

**Field considerations**: Working in the field presents additional hurdles to overcome. Being at a hotel, would make some participants suspicious as to whether we were trying to scam them. Given that there have been many disaster-related scams, this was understandable, and we would do our best to explain the situation. We would say that we absolutely did not want any personally identifiable information from them, and would always give simulated data when needed. Perhaps related to this, we had a higher than expected no-show rate, and would always need to over-recruit more than usual. Frequently, we had participants who showed up too early, so since we didn't have a waiting area, we set aside some chairs just outside the conference room where the early participants couldn't hear what was going on and could wait.

**Emotional impact**: These studies were the most emotional studies of any research I'd ever conducted in my 20 years of user research. Participants would sometimes get teary as they related their experiences, and sometimes they just wanted the opportunity to express their frustrations with what had happened. Many times I found myself struggling with wanting to comfort them while they talked while still trying to be a neutral and unbiased test facilitator. I remember one woman started crying as she talked about almost losing her disabled mother in a flood. I was not able to focus on the words of script, and instead went off-script to comfort her. As I watched the recording later, I reflected on whether I should have done that—but ultimately concluded that I didn't harm the research and that while it is important to be a good researcher, it is also just as important and critical to be human. For the most part, with this woman and many other participants, there was a lot of appreciation with the organization's role in helping after the disaster.

## Reporting on Sessions

We produced traditional Microsoft-Word-based reports where we detailed our findings and made recommendations. Along with these, we also created a PowerPoint version that was suitable for the presentation of the findings to the stakeholders, and we always tried to make in-person presentations of those findings.

**Value of videos**: We looked back at the recordings to points we had flagged for subsequent review and turned some of these into highlights-clips. We found that of all the reporting formats, the videos had the most impact on the Web development team, as they could really get a feel for what happened during the research. Although we encouraged stakeholders to attend and could even broadcast the sessions to stakeholders electronically live (and allowed them to provide additional questions via instant message), it was much more time efficient for them to watch the key clips as opposed to the 10-12 h of sessions.

**Findings that got lost**: Sometimes the research resulted in very salient findings that brought about immediate changes to the Web site. Other times, findings were put on the back burner, particularly those that were not able to be included in the most near-term code release. I found myself in the position of UX advocate, and would review the issues myself periodically and distill them down to those that were remaining and important. Due to the longevity of the project and people's changing Web responsibilities over time, sometimes changes the that that had been made to the site based on research findings were undone, when someone new who wasn't aware of this fact made alterations. I'd then have to make the case again to the new stakeholders.

## A Valuable Experience

Overall, this research was an incredibly valuable and meaningful experience for me, as I had such a phenomenal opportunity to have a large impact on the way that survivors of future disasters have electronic interactions with the organization to gain critical information. And I was able to see visible improvements over time, a better "scent of information," and a more direct path for survivors to get to the information that they needed. I saw improvements in terminology and wording, better use of plain language, and a reduction in the use of acronyms and jargon. I also gained skills personally in handling challenging field situations and emotional participants, and gained confidence in my ability to be flexible and go with the flow in unusual situations. I also became stronger as an advocate for those groups that need a good user experience the most.

# A Case for Quant

The large amounts of empirical data that are the result of quantitative studies can be used to validate designs. The risks are that they can sometimes be too narrow and not holistic enough, so they leave out important factors that are part of the bigger picture. This can be mitigated by using quantitative data in a strategic way, keeping the overall user and business goals in mind while still analyzing the details in the data.

In the many successful cases, quantitative data can be triangulated with qualitative data to deepen the understanding of the user and the system. This combination can provide rich data that can identify the big picture issues, patterns, and more detailed findings for specific issues.

The following case study is an example of the power of triangulating data. This case study considers many user touch points. Furthermore, it provides a case for biometrics, using eye-tracking and galvanic skin response, combined with qualitative feedback and self-reporting to better understand users' emotional engagement with a product.

## User Experience Across Platforms

Amanda Davis and Lydia Sankey

### Background

Users interact with products across Web-based and desktop applications, mobile apps and through person-to-person contact (e.g., phone, text chat, in-person). Designers must consider the complexity of the user interactions across these interfaces and strive to unify the experiences across visual design, content, and interaction design. Understanding users' emotional responses to these interfaces moves design beyond intuitive interactions to satisfying interactions. By understanding when and what emotional responses users have, designers can construct the user experience appropriate to the context of the interaction, resulting in a more unified whole.

## Use Case

Our client for the project was a leading sunscreen manufacturer, rated #1 by Consumer Reports Magazine. We had two main goals for the project. The first goal was to understand what engages consumers on both the client's product packaging and Web site when considering natural, outdoor skincare products. The second goal was to make recommendations for the branding and Web site design of their products based on participant feedback. The study was conducted in a formal usability lab setting at the Design and Usability Center at Bentley University.

This project provides a case study for researching emotional responses in participants to inform design recommendations for an enhanced and consistent user experience.

Our study addressed the multiple contact points of consumer product purchases, spanning the physical product packaging, printed and digital advertising, and online Web platforms. The client wanted to provide a unified product experience across the platforms and to understand the emotional responses to these experiences in order to iterate on their branding to address the context of their consumers' purchasing decisions.

## Persona Description

The study focused on mothers with young children (under the age of 18) living at home, who shopped at Whole Foods grocery store and who had purchased sunscreen and insect repellent in the last year. We wanted to understand how current consumers perceived the product in relation to other natural skincare products before transitioning into a more competitive market that included non-natural products.

### Issue or Problem

Emotions are often instantaneous and may be unconscious, so researchers should not depend solely on self-reported responses (Gonyea, 2005). With no single physiological measurement directly assessing emotions, researchers must measure affective responses with a variety of tools. The combination of these data and self-reported qualitative data provides richer insight into emotions.

## How Did We Use UX to Solve It?

We coordinated five tools—electrodermal activity (EDA), eye tracking, Microsoft Product Reaction Cards, net promoter scores (NPSs), and qualitative feedback—to understand the emotional impact of product packaging, digital ads, and Web site design.

### Tools

### Electrodermal Activity

The use of biometrics provides information about affective responses as they occur. EDA data were the most appropriate choice for this study, since the measurement device was non-invasive and mobile. The Affectiva Q Sensor is a wearable, wireless biosensor that measures emotional arousal via skin conductance. The unit of measure is EDA that increases when the user is in a state of excitement, attention or anxiety, and reduces when the user experiences boredom or relaxation (Figure 7.3).

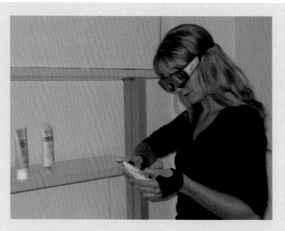

Figure 7.3 Eyetracking glasses and EDA gloves.

EDA, also known as skin conductance or galvanic skin response (GSR), is a method of measuring the electrical conductance of the skin, which varies with its moisture level. Sweat glands are controlled by the sympathetic nervous system (Martini and Bartholomew, 2003); therefore, skin conductance is used as an indication of psychological or physiological arousal.

### Eye Tracking

In addition to biometrics, eye tracking can be used to pinpoint emotionally charged experiences. Observers look earlier and longer at emotionally charged images than neutral images, perhaps to prepare for rapid defensive responses (Calvo and Lang, 2004). This study used both SensoMotoric Instruments (SMIs) RED computer monitor eye tracking system and mobile eye tracking glasses.

### Microsoft Product Reaction Cards

The Microsoft product cards were used to form the basis for discussion about a product (Benedek and Miner, 2002) and to access the participant's perception of her emotional responses. The main advantage of this technique is that it does not rely on a questionnaire or rating scales, and users do not have to generate words themselves. The 118 product reaction cards targeted a 60% positive and 40% neutral balance.

## Net Promoter Scores

The NPSs were used to understand the appeal of the interface. This surveying tool asks participants about their willingness to promote a company or product, indicating their loyalty and future growth (Reichheld, 2003).

## Qualitative Feedback

This research used a "think-aloud" protocol to encourage feedback from participants throughout the study.

We conducted a study on natural outdoor skincare products to:

understand what engages consumers on the client's product packaging and Web site relative to the competition;

make recommendations for branding and Web site design based on feedback;

improve the user experience across multiple interfaces by effectively addressing concerns of users.

During each 90-min, moderated session the participants wore the Q sensor, which monitored their EDA. Depending on the task, the participants either wore eye-tracking glasses or worked on a computer monitor with an eye-tracking system, both of which monitored their eye movements. Participants also performed the think-aloud protocol. They performed the following tasks:

*Analyze product packaging*. Participants were asked to view a shelf of four sunscreen products and then decide which product(s), if any they would purchase. They picked up and examined the product packaging while completing this task. The participants verbally indicated which product(s) they would purchase and why.

At the end of the task, they gave a NPS for each of the four products. Participants performed a similar task for insect repellents.

*Evaluate the Web site*. Participants performed several tasks on Web site A. At the end of the tasks, they gave a NPS for the Web site, and they chose ten words from the Microsoft Product Reaction Cards. Participants performed the same tasks on Web site B. The A/B testing for the Web sites was counterbalanced, with 50% of the participants viewing Web site A first, and 50% viewing Web site B first.

*Evaluate the effectiveness of magazine advertisements*. Participants viewed four images for ads.

We analyzed the data collected from the five tools that provided insight into what participants were thinking about the interfaces. The data from the research tools can be combined in many ways. On this project, we mainly used the following combinations:

First, moments of interest—or peaks—in the EDA data indicate where there is a heightened emotional response. While EDA data allow practitioners to pinpoint exact moments of emotions, it does not reveal what type of engagement or emotion the participant was experiencing. We needed to view the EDA data alongside data from other tools. These moments of heightened emotional response can be synchronized with eye tracking data to pinpoint what the participant was viewing at the exact moment of heightened EDA. Qualitative data can provide an additional level of understanding of the emotional response. Specifically, we reviewed the EDA data and identified the time of the peaks. Then the eye tracking data were reviewed for the specific stimulus the participants were viewing at the time of the EDA peak. Video recordings were then reviewed to hear what feedback the participants provided at the time of the EDA peak.

Second, the emotional activation level for a specific task or Web site can be combined with Microsoft Product Reaction Card data to determine the intensity and type of the emotional engagement.

Third, the participant's cognitive experience can be understood by combining data from the Microsoft Product Reaction Cards, NPS, and qualitative feedback. The participant's own interpretation of their emotional responses can be determined from this combination. Analysis of these three data sets provided insight into what the participants were thinking about the interfaces. We reviewed the most frequently chosen words on the Microsoft Product Reaction cards, and compared these positive and negative words with the NPSs and the qualitative feedback.

And fourth, aggregated eye tracking data can be analyzed to determine where participants focused most intensely.

Key Takeaways

In addition to providing key findings to our client, we learned several things regarding understanding and studying emotion in usability studies. First, the triangulation of data sources from multiple tools to explain and validate findings contributes more than any of the tools individually. Second, emotion is really important in interaction with interfaces, and it is not sufficient to rely solely on self-reported emotional assessment. And third, users' emotions can be understood through:

1. objective measurements of a participant's emotional response;
2. qualification of the type of the participant's emotional response through survey tools and qualitative data;
3. identification of trigger moments and sources of emotional response;
4. comparison of emotional response across tasks for each participant, to assess the relative emotional impacts of the interactions.

This method is ideal for testing interfaces to understand the type and severity of emotional reactions throughout interaction with a product. It provides insight into emotional reactions beyond what is articulated during a standard think-aloud usability study. Emotions are a key part of the technology experience. As user experience practitioners, we need to move beyond usability to emotional design. We can use these tools and methods in a strategic way to understand the emotions and behaviors of our users. With this knowledge, we can assess the emotional quality of our designs and whether or not we're truly supporting the emotional needs of our users.

## Usability Testing and UX Strategy

What makes usability testing successful is how much it influences development and innovation; especially of new products and services. Usability testing is successful when key stakeholders can observe a user struggling with an object, and understand that there is work to be done. This is true on the opposite side as well, if a key stakeholder can see a user enjoying their interaction with their products and services, then this helps the team to make the product better by building up the functions and affordances that bring the user back to the product.

Often usability testing is the first piece of work that the company will incorporate into their development process. Sometimes the company has a limited budget, sometimes they might want to get a better understanding of UX and will decide to try one usability test to see if the impact has enough value to warrant spending more resources on UX work.

A successful usability test is one that produces results that are helpful to the development team in improving the product, service, or technology. Even if the UX process is done with best practice, and creates clear and actionable design recommendations, it can't be considered successful unless the development team can make use of the recommendations. As we have seen in some of the case studies, a key element in all UX work is collaborating well with other team members. Any good strategy is sure to include good teamwork.

# REFERENCES

Benedek, J., Miner, T., 2002. Measuring Desirability: New Methods for Evaluating Desirability in a Usability Lab Setting. Proceedings of Usability Professionals Association, pp. 8–12.

Gonyea, R.M., 2005. Self-reported data in institutional research: review and recommendations. New Dir. Inst. Res. 2005 (127), 73–89.

Martini, F., Bartholomew, E.F., 2003. Essentials of Anatomy and Physiology. Pearson Education, New York.

Nielsen, J., 1994. Usability Engineering. Morgan Kaufmann Publishers, San Francisco, CA, p. 165.

Nielsen, J., Landauer, T.K., 1993. Usability Testing with 5 Users (Jakob Nielsen's Alertbox). useit.com (13-03-2000).

Reichheld, F.F., 2003. The one number you need to grow. Harv. Bus. Rev. 81 (12), 46–55.

# BIBLIOGRAPHY

Albert, W., Tullis, T., 2013. Measuring the User Experience: Collecting, Analyzing, and Presenting Usability Metrics. Morgan Kaufmann, Waltham, MA.

Bevan, N., Macleod, M., 1994. Usability measurement in context. Behav. Inform. Technol. 13, 132–145.

Dray, S., Siegel, D., 2004. Remote possibilities?: international usability testing at a distance. Interactions 11 (2), 10–17. http://dx.doi.org/10.1145/971258.971264.

How Many Test Users in a Usability Study? http://www.nngroup.com/articles/how-many-test-users/.

ISO 13407:1999. Human-Centred Design Processes for Interactive. www.iso.org/cate/d21197.html.

Sauro, J., Kindlund, E., 2005. A method to standardize usability metrics into a single score. In: Proceedings of the SIGCHI Conference on Human, dl.acm.org.

Seffah, A., Donyaee, M., Kline, R.B., Padda, H.K., 2006. Usability measurement and metrics: a consolidated model. Softw. Qual. J. 14 (2006), 159–178.

Usability. Usability.gov.

Usability Body of Knowledge. http://www.usabilitybok.org/what-is-usability.

Virzi, R.A., 1992. Refining the test phase of usability evaluation: how many subjects is enough? Hum. Factors 34 (4), 457–468. http://dx.doi.org/10.1177/001872089203400407.

# Chapter 8

## ITERATING ON THE DESIGN

This chapter explains the important of collecting data and using that data to redesign the product. The methodologies of Agile and Lean are explained and three case studies are included one from the early days of UX, one from NASDAQ, and one written as a lesson learned from a failure.

# Chapter 8

Arriving at one goal is the starting point of another.

**John Dewey**

## Iterating on the Design

The field of UX has been around for over 30 years. It is no surprise to discover that some theories and methodologies might appear to be newer versions of some older ideas.

In the early days of software development, products were built based on the old assembly line model. Each person was responsible for one piece of the whole. When one piece was completed it was "thrown over the wall" (a term that came from software developers sitting in cubicles with low walls), where another person did what? The cycle became known as a waterfall model—with one step moving logically to the next—that's how the product was put together and then shipped. Marketing was responsible for identifying opportunities that development teams would build and ship. In this model, cycle time between releases could take years; marketing requirements were often changing whilst the developers were building the software. By the time the product shipped, it was often out of date.

In the 1980s, as digital systems were coming into being, companies started to realize that the waterfall method was not producing as successful products,. This is when iterative approaches to product development started to be incorporated into product development. The iterative development processes incorporate stages of listening to customers, developing requirements that are then tested in a prototype stage with real users, and redesigned before the product is shipped. These iterations provided for the incorporation of user needs and goals into the production of more successful outcomes.

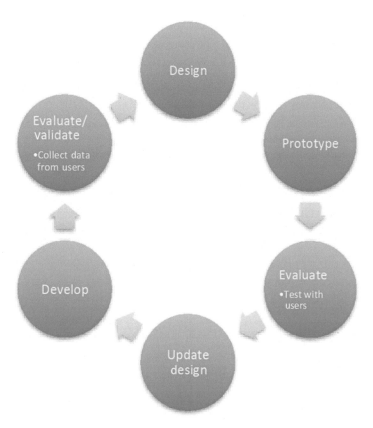

Figure 8.1 Iterative design.

Once the internet became widely used in the mid 1990s, the development cycles had to become even shorter and that's when Agile came into being (Figure 8.1).

## Agile

Agile development is a term that encompasses several iterative software development methodologies and processes. Common Agile methods include the following:

- Extreme programming stresses customer satisfaction and focuses on getting results through team work.

- Scrum recognizes that user needs can change during a development process and teams work together to find solutions.
- Lean software development is based on the principles of Lean manufacturing, which is essentially a very efficient method for creating robust operations for developing products. Lean processes work to eliminate all waste with the goal of improving quality.
- Dynamic Systems Development Method (DSDM) is a delivery framework based on the Agile methodology. DSDM sets the schedule, budget, and milestones at the outset of the project and maintains the scope by prioritizing the deliverables.

The different Agile methods have several things in common, primarily the iterative and incremental approach to development. In 2001 a small group of software developers met and published the Manifesto for Agile Software development, which is summarized below.

## Manifesto for Agile Software Development

We are uncovering better ways of developing software by doing it and helping others do it.

Through this work we have come to value:

**Individuals and interactions** *over* processes and tools
**Working software** *over* comprehensive documentation
**Customer collaboration** *over* contract negotiation
**Responding to change** *over* following a plan

That is, while there is value in the items on the right, we value the items on the left (shown in bold) more.

While this book is about successful user experience, it would not be complete without some discussion of failure. The next case study describes an Agile development environment. Even though UX methods were used, UX was not always successful.

This next case study describes and Agile UX project that did not work as expected but resulted in key learnings.

We do not learn from experience, we learn from reflecting on experience.
**John Dewey**

# Agile UX Failure

Diana DeMarco Brown

Introduction

I have been lucky enough to work on Agile projects at several different companies and with multiple teams within each organization. This has given me a deep appreciation for the fact that each Agile team is unique and needs to be approached in an adaptive way.

Several years ago, I had a few Agile projects under my belt and was feeling pretty good as I approached a new effort. My experiences had been very positive and I was turning into an Agile convert. I had done an Agile project at my previous company and been exposed to a variety of training specific to UX and Agile. That project had been on a new piece of functionality within some legacy software with upstream and downstream dependencies. The team was also spread across several locations—all challenges to an Agile newbie. But the project had been successful and I learned a tremendous amount from the process. At my new company, I was part of the first Agile pilot project and worked on an iPhone app that was brand new and allowed a user to access a subset of functionality of the desktop version. It was a well-defined project, with a very high functioning team that was largely co-located. Additionally, I had been doing research on Agile methodologies and how other user-experience practitioners were applying it for a book that I was writing "Agile User Experience Design: A Practitioner's Guide to Making It Work." I was ready for anything. Or so I thought.

This new project had a lot in common with my previous work in the same organization. Tight deadlines, a high-profile project, and offshore team members were all in play. While these are never part of the textbook descriptions of Agile and are rarely mentioned in most success stories, I was not concerned. These factors and the work involved were familiar old friends to me. I was comfortable with designing along with the development team and adopting their rhythm, doing some minimal documentation of design intent to support the efforts of the offshore teams and managing the laser-like attention of the executive team. The project team I had just worked with had no trouble managing those exact same challenges and it was very easy to integrate my UX efforts into the process. I had precedent on my side and was ready to create an awesome design.

## The Project

I met with the scrum master, who also happened to be a development manager, and the lead developer on the project. I explained to them how I had worked with my other team and solicited their feedback on whether or not this approach would be a good fit for their team. We agreed to some minor tweaks and got ready to kick things off. Everything was rainbows and sunshine. In retrospect, that should have been my first red flag. It would be natural for a team who has never done Agile nor worked closely with a UX resource to have at least some questions, if not some concerns.

Our first planning meeting went well, with a few normal hiccups happening throughout the first sprint. This application was an online way to view and explore complex files. It had some dependencies on existing software, but was largely a separate application. I was designing some basic screens ahead of implementation; other items had already been designed as part of a proof of concept demo in order to secure "funding" and were being redesigned for implementation. While some of the high-level interactions were still valid, there was some re-work to do on the look and feel, and some workflow refinement to be considered. By the second sprint, a few stress points started to show. Most of our QA team was offshore and they were having trouble finding out which UI elements were being redesigned and which were the final products. In order to support their understanding, I was creating tasks in the system, flagged with keywords and screenshots so that it would be easy to find which UIs had been "designed." In order to help out our documentation person, who was remote, I collected all of these images together on a wiki page so that she could get a good sense of the overall picture. I added some descriptive text to describe workflow.

While I was trying to be a good citizen by supporting my remote team members with documentation and letting the development team drive what I should be working on, both of these solutions had some flaws. The QA team would have to go into the system and search on the keywords and sprint to find the information. That is a lot of work for a fast-paced project and it was not always possible for them to invest that time. Additionally, the team would agree on a design in one sprint and it would get revisited and changed in another sprint. This made it hard to communicate changes to folks who were not in the room went it happened, and it was impossible to find this information in the system. Without being part of the discussion around how, why and the full scope of the changes that came up, it was difficult to keep track of what was changing and what it was changing to. The cycle of repeatedly revisiting the same issue was also a symptom of a bigger problem, in that the team was not really on the same page and agreements were not always genuine commitments. My fantastic wiki page also did not provide a way for my documentation person to provide me with any feedback or make it easy for her to ask questions. Late in the release, when we had a short session where we reviewed things together and had a great conversation I realized just how much I had been inhibiting communication.

Once we were a few sprints into the release, things really went off the rails. I was supporting multiple teams, and was routinely being tasked well over 100% of my capacity. The first time it happened and I raised the issue I agreed to juggle my other work, thinking that it was an isolated event. It was not. And I wasn't alone. Several key members of the team, from all functional areas, were consistently assigned work far beyond their capacity. It even became a team joke. Finally, during a team retrospective at the end of the sprint (a scrum event in which the team talks about what went well during the sprint and what they might like to see go differently in the next sprint), the lead developer and I both raised concerns about the sprint length. We were having 2-week sprints and we both felt that was not long enough to accommodate the production work and the overhead of the meetings related to sprint activities. Not surprisingly, our planning meetings and daily standups were routinely taking longer than they should have, which we also flagged as a concern. It was not unusual for fifteen minute standups to go 30 min or longer. Granted, extending the sprint to 3 weeks was unlikely to address some of the underlying issues that none of us seemed quite ready to talk about, but at least it would accommodate the realities and maybe allow us to meet our goals. Not everyone on the team felt comfortable speaking up, so it was largely the two of us advocating for change. Our scrum master, with the best of intentions, did not want to make a change to the sprint length. He felt we could more aggressively time box the other activities and continue on. In his defense, this had a lot to do with the tremendous pressure on the team to deliver for a specific date that could not slip. He believed that shorter sprint would get us there. His intentions were good. Unfortunately, that was the last time I raised an issue in a retrospective, and don't recall that anyone else ever did either.

Not so surprisingly, things continued in the same way and there were a few meetings that got so heated that tempers flared for even the most reserved team members. In the end, the "last" sprint was of an indefinite length and the release did not include many of the required features that had been planned. No one left that project feeling good about the process, which was especially disappointing for those for whom this was their only experience of Agile.

## Conclusions

Things had felt so promising at the start, what could I have done differently to help keep things on track? While it would be easy to point at other functional areas for being at fault, every team member on an Agile team is empowered to inform the culture, regardless of whether or not they use it. And as the UX person, it was my responsibility to speak up and advocate for changes when it came to my deliverables.

In looking back, I would have tried harder to continue speaking up in retrospectives and trying to encourage healthy communication. I am a huge believer in modeling behavior to influence change, and if I let my frustration get to me how could I expect anyone else to react differently? I also would have pursued concerns with the scrum master and development lead offline where we might have been able to address unexpressed concerns in a less public way. Is that taking a page from an Agile textbook? No, it is not.

But there was a lot of subtext going on and healthy communication might have been more likely to happen in a one-on-one situation.

It can be hard to change course mid-stream, especially on a project with such intense pressure. And that is why the main thing I wish had done differently was the way I approached defining my role with the team. Rather than just telling them what had worked with an entirely different group, I wish I had sat the scrum master and the development lead down and asked them how they saw me working with them. That might have allowed some issues and expectations to surface in a way that saying "hey, let's do it this way" did not. I also would have used the definition of working with the UX team (me) as an opportunity to discuss the Agile process with the whole team. Not everyone on the team had Agile training, although a few had received some really great training, so the phrase "that's not Agile" was often used and generally went unchallenged. I would not have looked to replace training, but in talking about how my work might dovetail with theirs, I might have at least been able to uncover potential obstacles.

I think this team was challenged by many internal and external factors, which would have made the project a challenge regardless of process. The benefit of Agile is that many of the risky behaviors were identified early enough for us to react to them; the problem was that we didn't recognize them for what they were and resolve them. And that can be a risk, in an environment where the whole team is hurtling toward a date as fast as they can, taking a step back and reflecting on process can feel impossible.

## Lean UX

Lean UX is a practice that focuses on the actual experience that is being designed and less on the specific process deliverables such as reports. Both Agile development and Lean developing processes inspire Lean UX.

Lean UX focuses on the design stage of product development, getting feedback early and integrating it quickly. Jeff Gothelf explains it well in his article in smashingmagazine.com on March 7, 2011. "Lean UX is the practice of bringing the true nature of our work to light **faster**, with less emphasis on deliverables and greater focus on the **actual experience** being designed."

Lean product development is built on the foundation of Lean manufacturing, which looked to improve product manufacturing through the elimination of waste, while improving quality and managing the process toward perfection. The Lean software development is based on the seven principles listed below:

- Eliminate waste, taking away anything that does not add value to the user;
- Amplify learning;
- Decide as late as possible;
- Deliver as fast as possible;
- Empower the team;
- Build integrity in;
- See the whole.

This process helped the software development community streamline the development process and lead the way for the Lean UX movement, which includes rapid user testing and design improvement, without the use of project reports and deliverables. The Lean UX movement is the next step in the evolution of the field of UX. It makes sense, to integrate the team, to provide a process that brings software development and UX work closer together.

Lean UX is built on three principals:

1. Design thinking, which applies design principals to all aspects of business;
2. Incorporation of Agile development principals;
3. Lean startup methods.

Incorporating design, development and business processes with UX makes sense because it brings the evolution of UX, almost, to a full circle.

# Design at Compugraphic

Elizabeth Rosenzweig

In 1985 I was working as a Senior Graphic Arts Specialist for Compugraphic, a phototypesetting company that was eventually acquired by Agfa Gavaert, an imaging company. The company was in the commercial printing industry, one that was slowly evolving toward fully digital systems. The whole prepress market knew that everything was going to be digital, and it was just a matter of time before the manual processes of design, layout, color correction, and color printing would become digital. The printing systems companies were competing to create the best digital prepress systems, while Compugraphic was trying to evolve. Knowing the printing industry was becoming more digital, the company planned on producing a new prepress system for the printing industry. Compugraphic had been successful at producing typesetting equipment and knew that as systems became more digital, they would have to start producing more digital systems to stay competitive.

The mid 1980s was an exciting time to work in the field of design but there were no formal UX methodologies, let alone any awareness of the value of creating usable systems. As a Senior Graphic Arts Specialist (SGAS) I was designing user interfaces for graphical user interfaces (GUI). The role was new and it was not clear where we would have the most impact, so the company kept moving the role between the development, marketing, and quality assurance departments. Because the printing industry was full of designers, the company knew that in order to get market acceptance, they needed a well-designed system. As a SGAS, I was asked to design the GUI for a new prepress system that Agfa was developing. This included not just the screens but also the workflow and user requirements. Although no specific UX processes were in place for this, it was clear to the product team that they needed to talk to real customers. Since the prepress systems had not migrated to digital, the development had to start with the analog systems that were originally in place.

I was on a team that included one other designer, several developers, a marketing manager, a product manager, and a quality assurance engineer. I pushed to have the team hear the voice of the customer, directly from the customer. I wanted the team to understand the psychology of the user. The solution was to take the whole team into the "field" to see how people carried out these tasks in their everyday lives. It was a tough sell; people did not want to start talking to users or listening to what they had to say. In order to make this successful, we needed a team approach and so the idea was put to everyone—we need a field trip to go talk to people who are currently carrying out the tasks that we want to improve with our product (Figure 8.2).

Figure 8.2 Field visit to commercial printer.

Although I did not realize it at the time, my team field trip solidified the team's understanding of UX. The team saw the value right in front of them. They knew enough to hire user interface designers, but did not also realize that they needed to incorporate this direct voice of the customer to the product development cycle. Once they saw how much impact UX could have, they made it a part of development.

The biggest question at the time was, how would we design a system that had existed previously as many separate pieces but not as a whole. Some prepress systems allowed printers to lay out pages or do typesetting, color correction, and other prepress functions, but none had done it all on a single workstation. We had no legacy system to build on and no single technology already in place that would provide a model for design. I knew the next step had to be to talk to the potential users. My plan was to take the developers and marketing researchers to the field, to visit print shops. After careful planning, we made field trips to six local printing sites and talked to them about their workflow, pain points, and key markers for success. These potential users provided so much valuable information that the entire team worked together, quickly, to produce user requirements, software and hardware components, and extensive user documentation. There were no specific test processes, no UX methodologies, and the only deliverables were screen designs, hardware prototypes, and beta software. While the terms Lean UX and Agile had not been thought of yet, the seeds were being planted. The basic principles of putting the user at the center of the development process, observing them and iterating on the design were in place at Compugraphic. Several early versions of the system were put in front of some of these prepress print operators whose feedback was incorporated into the system design before the final product was shipped.

These informal iterative processes were the precursors to the more formal methods in the field at this time.

The technical writers turned out to be close allies to the SGAS, because the writers already knew the importance of focusing on the user. Documentation was written for the user, so in order to be effective, technical writers had to be able to fully understand and empathize with the users. This proved helpful after the product passed the beta stage. Since usability testing was not a key part of the development process, no one actually spent time observing the user perform the tasks on the system until after the first few systems had been sold.

## Agile and Lean Practices Today

The Compugraphic and Agfa prepress systems were eventually replaced with more integrated digital systems, but the development processes are still around today. The idea of co-locating UX professionals with development and marketing teams still proves to be an effective way to produce products that put the user at the forefront, meeting their needs and becoming more efficient in the process.

Salesforce success with implementing Agile and Lean development practices shows the value of the new approach. Salesforce is a software company that grew quickly and produced software at the rate of four major releases a year. 7 Years of growth helped them develop a customer base of over 35,000 with 110,000,000 transactions a day. Salesforce had developed software with the usual waterfall method which worked when the company was small but did not scale up as the company grew. The company tried a major enterprise-wide transformation to Agile in just 3 months. One of the reasons cited for the successful transformation was that the Agile method operated on principles that mapped directly to the company value:

- Keep It Simple Stupid (KISS);
- Listen to your customers;
- Iterate.

The transformation required a lot of work to introduce the new iterative cycle of development with dedicated cross-functional teams. Developer and designers were sent to Agile training and after running one successful project using the new methodology, the company decided to roll out Agile development methodology to all product teams. The results were positive; Salesforce has held its position as one of the world largest providers of customer-relationship-management software.

Agile and Lean methodology works especially well for software systems, since the costs to revise is less expensive than reworking hardware. The next case study demonstrates how Agile and Lean UX can be used successfully in a busy hectic environment that is seen in large financial software systems.

## Lean and Agile at Work: NASDAQ IR Mobile

Chris Avore

### Overview

Following the recent acquisition of a significant competitor, we at NASDAQ Corporate Solutions were faced with the challenges of integrating two different product portfolios while continuing to build new features and products for our existing customers. Many of these customers were regularly contacted by the competition claiming we'd be tied up with just managing the after effects of the acquisition instead of innovating our product line. We had to act fast.

Management began identifying opportunities to provide customers with useful updates that wouldn't take years to ship. Following both internal auditing and competitive analyses, we proposed the hypothesis that redesigning an existing mobile app would increase client retention and act as a bridge until the comprehensive system was launched later in 2015. In addition, we also knew that shipping an app first would allow us to monitor the usage analytics to inform our full desktop design roadmap.

As a result, we shipped a redesigned and rethought, mobile-optimized, investor-relations web app called *IR Mobile* in April 2014, June 2014, and November 2014. The newly introduced Agile and Lean approach enabled the product management, product design, and development teams to explore new directions, validate and refute assumptions with just enough research, and modify the roadmap throughout the process (Figure 8.3).

The initial release of IR Mobile—designed by the recently acquired competitor prior to the close of the deal—was effective in that it successfully displayed content previously unavailable on a mobile device. But it didn't use generally accepted mobile interaction design patterns nor summarize important data and activity when people first opened the app. Our customers weren't frustrated by the product, but it wasn't what it could be.

Like every project underway at NASDAQ Corporate Solutions, our first steps were those of reaching a shared understanding of the vision of the project with our business stakeholders, identifying what we needed to learn from our primary customer base, and determining how we would measure success.

Figure 8.3 NASDAQ IR Mobile tablet.

A few months prior to kicking off the IR Mobile work, we had completed a significant discovery research campaign. As a result of interviewing over a dozen investor relations professionals at their offices, and conducting another five interviews over the phone, we could focus the mobile research campaign on understanding what was missing in the mobile experience.

To source our next mobile-specific research campaign, we sent an online survey to early IR Mobile users to probe baseline expectations.

We then targeted six IR Mobile user interviews to discuss more mobile-likely contexts and workflows. The most glaring customer need was a bird's eye view of their day—whether they were starting their day while still at home, commuting to the office, or traveling to meet investors (Figures 8.4 and 8.5).

But while designing a new dashboard and user interface may seem like straightforward needs to address, we still needed more flexibility in our approach than would be possible following a waterfall methodology.

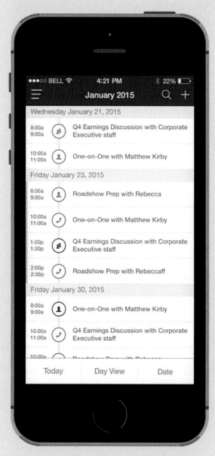

Figure 8.4 IR Mobile phone calendar list.

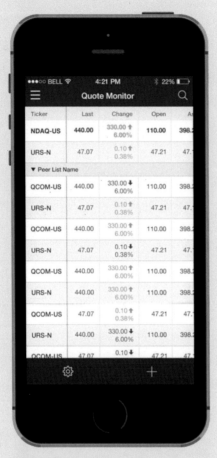

Figure 8.5 IR Mobile phone quotes.

The Agile approach allowed us to iterate and evaluate features and functionality that weren't scoped when the project was initially planned.

For instance, some early plans called for large tile-like buttons to navigate users to the respective panels. But as we continued to design the tiles, and simultaneously talk to clients about what information they were seeking by tapping the tiles, we prototyped summarizing important data into the tiles themselves.

The business mandate to launch in a matter of months required an approach to reduce relying on requirements, approvals, and rework. Our own decision to use Lean practices—just enough research, validating design decisions in the marketplace, never fixating on an idea, and a reduced reliance on high fidelity deliverables—led to a successful product launch in only 4 months.

Measuring success was both a qualitative and quantitative exercise. For instance, sales and account representatives eagerly shared client accolades for the new layout and the prioritized information on the dashboard. But reviewing our usage analytics also suggested more people were using the redesigned product. The redesigned IR Mobile logged more than a 50% increase in usage over the first 3 months of being released.

This increase in activity tied directly to the business mandate of satisfying customers who were anxious to put to work the fruits of the acquisition.

## Key Takeaways

- Agile methodology produces quick turnaround times, teamwork and directly supports iterative design.
- User research can provide insights without being expensive or time consuming. Online surveys, compared with usage data, informed more formal discovery interviews.
- Cross section of users interviewed: investor relations professionals ranged from administrative level to senior vice presidents; as such the expectations of IR Mobile were vastly different depending on the role of the user. By interviewing people across the spectrum of responsibilities we confirmed our product would serve those differing needs.

- Diverse prototyping yields better, faster results:
  - High-fidelity mockups and iPad prototyping software enabled the product design team to test gestures and interactions directly with clients
  - Prototyping the product directly in code enabled faster a turnaround time between product design and development, and reduced ambiguity.
- Discovery documentation only focused on learned insights—not summarizing the current state, for example , to reduce preparation time.

# BIBLIOGRAPHY

Bias, R.G., Mayhew, D.J. (Eds.), 2011. From Cost-Justifying Usability, An Update for the Internet Age, second ed. Interactive Technologies, pp. 489-518.

Fry, C., Greene, S. Large Scale Agile Transformation in an On-Demand World. Salesforce. com (company report).

Gothelf, J. Lean UX: Getting Out of the Deliverables Business. http://www. smashingmagazine.com/2011/03/07/lean-ux-getting-out-of-the-deliverables-business/.

Medlock, M.C., Wixon, D., Terrano, M., Romero, R., Fulton, B., 2002. Using the RITE method to improve products: A definition and a case study. Usability Professionals Association, 51.

Ruffa, S.A., 2008. Going Lean: How the Best Companies Apply Lean Manufacturing Principles to Shatter Uncertainty, Drive Innovation, and Maximize Profits. AMACOM, New York. ISBN: 0-8144-1057-X.

# Chapter 9

## MOVING PAST THE LAB

This chapter is about field studies and focus group, methods outside the formal setting of a lab. One case study describes a field study at a hospital and one describes a focus group done for the Medicare.gov project.

# Chapter 9

The environment is everything that isn't me.

**Albert Einstein**

## Field Studies/Contextual Inquiry

Visiting a person at their office and observing how they work and what the environment looks like can tell us so much more than simply talking to a person in a lab or over the telephone. These site visits allow us to see the context in which people are using things. Even a single visit can provide a large amount of information to help improve a product or systems.

The following are two examples of the power of a single field visit:

The first story comes from a professional in the field, Diana DeMarco Brown: "I worked on a product that I knew had too small a font. When I went on a site visit for a beta, I watched the user adjust the browser zoom to 150% (which was actually lower than her usual 175%). I immediately saw that it caused some of the control buttons and navigation to fall off the screen, which defeated the purpose of using small font to squeeze everything in. This made us focus on the problem of the font. It opened the door to more research and to asking other customers about what they did. This work provided the data to rationalize the change in the subsequent design."

The second story is from a study I did for a company that was developing a large prepress system. We did not have a lab and made use of field visits to help us get data about our users. The prepress systems were designed to do a full page layout, including functions that had previously been part of a typesetting system.

Since the system was so complex, many functions were hidden in the complicated menu structure. As soon as I arrived at the site, I saw a workstation covered in sticky notes. In fact, there were so many sticky notes it was almost impossible to see the screen. I asked the user to tell me about the sticky notes she had in her work area. She replied that the menu structure was so complex she could never remember how to get to the functions she used the most. The sticky notes provided a way for her to quickly get to the functions she needed. This single visit illustrated how complex the system had become. We were able to spend time with her and other users, taking pictures of their sticky notes and using the information for another study that dug deeper into the complexity of the system.

Contextual inquiry shows us:

- what a person's environment is like;
- how the environment influences the work;
- whether the user has to make accommodations for poor design or a difficult working condition: Do they have to yell across a room to get help to do a task?
- what equipment they are using: How have they set up their workspace? Does their office has a lot of sticky notes up, and if so, why, what do they say? Perhaps the system is not providing the information they need, so they are posting notes to make sure they have that information readily available;
- what opportunities these environment present for innovative thinking.

## Field Research

Field research is quite similar to contextual studies. Both focus not only on the user, the persona and use case, but also on the context of use. There are often many reasons why a site visit might be useful. Perhaps the product is a system that works only in a specific environment, in which case the site visit would focus on the actual physical environment to understand how that influences the user experience. Perhaps the product team is looking to move the product to a different platform or create a new service. In that case, a site visit can show them, first hand, the specific issues a user is dealing with as they perform their tasks with the current product(s). These types of site visits are most successful when they are planned ahead, just like in any other study. A moderator's guide is needed, as well as a checklist for the UX tools, such as a recording device, questionnaires, etc.

Field research has been a staple methodology for anthropology, market research, and psychology as a way to gain an understanding of how people behave. UX field research also seeks to understand how people perform tasks, and what, if any, restrictions their environment put on the process. The next case study demonstrates the value of getting out of the lab and into the world where people live and work.

# A Site Visit at Buffalo General Hospital Researching Use of a Cardiac Workstation

Victoria Morville

## Introduction

In 1997, as some hospitals were converting from analog to digital technology, Eastman Kodak was marketing the Cardiac Direct Connect Workstation. This digital alternative to projectors and film was designed for viewing and sharing cardiac catheterization videos.

Cardiac Catheterization is the process of injecting a dye into the patient's blood vessels and viewing that dye's {progress/pathway?} to find plaque buildup and blockages.

My role was to gather user feedback on the workstation and provide design recommendations for the next release. A standard usability test, however, was not the right approach for several reasons. First, the cardiac viewing environment was not in a standard office setting—instead, it was in a meeting room with diverse lighting, sound levels, and user types. Second, it was important to understand existing viewing tools and procedures so that the transition to a digital platform would be as seamless as possible. The best approach was to observe users in their own environment. I set out on a 3 day site visit with a potential customer—Buffalo General Hospital.

## The Product

The Cardiac Workstation looked like a digital version of the projectors used at the time (refer to Figure 9.1). The workstation's main input device, humorously called the RAT, was a large roller mouse that controlled video playback and simulated the existing projector control panel. The workstation screen was smaller than the projector screens and angled for a standing user. It all rested on a standing cart with no wheels.

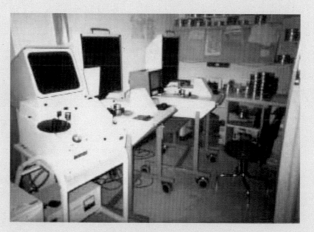

Figure 9.1 Viewing room with Kodak Cardiac Workstation (far left) and projectors to the right of the Kodak Cardiac Workstation on the tables with wheels.

## Site Visit Members

A Kodak sales person insisted that he join me for the site visit—not an ideal arrangement. Although we were both there to meet the users and observe their working environment, our goals were very different. My goal was to discreetly observe, while his was to pitch the product. We found ourselves competing for the users' time.

## Site Visit Process

Before the site visit, I generated a moderator's guide to ensure that the critical questions would be answered (refer to next section, Moderator's Guide). While observing the cardiac unit work environment, it was important that I interfered as little as possible, so as not to disrupt the users' natural flow. I ran fast, efficient usability tests with several volunteer cardiologists throughout the day, and many times had to rearrange or shorten tests depending on their ever-changing availability. Since my participants had only about 15 min to spend with the workstation, my moderator's guide was high level and flexible. During the rest of the time, I stayed in the background taking notes, taking photos, and asking questions when necessary. My goal was to make the doctors feel as comfortable as possible. I wanted them to confide in me their daily challenges and allow me to understand their needs.

Since the doctors were often too busy to answer lengthy questions, I learned a great deal about the cardiac department from the film librarian and technicians. With their help, I learned the process of performing a catheterization, sharing, and viewing the video results, as well as every staff member's role in the unit. I asked questions about catheterization viewing, film organization, and equipment usage. Over time I also learned the "behind the scenes" information—what did the staff complain about the most? What would make their jobs easier?

## Moderator's Guide

This guide was used as a reference to gather profile data on each participant, capture each user's feedback, and answer general questions about the working environment.

### User Profile Data

- Novice or experienced computer user?
- Is this an occasional use product? Is it integrated in daily activities?
- How did users do this work before? Are there transferable skills?

### Environment

- What's the environment like? Light or dark? Lots of open space or cluttered? How many people view the injections at a time?
- How is the review station set up? Where's the keyboard, monitor, CPU, RAT?
- How many studies do the cardiologists go through in a day? Will this system make them work efficiently given these numbers?
- Is there anything that they liked about the old system that they don't have with Direct Connect?
- Would they like to use the injection images to convey information in reports and, consulting with other cardiologists, provide patients with an image? If so, how would they like to be able to transmit these images?

### Workstation

- How do they interact with the system? What's at their fingertips? What do they need to reach for?
- RAT: Do they lift it in order to be able to see the labels? Do the lights on the RAT show up clearly?

- Does the system always keep them informed on what it is doing? Do they have issues with waiting for images to load, etc.? When do they get confused?
- What information do they look for when they sit down to review a catheterization?
- How well are the following features working?
  1. Opening studies from network and from CD—which do they do more often?
  2. Zoom;
  3. Viewing order;
  4. Playing injections;
  5. Moving across injections.

## Working Environment

The cardiac unit was certainly not a typical office environment. All cardiologists performed catheterization reviews in one small common viewing room using one of two large projectors in the center of the room (refer back to Figure 9.1). The Cardiac Workstation was placed next the projectors. The walls contained bookshelves stuffed with film reels (refer to Figure 9.2). The counters in front of the shelves were used to hold the most

Figure 9.2 Shelves of film managed by the division's librarian.

recently processed films. Each doctor had either a bin or a "spot" on the counter on which designated films were placed every day. Although none of the "spots" on the counter were labeled, each cardiologist knew his designated counter area, and the librarians and technicians could recite each doctor's name while pointing at random places on the counter.

The space felt cluttered and claustrophobic, but there was a kind of organized chaos when dealing with these films.

Space in the room varied as throngs of cardiologists, surgeons, and technicians swarmed in and out. At times they were crammed in, each doctor searching for a film reel or standing around a projector, discussing diagnoses.

Other times, the room was quiet as straggling cardiologists or surgeons visited to review cases.

## Users in Their Own Words

The cardiology division at Buffalo State Hospital was comprised of about eight cardiologists, eight cardiovascular surgeons (CV surgeons), eight technicians, and two librarians. In order to give the Kodak team a good understanding of who was using this product, I observed and interviewed each type of user. Some important elements to capture were their day-to-day tasks, job goals, and requests. In my report, I assigned a characteristic quote to each type of role. This gave each user a tangible personality and voice.

The following is a list of each job and typical quotes from the individual groups:

## Cardiologists

"Waiting ten minutes for my images is ten minutes too long. What I want most is speed and convenience."

## Cardiovascular Surgeons

"I want easy access to the cases in the cardiology division, and fast copies of these images to take with me to the OR."

## Technicians

"I think that I can process film faster than the Review Station can receive the images."

"I'm worried that CD's will get lost more easily than film."

## Librarians

"Our biggest problem is storage."

## Main Feedback

These were the main takeaways from my site visit:

- *Height of the workstation*: doctors would either sit or stand while reviewing a catheterization video, depending on their time and how crowded the room was. The input controls were too low to reach if the user was standing, and the monitor was too high for ideal viewing while sitting. The screen and controls needed to be adjustable.
- *Portability*: sometimes the doctors needed to present their findings in other locations in the hospital. Like the projectors, the workstation needed to have wheels for easy portability.
- *Viewing*: videos were viewed in the dark as well as in bright rooms. Screen brightness and contrast needed to accommodate both viewing environments.

Also, the screen needed to be large enough for several people to see the details comfortably while standing around it.

- The fact that the digital workstation was much quieter than the projectors was a big bonus in a small, sometimes crowded observation room.
- Cardiac surgeons very much wanted a print feature, which would allow them to take a screen shot into the operating room.
- The workstation's input device, the RAT, was very well received because it simulated projector controls.

## Lessons Learned

Overall, this site visit was very informative and provided a lot of insight for future design ideas; however, it should be noted that different hospitals work at a different pace and have unique procedures. As part of my results report, I recommended additional site visit studies in different hospitals.

There were several factors that helped make this study successful. First, I was able to connect with a few staff members who were willing to spend time explaining the department's processes and issues. This saved a lot of time and helped me get a good grasp of the environment in a short period of time. Also, although I had a site visit plan, I was willing to be flexible. Due to the hectic environment of a cardiac unit, I was willing to dynamically rework the plan and schedule based on what was happening at the time and who was available.

If I could have done something differently, it would have been to conduct the site visit alone, without a salesperson's accompaniment. Although both sales visits and usability site visits are very important and serve their own purpose, they should not be combined. The two have very different approaches and may confuse users or make them defensive.

Nevertheless, it was a fun, informative study.

# Focus Groups

Although many focus groups occur in a lab-like setting, many of them take place in the field, where the users work or gather. Focus groups provide researchers with a tool to probe into large conceptual issues, as well as drill down into some specific details of a domain.

The Medicare.gov study that I have been discussing in previous chapters also included several focus groups. The following case study describes a focus group that was both successful and unsuccessful.

## Focus Groups with Nursing Home Providers

Fiona Tranquada

### Background

In the fall of 2012, I led a project with a team of graduate students at the Bentley University User Experience Center (UXC) to run focus groups with nursing home providers. The focus groups were part of a larger strategic effort that a fellow consultant—Elizabeth Rosenzweig, also from the UXC—was coordinating for ABT Associates on behalf of their client, the Centers for Medicare & Medicaid Services (CMS).

CMS had recently redesigned Nursing Home Compare, their Web site that allows consumers to compare different nursing homes within a geographical location. Elizabeth asked me to lead the effort to gather feedback from nursing home providers about their experience with Nursing Home Compare (NHC). These providers use the NHC site to compare themselves with other nursing homes in their area, and also to understand what information a potential customer may have seen about their facility ahead of time.

The feedback would then be incorporated into the strategic UX plan that she was developing for ABT to address all of NHC's target audiences. Since I hadn't been involved with the on-going strategic effort, I had to quickly get up to speed on the existing relationship and expectations that had already been set with ABT, in addition to making my piece of the project successful. I also needed to understand the larger context of how my work was going to be used within that larger plan. Throughout the project, my team collaborated as closely as possible with Elizabeth's to create a consistent experience for ABT.

## Research Method

We identified a focus group as the best research method for gathering feedback from the providers. Focus groups would let us have focused group discussions about the NHC site, and also offer providers a chance to share feedback with their peers. Since NHC wanted to establish itself as the most credible source for nursing home information, an informal conversation would ideally build goodwill toward NHC while also allowing our team to gain additional feedback that could be incorporated into our findings.

Because it would be difficult to schedule enough participants in any given city, we decided to hold the focus groups at the 2012 American Healthcare Association (AHCA) conference, which would have a large number of nursing home providers in attendance. The team hoped that it would also be easier to schedule multiple conference attendees for a single time slot than to find multiple time slots for individual attendees. To find participants, an email was sent to conference attendees to gauge interest. Respondents were then screened by an external recruiter to see if they held the desired role at their nursing home (Administrator, Director of Nursing, Chief Clinical Officer) and to establish the size of the nursing home so we could include a mix. We scheduled 2 focus groups, with 10 participants each.

While focus groups are valuable for developing an understanding of a domain or product, we wanted to make sure we captured individual reactions in addition to group discussions. As we worked through the research plan for the focus group, we built in paper surveys that participants would complete individually before the group discussion to ensure that we'd get robust feedback.

## Project Setup

Our team prepared a facilitator guide that included large screenshots of the key screens within the NHC Web site. In these screenshots, which would be projected for all attendees, we blurred out content to keep the facility anonymous. However, since it was important to understand how each provider viewed the data listed on the site about their facility, we supplied each participant with a hardcopy of their facility's current ratings from the Web site. This information reminded infrequent site users about how their facility was represented on the site while also providing a private way to get feedback on the quality and quantity of data listed.

The hardcopy was included in a folder provided to each participant. The folder also contained several surveys. After the facilitator walked through how a user would get to a specific screen on the NHC site and provided a brief overview of the screen, participants would complete the survey that corresponded to that screen. Each survey asked for feedback on:

- Usefulness of the data;
- Accuracy of the data;
- Any other thoughts about that section of the site.

The folder also contained a participant consent form (explaining the goal of the focus group and the participant's rights), an envelope containing the compensation, and a cash receipt to indicate that the participant received the compensation.

In the room, we set up a screen at the front that the facilitator guide was projected on to, and the desks were arranged in a U-shape facing the screen. We set up a camcorder on a tripod in the front corner of the room that was able to capture the full U-shaped setup. A portable audio recorder was placed toward the middle of the tables as a backup recording device, and a note taker (using a laptop) sat by the camcorder.

Once we saw our room's location—which was remote in a way that didn't come across on the maps of the facility—we posted additional signs, hoping to keep participants from getting frustrated and lost.

## Key Findings

Providers felt that the NHC Web site was a good first step for consumers trying to educate themselves about nursing homes and finding a facility. However, our main finding from this study was that nursing home providers felt that the NHC Web site and its 5 star rating system did not provide consumers with an accurate or complete picture of their facility. For example, a consumer has no way of knowing when information listed on the site about a facility was last updated, which means that they may make a decision based on out-of-date information.

Providers also felt that key information was missing that would help consumers decide if a facility could meet the needs of a resident, such as details about level of care offered, quality-of-care ratings compiled via resident satisfaction surveys, and a lack of consistency due to differing state regulations.

Based on the findings, we identified key opportunities for the site:

- Provide additional filters to allow consumers to easily find nursing homes that support specific specialties (e.g., memory loss, mental health), length of stay (e.g., short term, rehab care), or meet other criteria (such as size or number of residents).
- Bring more visibility to how the 5 star ratings are calculated.
- Move the date that each section was last updated to the top of the page.

## Challenges

Our team encountered several challenges throughout the project.

*Providing a consistent experience for client*: While Elizabeth had a pre-existing relationship with ABT, this study was my first time working with them. My goal was to have the project go as smoothly as possible so it would feel like a continuation of the existing work rather than a separate piece of work. To help with this, I had one of the graduate students who had worked on Elizabeth's earlier research support this project as well, and she was able to share her experience and point me to documents that had been used before. We adapted those documents—including the recruiting screener and facilitator guides—to ensure that we were starting from a point that had already met ABT's approval. We also met with Elizabeth's team on a regular basis to ensure that we were aware of any other issues with ABT that might affect our project. This solution worked well. The student's work on both teams provided continuity and meeting with Elizabeth's team regularly helped keep the projects connected.

*Minimal control*: ABT insisted on handling the facility logistics for us. On one hand, this was helpful because they had contacts among the conference organizers already. However, we were not able to enforce some of our desired accommodations, e.g., rooms for the focus groups that were close to the main conference events (instead of in an isolated area far away from everything), and we had no control over when the groups were scheduled during the conference.

*Difficulty contacting participants*: Because almost everyone had traveled to the conference, the recruiter had difficulty confirming sessions with participants the night before the focus groups and getting in touch with the missing participants on the day of the study.

*Poor show rate*: For our first focus group, 6 out of the 10 scheduled participants showed up. For the second focus group, only 1 out of 10 showed up! Even though our recruiter had confirmed with participants before the conference, less than half of them made it to our session. As mentioned in the earlier challenge, the recruiter had difficulty getting in touch with participants on the day of sessions, so it's difficult to tell whether participants had difficulty finding the room or were distracted by other events at the conference. Having only 1 participant for a focus group meant that we had to change the format into more of an interview. This meant that we were able to cover the same questions as in the earlier focus group, but we missed out on the discussion with other providers.

Conclusions

Luckily, the client attended the focus groups in person so saw our poor location and our attempts to contact the missing participants first-hand. Our client was satisfied with the results of this research, and our findings added the necessary context to the larger strategy project. We also came away with some important takeaways for anyone performing similar research:

- When performing research within a larger group effort, try to include at least 1 person who's been involved in other research for that project. This will help provide a consistent experience for your client and also expose you to previous findings that you might otherwise be unaware of.
- Review the documents and deliverables provided for those other project phases, and use a consistent approach for your research. This helps reassure your client that you're not operating in a vacuum.
- Be prepared to adapt, no matter what kind of session you're doing. No-shows are a common problem, even if you do everything right—confirming multiple times, offer appropriate levels of compensation, etc. Think ahead of time about what you'd do for different levels of no-shows. We were able to convert a focus group into an interview fairly easily, but it would have required additional forethought had there been more group activities requested of the attendees during the focus group. This advice is appropriate for any research, but is especially important when you have tight constraints on your ability to find participants (e.g., because you have to rely on your client to recruit, or because your participants will all be at a specific conference).

# BIBLIOGRAPHY

Beyer, H., Holtzblatt, K., 1998. Contextual Design: Defining Customer-Centered Systems. Morgan Kaufmann Publishers, San Francisco, CA.

Contextual Inquiry. http://www.usabilitybok.org/contextual-inquiry.

Contextual Inquiry. http://www.usabilitynet.org/tools/contextualinquiry.htm.

Gaffney, G., 2004. Contextual Enquiry—A Primer, http://www.sitepoint.com/article/contextual-enquiry-primer.

Holtzblatt, K., Wendell, J.B., Wood, S., 2005. Rapid Contextual Design: A How-to Guide to Key Techniques for User-Centered Design. Morgan Kaufmann, San Francisco, CA.

The Use and Misuse of Focus Groups. http://www.nngroup.com/articles/focus-groups/.

Whiteside, J., Bennett, J., Holtzblatt, K., 1988. Usability engineering: our experience and evolution. In: Helander, M. (Ed.), Handbook of Human Computer Interaction. North Holland, New York, pp. 791–817.

Wixon, D., Ramey, J. (Eds.), 1996. Field Methods Case Book for Software Product Design. John Wiley & Sons, Inc., New York.

Wixon, D., Holtzblatt, K., Knox, S., 1990. Contextual design: an emergent view of system design. In: Proceedings of CHI '90: Conference of Human Factors in Computing Systems, Seattle, WA.

# Chapter 10

## GLOBAL UX AND ONLINE STUDIES

This chapter addresses issue that come up when doing UX work globally. It describes how to integrate different cultures and uses a case study to show a project done in Switzerland and one in China as well as, World Usability Day's goal of creating a more usable world.

# Chapter 10

We must create a kind of globalization that works for everyone… and not just for a few.

**Nestor Kirchner**

## Global UX

The World Wide Web has grown quickly into a global Internet, with approximately 40% of the earth's population or roughly 3 billion online. It has, in many ways, made the world smaller, since we can connect with people on the other side of the planet in a matter of seconds. Although not everyone has access to the internet many people do. At the time of writing the distribution of Internet users is roughly:

- 48% Asla;
- 22% Americas (North and South);
- 19% Europe;
- 10% Africa;
- 1% Oceania.

This means people have access to other cultures, experiencing them in different ways online. The mixing of cultures is a common occurrence. We don't know what we don't know and therefore sometimes we might offend without even knowing. This certainly gets in the way of the UX and provides many barriers to entry. On the positive side, people have learned about other cultures and the Internet has informed us as to how to interact with those who might be different from us.

When the Kodak Brownie camera became available fully loaded for $1 in 1900 people were given the power to see more of the world than ever before. The Brownie provided people with images of family and friends, and scenes from places all around the world. This changed the world by making it a bit smaller, through the connections people made with the images.

While there are many challenges for creating usable global experiences, there has been a lot of good work with the creation of standard methodologies.

Communities have been developing online for many years at Web site such as Facebook, Twitter, LinkedIn, and other social media platforms. The advances make it easier for people to be able to connect from anywhere to anywhere. The possibilities are increasing every day. The most successful systems will be the ones that were developed with the user at the center.

The same methodologies and principles of good user experience design apply to global UX design. Global UX design requires a deep understanding of the user, where the persona includes cultural awareness, especially as it relates to design. These considerations can be broken down using the following guidelines:

- All UX design methodologies apply, but with more care directed at creating personas, including attention to global demographics;
- Areas of cultural differences which may impact both the user and UX design include the following:
  - Education is highly prioritized in some cultures, while others might balance book learning with experiential interactions with the real world.
  - Standard of living has a huge impact. Citizens in developing countries might not have the same access to technology as those in developed countries. These different levels of familiarity with technology could impede adoption and use, if one were not aware of the other.
  - Modes of interaction may be verbal, visual, and/or sensory.
  - Ways of thinking may be holistic or linear.
  - Relationship to time is important. Some cultures have a structured adherence to the clock while other cultures think of time as a suggestion, and not rigid. If one person from a culture that is structured around time had a meeting with someone who thought of a clock as a suggestion, they could easily frustrate each other with the pace of the interactions.

## Internationalization and Localization

Technology development that aims to serve a global audience must make sure it is addressing the need of people from the targeted geographical region. This means the design must understand and incorporate the customs, culture, and language from each region. For example, if you are displaying a map of restaurants in Shanghai, China, use icons that map to objects in the Chinese culture. Do not use an icon that represents a fork and knife to represent the restaurant because in China restaurants would provide chopsticks as their utensils of choice.

The process is often called localization and/or internationalization. Many companies have strict practices to translate and localize their user interface and documentation for each market. Best practices for user groups that are not from a single culture or geographical location include:

- Always have a native speaker review translations before the people of the culture use them.
- Compilation of multicultural teams helps ensure that different points of view are taken into account while designing and developing products and systems.
- If English is your first language, use caution not to take English for granted. The version of English spoken in the United Kingdom is not the same as the version spoken in the United States of America.

When designing for an audience outside of their local area, teams need to pay great attention to cultural differences. This can be done during user testing by asking the following questions:

- Where do you live? Tells us about their current culture and language.
- How much do you travel? Where do you go? This tells us how much exposure the user has to other cultures.
- Where did you grow up? Tells us about their culture and language of origin.

The following case study examines a specific UX process for redesigning a traffic-management system. Switzerland is made up of citizens who speak several languages—German, French, Italian, and Romansh.

The Swiss federal government must take care to offer verbal and written information, e.g., signage, in the critical languages to reach the entire country. The following case study shows how a country such as Switzerland, whose citizens are so culturally diverse, can incorporate best UX practices to redesign a basic transportation system.

# The Redesign of the Swiss Traffic Management

Silvia Zimmermann

Switzerland is a landlocked country in the middle of Europe consisting of 26 partly self-governing cantons[1], all under a central federal government. It spans an area of 41,282 km$^2$ (15,940 sq mi). Switzerland has currently a population of approximately 8 million people. The traffic volume on the Swiss roads is, like in other countries, steadily increasing. Between 1990 and 2000, the number of kilometers traveled on the road network increased from 50 to 58 million. According to the Federal Office for Spatial Development (ARE) it is suggested that traffic will further increase by another 25-30% by the year 2020.

The consequences of increased traffic are known: higher pollution and noise emissions, more accidents and congestion, and longer travel times. The whole transport system as such becomes more vulnerable to disruption. The already inadequate "roads" will be even more inadequate in the future. From an economic, environmental, and social perspective, it is useful to counter these tendencies by taking appropriate measures. The Swiss Traffic Management (VM-CH) plays a central role in this endeavor.

## Reasons for the Redesign

Historically, each and every canton had its own system to monitor and steer its cantonal highway traffic. Since these systems were developed independently from each other during different periods of time and also with different providers, an almost countless number of different user interfaces with a variety of different usages and design patterns existed (Figure 10.1).

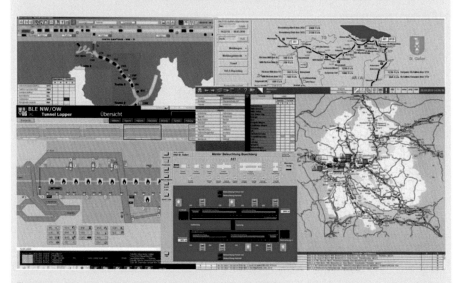

Figure 10.1 Excerpt from different system graphical user interfaces.

Back in 2008, the ASTRA (Federal Roads Office—FEDRO) received sovereignty for the entire Swiss highway network as well as for the VM-CH. Shortly afterward, the FEDRO launched a project to develop one common system for steering and monitoring the entire Swiss highway traffic control. They laid out a vision called *System Architecture Switzerland* (SA-CH) and divided the project into two main phases: phase 1: INA (Integrated Applications) on a Service Oriented Architecture (SOA) and phase 2: SA-CH.

The entire system should eventually consist of a harmonized, fully distributed communication and service network that delivers data to both local Web servers as well as to the servers in the traffic control centers, i.e., to all users involved. In the light of this harmonization process, there was also the idea that all users within the different cantons use the same system with an identical set of user interfaces, i.e., to use cross-cantonal synergies.

## UX Design Process

During the first kick-off of the project a consulting firm applied the method of **story telling** to gain insights about the necessary functions and features of the new system. Why this method was applied is to-date unknown. But what happened was that the method produced far too many and far too detailed requirements. As a consequence the project team was not in a position to derive the new **conceptual model** from the requirements. As a result the project was put on hold.

During the second kick-off our company was invited by the general contractor leading the project to help frame how the UX process should be applied. After a first analysis of all existing interfaces and based on our experience with strategic projects of that size and complexity we suggested applying **a top-down user-centered** approach. Hence, after an in-depth analysis of the current state we conducted intensive field research, including **shadowing and interviewing activities** at the different control centers to gain a better understanding of how the operators worked with the system during their daily work routines. At that point we realized that a variety of different user groups existed and that the new system should be as flexible and scalable as possible.

We developed 10 different **personas**, ranging from Peter, the traffic operator on duty, who is event-driven and has to react in case of an incident (fire in a tunnel for example) to Paul who maintains the traffic network (fixing a light in a tunnel or mowing the grass by the roadside for example). After reviewing and approving the personas we started to develop the **conceptual model** for the new system, including **sketching** the first user interfaces in Adobe InDesign.

To give you some more insights let me share some of the complexities we were facing. We had 10 different personas all working with different devices and with different screen resolutions, ranging from $1024 \times 768$ to $1920 \times 1080$ pixels, and from 15″ to 27″ monitor sizes. The users were also working in very different contextual situations, i.e., ranging from a modern operating room with large monitor displays to a console in a tunnel where the user couldn't even use a mouse due to the environmental constraints. From a scalability point of view the user interface also had to present users with different views, i.e., a map view (traffic) as well as a schematic view (tunnel) and text views (for manuals). Moreover, the system also should allow users to individually drill down, i.e., from the entire Swiss area down to the tunnel aggregate. It's like drilling down Google map, only that the drill down goes inside the tunnel and shows all tunnel objects and aggregates in detail. Given this complexity we decided to adjust our user-centered design activities in a step-by-step manner, based on the outcome of the previous UX activities.

After we had developed the first sketches we decided not to run user studies on them as you would normally do, but discuss them with the different user groups in large, one-day **workshops**. We aimed to get initial feedback on the conceptual model and at the same time more insights into the layer concept we had developed. We also wanted to understand how users perceived navigation through the different views and how easily they managed to understand the alarm concept in the user interface.

The results were encouraging and based on the outcome the general contractor generated Visio mockups on which we performed **usability tests** in the different areas of Switzerland with different user groups. After successful completion we developed a mockup for the new workplace in the operator room, i.e., we created a real-life workplace with cardboard display mockups of the user interfaces. We let the user who work shift work test them over a period of time and asked for feedback with a detailed **questionnaire**. It was only after completion of the analysis that we started to create **Axure prototypes**. We used Axure to lay out the entire system, based on the general **design style guide** of the Swiss Government.

Since it was the aim of the FEDRO to apply our conceptual model to all new developments, we were then tasked to write the **SA-CH$^2$ Style Guide**. This was one on the more intense steps in the entire process, since we had to measure out every UI element (buttons, checkboxes, text entry fields, colors, icons, and so on) on a pixel level. Based on our style guide the user interface was built for a first pilot highway section in 2014.

## Learnings

The decision to apply a top-down user-centered approach was the right one. Applying storytelling methods might work for smaller projects, but for a project of such size and complexity it definitely did not work. We also found, that compromising on the user-centered design process by dynamically adjusting it based on the project needs was a good decision. The theoretical UCD would have had many more UX activities, but we felt comfortable leaving them out since the conceptual model gave us confidence that our initial sketches would eventually provide all user groups with the functions and features needed. And also, that the user interfaces would be flexible, scalable, and easy to use. The fact that the sketches were already done in Adobe instead of using an easy sketching tool, as we would normally do, also paid off. I was skeptical myself in the beginning, but the sketches really helped us to have the right level of discussions with the users very early on in the project. Paper pencil sketches wouldn't have helped us at this point because of the lack of detail. So all in all it can be summarized that a top-down user-centered design process was the right approach for a project of such size and complexity.

---

[1]http://en.wikipedia.org/wiki/Swiss.

[2]SA-CH = System Architecture Schweiz.

## Storytelling and UX

The storytelling approach described above is a good way to understand the cultural issues that might be relevant to a person in a multi-cultural location such as Switzerland. It is clear that the storytelling helped visualize issues for simpler systems, but it is not sophisticated enough for complex systems. In those cases, flexibility, and awareness of the deeper issues helped create an approach that was able to satisfy the project needs.

This next case study illustrates the issues that arise when moving a Web site from one culture or country to another. The project includes a large series of tests, across five cities in a very large country. As in the prior case study, a country can present different cultural issues within its borders and that results in UX issues that must be solved. In both cases UX practice and methodology provides the tools to find evidence-based solutions.

# Cross Channel e-Service Design in China

Jason Huang

## Introduction

Founded in 2007, Tang is a user experience consultancy and design studio based in China. With studios in Shanghai (headquarters), Beijing, Xiamen, and Shenzhen. Tang has established itself as a leader in the Chinese user experience industry and it employs the "X Thinking" approach (http://www.tangux.com/).

Intercontinental Hotels Group (IHG) is a multinational hotels company headquartered in the United Kingdom, with regional operations offices around the world. The IHG brand comprises 11 hotel brands, including Holiday Inn, Crowne Plaza, and Hotel Indigo.

IHG first came to Tang looking for usability testing support in 2011, to evaluate a Web site concept designed for the Chinese market. The design Tang was presented with was created in the United States, by an American design studio. The importance of the Chinese market was clear to IHG from the beginning, but the choice of what approach to take was a point of confusion. IHG maintains a global Web site which is translated into a number of languages and used by guests around the world. Even from the beginning of our collaboration with IHG, it was decided that the Chinese market would benefit from a tailored design due to the differences in culture, language, and habits of Chinese guests.

## The Importance of Localization

After carrying out a series of usability tests on the design concept with 40 users in five cities across China, the research team at Tang found close to 50 usability and localization issues with the design across four dimensions: content, interaction, navigation, and presentation. It was clear that the design concept would not deliver the business gains IHG was hoping for by developing a specific Web site for the market. After a period of close collaboration, IHG agreed that the design concept would not be appropriate for use, and in turn decided that Tang would be the most suitable partner to design a truly localized concept.

And so began the project to fully re-design the IHG China Web site. Given that the originally proposed design did not satisfy user needs, Tang proposed a period of in-depth user research at the beginning of the project, to provide inspiration and insights to IHG and the design team. It would not simply be a matter of understanding visual preferences, and identifying pain points, but rather a complete vision of the ecosystem, and where a hotel's official Web site fits in. We needed to identify the different channels users interacted with, and when and why they would use these channels. With the huge rise in smartphone popularity in China, it was of great importance that not only did we paid attention to the role of mobile devices within the ecosystem, but also that we tried to understand when users are most comfortable using their smartphones, and which tasks they use them to perform.

In-Depth User Research

This would be the second phase of user involvement that Tang had facilitated for IHG, although this time the focus was on user perceptions of the IHG brand, user habits, and needs, rather than evaluating an existing product. We worked closely with users from both Western and Eastern China for this part of the project. It is worth noting that it is difficult to describe a typical "Chinese user." Preferences, cuisine, and even language vary greatly across China, and it is important to understand users from all regions and cities with different levels of development, in order to create a truly localized solution. Each user was asked to complete a diary in a template we provided, in which they provided details of their last traveling experience, the pain points they experienced, their mood at each stage of the process, and the channels they used (Figure 10.2). As well as facilitating the diary work with users, the researchers also conducted user interviews and data analysis, and evaluated IHG's competitors. After gathering almost 20 user diaries, the research team at Tang was able to develop three personas: hedonist, materialist, and pragmatist.

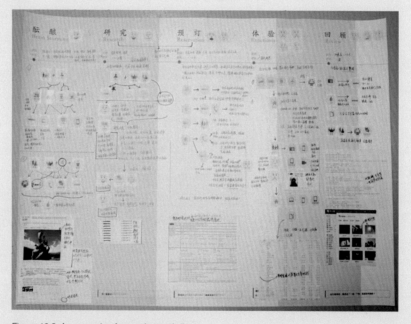

Figure 10.2 An example of a user's travel diary.

Put simply, our three personas describe: people who do not spend a lot of time preparing and planning their trip (Hedonist—Figure 10.3); those who like to plan and research many aspects of their itinerary before they travel, typically on a budget (pragmatist); and those who expect perfection during their trip, and enjoy trying new things (materialist). We summarized each of these personas by outlining their age, occupation, income, education, typical hotel choices, their attitudes toward traveling, and what they usually experience whilst on a trip.

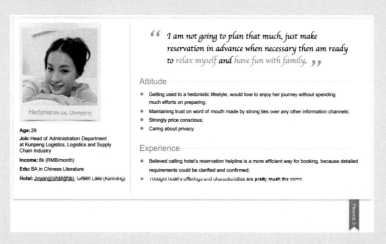

Figure 10.3 The Hedonist persona.

A combination of all our findings allowed us to develop a detailed travel experience journey map, which organized travel experiences into five main processes: inspiration, research, reservation, experience, and review and share. At the time we created the travel experience journey map, it was the first time IHG had seen the full scale of its touch points with its guests. Our journey map outlines the channels users generally interact with in each of the five main processes, and which devices they use. Not only was this of importance for the later design conceptualization, but also in determining future strategies for IHG. We were able to demonstrate that the current channels offered by IHG did not meet the needs of guests throughout the different parts of their journey, and IHG acted upon this in the planning of their future business strategies. It is important that IHG saw its channels and the relationships between them, from the guest's point of view, rather than an organizational one.

Our design for the IHG Web site needed to satisfy the three personas in completing a number of tasks such as destination research, hotel selection, and reservation. In addition, our experience journey map outlined another objective we needed to accomplish. We had observed that many of the users frequently used online travel agencies. Popular OTAs in China include ctrip.com, elong.com, and qunar.com. Such Web sites are becoming increasingly popular as a quick and convenient way to make travel arrangements, so a challenge we faced was ensuring that our Web site design not only stood out from competing hotel groups' Web sites, but also offered greater value than the range of OTAs.

To give just one example, we found that many Chinese users were almost completely unaware of the IHG brand, although in contrast, they were familiar with the individual hotels, and many users we interviewed had stayed at some of the IHG brand hotels before. When faced with the global IHG site, users are also unclear about the relationship between the hotel brands and their positioning. As a result, we felt that our design should also take into consideration branding.

At the end of our user research phase, we arrived at four design directions and strategies that we would focus on. These were: optimizing the reservation system, brand building and promotion, in-depth content creation, and a brand new sharing system (Figure 10.4), and we determined that we would achieve these by creating a seamless experience, a multi-channel experience, building a stronger brand image, and designing an exciting visual experience.

Figure 10.4 Tang's four design directions for the IHG project.

## Beyond Design

With our journey map and design strategies, we went about creating two design concepts in parallel. Two teams created sketches, wireframes, and visual designs concepts, which we later shared with IHG to hear their feedback. Whilst IHG came to Tang for our knowledge of the Chinese market and ability to conceptualize and design solutions based on our user research, it was always agreed that IHG would leverage their global development team based in the USA and India to implement the designs we created. This presented one of the major challenges of the project. Working with teams with different cultural backgrounds will present difficulties, and working in different time zones only adds to the complications. In addition, the importance of collaboration between the design and development teams cannot be underestimated. The design team must be aware of the developers' capabilities and working styles to ensure that the design concept is feasible and understandable. Having not worked with IHG's development team before, this rapport was built from scratch, but was absolutely necessary in order to achieve the product we see today. Regular communication was indeed the most effective way to achieve this.

Just after the site had been implemented, some initial statistics were collected in order to validate the design. In terms of reservations, the original site had a bounce rate of approximately 80%, whilst the latest design lowered that by 25%. We achieved this by simplifying the reservation process into just three steps, providing the specific information requested by users when making a booking, and ensuring the page was well localized, which included all details from form design to offering appropriate payment methods (Figure 10.5).

Figure 10.5 Reservation page before (left) and after (right).

Whilst the design of the new Chinese Web site was a great success, the Web site was just a single piece of the puzzle in transforming the user experience for IHG guests in China. We also worked with IHG on their membership program, social media, special offer campaigns, and customer service channels. Tang and IHG are still striving to continually improve the guest experience in each stage of the experience journey map.

Key Takeaways

- Successful localization requires a deep and combined understanding of users and the problem space.
- Creating an experience journey map can help structure a project.
- A translated version of a global Web site in unlikely to deliver the same ROI as a truly localized one.

The IHG China Web site can be found at http://cn.ihg.com.

Online Studies

- **Why do them**? They can save money; they can include participants from many geographic locations.
- **When to do them**? When you want to reach a lot of people in a short time, if you have a great number of personas, or if the product is online and you want to test it in a natural scenario:
    - **All in one country**. Big countries still have the issues of getting participants to travel great distances. In some situations, there is wide latitude for personas and the online testing makes it easier for everyone to participate.
    - **Multi-country** studies lend themselves nicely to online execution. This is because of the potentially high number of personas generally included in multi-country studies.

We're still in the first minutes of the first day of the Internet revolution.

**Scott Cook**

# World Usability Day

A chapter about UX and usability in the world would not be complete without mention of World Usability Day.

World Usability Day was started as an initiative of the Usability Professionals' Association in 2005. I came up with the idea when I was on the UPA Board of Director and working with Nigel Bevan on Outreach. I was (and still am) concerned when I hear people tell me that they are not technically literate, or not smart when it comes to technology. I wondered why people automatically blamed themselves if a piece of technology was hard to use. The complete faith that the technology had been designed in a thoughtful way baffled me. I have carried out user research with some very intelligent people such as doctors, professors, scientists, and even some of them would tell me that when it came to technology, they were not very smart. I thought maybe part of why so many products, services, and technology were developed as difficult to use was because no one had complained. Of course people call customer service to ask for help in figuring out how to do something, but people always assume that they are at fault. I thought we should change people's thinking about how technology should work. Why blame ourselves when we can push back? Speak up to the companies, complain, or, better yet, simply stop buying products that don't work. I wanted to change the dynamic of technology development and put the person at the center, create a UX that does start with the person. Maybe we could start a usability revolution, the way Earth Day brought about the awareness that we need to take care of our environment, recycle our waste, and create a more sustainable future.

I had hoped the World Usability Day could be the start of that. By 2006 more than 135 events were organized in 35 countries. And finally our numbers rose to 44 countries with 40,000 people involved. But it did not turn out to be a usability revolution. No one has stopped buying products because they are not usable, but the message is getting out to corners of the world that had previously not thought about developing products by putting the person at the center of all the technology and marketing.

Events were held at museums and malls around the world with activities such as:

- "Sorting Socks" where piles of socks were on tables and people were encourage to simple sort them to any category that made sense. People observing could see that participants would use categories such as size, color, pattern, and more. Not everyone thought of sorting them in the same way. The World Usability Day people standing by would.

- "Walk of Signs" where teams of people would take a walk around their town and photograph signs that was either incredibly helpful or incredibly confusing. I recall one set of pictures in Boston, during the time of the Big Dig, showed several signs on a single street giving conflicting directions: "Right Turn Only" and a few feet down "No Right Turn."

- "Alarm Clock Alley" was a favorite at science museums, where kids would race each other to set an alarm on different clocks. The adults looking on inevitably would say "Wow, I always thought it was me who could never figure those things out."

- One free hour of consultation: UX professionals would be on hand for a one-hour consultation to a nonprofit organization working in the area. They would schedule the consultation and come into the event to meet with several UX professionals who would do an expert review on their Web site or product for 1 h.

At the time of writing, World Usability Day has opened up new work in regions of the world such as India, Eastern Europe, and the Middle East. And it seems to be taking on a life of its own. The global network the makes up World Usability Day is now run through the hard work of volunteers. The Web site www.worldusabilityday.org is a repository for people to connect and register their events around the world. The events are always held on or near the second Thursday in November.

The idea that people have come to accept is that when they have a hard time figuring out how something works, something is wrong with them, made me think we needed to get our message out. It needed to reach beyond the fields of computer science, engineering, and marketing: to the greater world and the common person. This gave birth to World Usability Day (WUD) in 2005 whose mission was to raise awareness of the importance of putting people's needs in front of market drivers. WUD has been successful in growing the field in developing countries, but the average person still thinks they need to be smart or have technical skills to be able to use technology. WUD's primary mission is to change this thinking, so that the average person would blame the technology if there was a problem and not themselves. WUD was formalized in 2006 with a charter (Figures 10.6 and 10.7).

# World Usability Day 2006
14 November 2006 • Making life easy!

# World Usability Day Charter

Technology today is too hard to use. A cell phone should be as easy-to-use as a doorknob. In order to humanize a world that uses technology as an infrastructure for education, healthcare, government, communication, entertainment, work, and other areas, we must agree to develop technologies in a way that serves people first.

Technology should enhance our lives, not add to our stress or cause danger through poor design or poor quality. It is our duty to ensure that this technology is effective, efficient, satisfying and reliable, and that it is usable by all people. This particularly important for people with disabilities, because technology can enhance their lives, letting them fully participate in work, social and civic experiences.

Human error is a misnomer. Technology should be developed knowing that human beings have certain limitations. Human error will occur if technology is not both easy-to-use and easy-to-understand. We need to reduce human error that results from bad design.

We believe a united, coordinated effort is needed to develop reliable, easy-to-use technology to serve people in all aspects of their lives, including education, health, government, privacy, communications, work and entertainment. We must put people at the center of design, beginning with their needs and wants, and resulting in technology that benefits all of us.

Therefore, we, the undersigned, agree to work together to design technology that helps human beings truly realize their potential, so that we can create a better world for ourselves and future generations.

**We agree to observe World Usability Day each year, to provide a single worldwide day of events around the world that brings to get communities of professional, industrial, educational, citizen and governmental groups for our common objective: to ensure that technology helps people live to their full potential and helps create a better world for all citizens everywhere.**

Figure 10.6 World Usability Day Charter.

### Article 1: Education

Wired and wireless schools are appearing everywhere. Students around the world benefit from low-cost, easy-to-use, reliable computing, Internet access, and telecommunication. Educational technology must be not only affordable and available, but must be usable by teachers, students and parents.

### Article 2: Health

Healthcare must be available to everyone around the world. Medical technology can improve health, but it must be easy-to-use: error in this arena is costly. Because we are what we eat, we need healthier food supplies that will improve the well being of people everywhere. Technology that produces better food for all must be built on research that keeps the whole person in mind.

### Article 3: Government

Governments around the globe seek to use new technology to better serve their citizens and increase participation in the civic experience. Citizens can pay taxes and take care of business online in many countries in the world; this same capability should be available to all, eliminating the digital divide that separates rich from poor or isolates social groups. Voting systems must ensure trust and confidence in elections. Technology that supports civic engagement must give all citizens equal access and opportunity, and must be easy to use and easy to understand by all citizens, including those with disabilities of any kind.

### Article 4: Communication

People need to connect with each other. We have more means than ever to communicate: phones, Internet, messaging and the printed medium. Technology that facilitates communication between people must be intuitive to use. It should have instructions that are easy to understand, and knobs, dials and buttons that do not require constant tuning.

### Article 5: Privacy and Security

As the use of technology grows, so do concerns about new forms of e-commerce, e-government and e-communication. We must build in appropriate safeguards to ensure that our interaction is secure, that children and others are protected, and that our systems are trustworthy.

### Article 6: Entertainment

Entertainment is not just for our spare time. People use entertainment for many reasons throughout their daily lives. The world of entertainment has embraced technology to give us photos, movies, music and games in new ways and on new devices. But, even amusement benefits from usability! Incomprehensible remote controls, confusing instructions and blinking VCR clocks speak to the need for improvement in out media. Usable entertainment systems will make the experience less tiring and frustrating.

Figure 10.7 World Usability Day Charter, section 2.

# What is Common?

Global UX means really looking at the big picture. We are all people and working together to fix problems will make it all work better. We can provide the principles of UX to almost all we do. UX really can change the world.

## Why Clutter Up the World With Useless Devices?

**Accidental usability** is the state that good developers create when thinking of the long-term use of a device. The reason it is accidental, is that the goal might not have been to create a more usable product, but because of other goals, such as creating products that are recyclable and sustainable, they also create a better user experience. For example, if a device is built so that it lasts, perhaps as a modular device or one that is open to updates, then it won't need to be replaced as often, creating more sustainable products. This creates a better world, which is inherently a better user experience.

Today many products and services are developed as a result of cutting edge technology or pushed by marketplace popularity. A new technology is invented, with a specific product goal, and the result is an object that might have some cool features, but is not creating a good experience for the user. Product developers do not really put the user at the center of the development; some assume that users are novices that can't understand the product, etc., assuming that if they can't figure it out, they must be stupid. Of course, that is a vicious cycle, since whenever a developer sees a user having trouble, they blame that user, and not the way the system was developed.

The "I am not technically literate" attitude affects the overall state of product development. Over the years, people have embraced technology, but many people assume that, if they have a problem with technology, it is their fault. "I am not technical" has been a comment made time and again by many smart people, always assuming the technology knows more than they do—that in fact, they should blame themselves when there are technical problems. Users are not trained to blame the technology. One of the reasons that World Usability Day was started was to educate the common person, so they would stop blaming themselves when they could not understand a new piece of technology.

# BIBLIOGRAPHY

Bedore, T., 2006. How About Make Things Easier Day? (HTML/Audio). American Public Media's Marketplace, (radio program) (Retrieved 27-12-2006). "Today is World Usability Day, a day to promote intuitive engineering and user-friendly design. Commentator and humorist Tim Bedore is all for it, if only we could come up with a better name…".

Internet Users. http://www.internetlivestats.com/internet-users/.

Kodak History. http://www.kodak.com/ek/US/en/Our_Company/History_of_Kodak/ Milestones_-_chronology/1878-1929.htm.

Quesenbery, W., Brooks, K., 2010. Storytelling for User Experience, Crafting Stories for Better Design. Rosenfeld Media, New York.

# Chapter 11

## SURVEYS, WEB ANALYTICS, AND SOCIAL MEDIA

This chapter describes the role that surveys, Web analytics, and social media have in UX. Case studies include research using surveys as well as Web analytics for Medicare.gov.

# Chapter 11

Knowledge is power. Information is liberating.

**Kofi Annan**

Opinions that are supported by data are always stronger than those formed through personal or anecdotal experience. Evidence-based work establishes a foundation of knowledge from which to make informed design decisions. It is not uncommon for design and development teams to spend hours arguing over their opinions, but without data, these opinions don't always hold up and can be based on wrong assumptions. Information provides us with evidence that might surprise us, but keeps us honest. In fact, if one can look at the evidence with an open mind, new ideas, and creative solutions emerge.

## Surveys

Collecting reliable information is the foundation for understanding any situation, and being able to make informed decisions. When it comes to UX and design decisions, getting reliable data about the users and how they are interacting with objects is key to a good design.

Questionnaires and surveys are tools for collecting large amounts of data from specific groups of people. The benefits of using surveys include:

- Ability to reach people in remote locations;
- Cost savings over other methods of collecting data;
- Online tools for easy data analysis;
- Statically significant results.

Surveys can be run in many ways including in person, on the phone, online, and by mail. Good survey design includes carefully identifying the target group and scientifically crafting the questions to be nonbiased. Surveys are good for running quantitative evaluations of technology products and services. Some UX strategies would include combining survey tools with usability inspection methods to develop a deeper understanding and validate usability issues. Surveys can use open-ended or multiple choice questions, as well as many other techniques.

## Online or In Person

Prior to the invention of computers all surveys were done on paper, usually in person. Sometimes they were handed out to participants who took pen to the paper and filled out the survey. Sometimes surveys included questionnaires as a tool for an interviewer to fill out while talking to a participant. These paper surveys are still used on occasion today, but they are slowly being replaced with online surveys.

Paper surveys often take longer to fill out and in the current world of instant access, online surveys are more aligned with people's lifestyles. There are limitations to online surveys, such as certain populations not having regular access to the Internet and computer technology, making it hard to reach them.

More researchers are turning to online surveys for their great advantages in reaching larger audiences within the shortest time and as a less expensive approach.

**Online surveys** can reach across time zones to get data from people. The UX researcher has many online survey tools to choose from, many of which provide services to help recruit respondents and analyze the data once it has been collected.

Some commonly used online survey tools are listed below:

- SurveyMonkey is a straightforward online survey tool that helps create surveys and analyze the data.
- UserZoom claims to be the number one platform for testing, measuring, and monitoring the user experience.

- Qualtrics is a more complex online survey tool that has the capabilities to do remote testing as well as surveys.
- Zoomerang is an easy-to-use online survey tool that helps create surveys and analyze the data.

Surveys have limitations, as any methodology might, and it is important to understand them before using them. The case study below demonstrates the risk of a participant being biased by their own personal beliefs, so much so that their bias changes their behavior.

## Does a Personal Belief Create Bias in User Behavior Online?

Liz Burton, Debra Reich and Yina Li

### Overview

The studies described here started as a group project for the Measuring the User Experience class in the Human Factors in Information Design master's program at Bentley University. The impetus for our team's project was to try to explore the effects of user bias on the results of usability studies. To that end, we decided to conduct a study of two Web sites—one hosted by the US Democratic Party and one by the US Republican Party—and then compare the results for three subgroups of participants: those who identified themselves as liberal, conservative, and neutral. Our hypothesis was that, if participants are biased by their personal beliefs, they may be inclined to try harder to complete tasks on a site that is aligned with their beliefs, resulting in systematic differences between the three groups on the two sites. To explore this question, we used UserZoom to conduct online, un-moderated tests to measure time on task and success rates of participants. Each participant completed a series of four tasks on both sites. They were also asked to rate their overall impression of each site.

## Background

There is a substantial body of research, conducted across a wide variety of contexts, on the various types of bias that can impact the results of behavioral research studies (see Podsakoff et al., 2003, for a review). Sources of bias include both methodological factors (i.e., factors arising from the design of the study and how the results are measured) and response biases (i.e., factors that cause participants to respond in ways that don't accurately reflect their true feelings or opinions). Within the context of usability studies, one of the most commonly studied methodological biases is the evaluator effect (see, for example, Hertzum and Jacobsen, 2001). Studies of this phenomenon have shown that multiple experts, evaluating the same system, and using the same evaluation method, can identify markedly different sets of usability issues. Other biases that can affect the results of usability studies include the Hawthorne effect, in which the simple fact that participants are being observed changes their behavior, and the possibility that a participant's sole motivator for taking part in the study is to obtain the honorarium, which can cast doubt on the value of the data (Sauro, 2012). Participants' response biases can also affect the results of usability research; in particular, social desirability bias (Holbrook et al., 2003; Nancarrow and Brace, 2000) may lead participants to express a more positive opinion than they actually hold, because they believe that's what the researcher wants to hear (Sauro, 2012).

For our study, we proposed to measure the outcomes of the usability test of each of the two political Web sites using performance metrics (task success rates and time on task) as well as quantitative attitudinal measures, and to evaluate the results using statistical significance tests. Within the body of research on bias, this approach appears to be unique. Therefore, we felt it could potentially represent a meaningful contribution to the research literature, as well as expand the body of research specific to the user experience field. According to Sauro (2012), "biases can never be entirely eliminated; so being aware of them and communicating their potential impact on decisions is often the best remedy." Since there are many subject areas and even companies that elicit emotional responses from users, it is an area of study that should be addressed. We felt our study could provide a useful first step for researchers to begin to understand the potential impacts of user bias and ensure that those effects are accounted for appropriately in interpreting results of user studies.

## The Initial Study

The initial study was conducted on Userzoom.com and ran from April 1/th to May 3rd, 2013. We used a within-subjects design in which participants were asked to complete a total of eight tasks, four on each site. In order to control for possible order effects, we used the randomization capacity that Userzoom offers to counterbalance the order of presentation of the two sites. However, within site, the goal was to present participants with a relatively easy task first and have subsequent tasks that increased in difficulty as participants progressed. Therefore, while the order of presentation of the two sites varied across participants, the task order within site remained constant. Our aim was to select a set of tasks for each site such that the overall level of difficulty was approximately equal for the two sites.

After the participants had completed the usability test for both Web sites, they were asked to indicate their personal political beliefs using a 5-point Likert scale, where 1 = *Democratic* and 5 = *Republican*. Participants who selected 1 or 2 were placed into the Liberal/Democrat group, those who selected 3 into the Neutral group, and those who selected 4 or 5 into the Conservative/Republican group. Our recruiting strategy was limited by the fact that we couldn't offer any incentive to participants so initially it consisted entirely of reaching out to our own personal networks. However, when it became clear that one end of the political spectrum was much more heavily represented among our acquaintances and families than the other, we added two more strategies: placing ads on the volunteer section of craigslist in 30 different geographic areas across the country; and emailing approximately 150 college Republican clubs. In the end, we had 69 participants complete the test: 65 from our personal networks, 4 from the craigslist ads, and 0 from the college Republican clubs. Sixty-two percent of the participants identified as Democrat, 13% as Republican, and 17% as Neutral; 7% of the participants declined to answer the question.

While the results of the study showed some interesting patterns, we felt the extreme disproportion in the numbers of participants in each of the three groups seriously undermined the credibility of the results. Therefore, we decided to redo the study with a broader (and, hopefully, more representative) set of participants.

## The Follow-Up Study

Despite our concerns about the validity of the results of the initial study, the group still felt that the research protocol we had used could yield some valuable findings for the field if we were able to address the major flaws of the original study. Therefore, we decided to conduct a follow-up study after the class ended. For the second study, we recruited participants using Amazon Mechanical Turk. We chose Mechanical Turk because it gave us access to a much larger pool of potential participants, while still enabling us to run the study very economically. However, because of the recruiting problems we experienced in the original study, we decided to put measures in place to ensure that the same thing didn't happen again. To accomplish this, we added a qualifying survey at the beginning of the process and implemented quotas to control the number of liberal and conservative participants that were included in the study.

The second study ran from October 14th to October 21st, 2013, again using Userzoom.com. Aside from controlling the number of participants in each political group, the only requirement for someone to participate was that they must live in the United States. There were a total of 153 participants: 58 Liberal/Democrat, 40 Neutral, and 55 Conservative/Republican. An examination of the demographic characteristics of the sample (age, gender, highest education level attained, and hours per week using the Internet) showed no substantial differences among the three groups. Ninety percent of participants indicated that they were registered to vote in the United States

The performance measures used to evaluate the results for each site were task success rate and average task time. The attitude measures were ease of finding information on the site (1 = very difficult to 5 = very easy) and general impression of the site (1 = hated it to 5 = loved it). In addition, after completing the tasks for both dems.gov and GOP.gov, participants were asked to indicate which site they preferred (1 = dems.gov to 5 = GOP.gov).

## Analysis and Results

For each of the summary performance variables (overall task success and average task time for each site), as well as each of the site-level attitude measures, an analysis of variance (ANOVA) was run comparing the performance of the three groups. In addition, using the same variables, a series of paired *t*-tests was run for each group of participants, comparing their performance across the two sites. A final ANOVA compared the site preference ratings across the three groups.

The results of the analyses showed no statistically significant differences— either among the three political preference groups, or between the two sites— on any of the site-level measures. The only significant difference was for the site preference question asked at the very end of the test. For this question, participants were not asked to consider the sites' respective performance or usability; instead, the question gave them an opportunity to express their personal preference for one site or the other. Unsurprisingly, on this question, Democrats stated a preference for Dems.gov and Republicans for GOP.gov. The significant difference in the responses to the site preference question suggests that the groups of participants did indeed have different personal beliefs (biases) that *could* have affected their performance on the usability test. However, the lack of significant differences for the remaining variables suggests that, in fact, their biases *didn't* affect their performance.

Even though the study only looks at one context (politics) and the results cannot be generalized to other contexts, the findings do appear to provide limited support for the belief that people are able to set aside their biases when participating in a usability study. However, a little scrutiny reveals some factors that raise doubts about the validity of the results, even within the context of political beliefs.

*Recruitment of Participants*: While we were able to recruit approximately equal numbers of Democrats and Republicans, it was necessary to keep the study open to Republicans more than twice as long as Democrats in order to get to that point. There are several possible reasons for this: (1) Mechanical Turk workers may be predominantly Liberal/Democrat; (2) Conservative/Republican workers may be more hesitant to participate; or (3) Conservative/Republican workers may be more hesitant to reveal their political leanings. Any of these possibilities could have affected the results of the study.

*Study Methodology*: as described above, participants first took a questionnaire that asked them about their political leanings and then completed parallel sets of tasks on the two sites. The design of the study made its purpose transparent in a way that may have affected the behavior of the participants, even if only subconsciously.

*Use of Mechanical Turk workers*: Finally, Mechanical Turk was designed to provide a way to crowd-source large numbers of small tasks that require a human being to complete. These Human Intelligence Tasks (HITs) are generally both well-defined and self-contained, and usually take only a few minutes to complete. For example, workers may be asked to transcribe the items on a receipt, apply labels to images, or judge the overall sentiment expressed in comments to an online newspaper article. In contrast, the average amount of time participants spent completing our usability test was nearly 30 min. While this average is artificially inflated by users who didn't complete the test in one sitting, it is clear that this test required a substantially greater time commitment than is usually required of Mechanical Turk workers. It seems likely that the mismatch between workers' expectations for HITs and the requirements for the usability test may have affected the results as well (Figures 11.1–11.5).

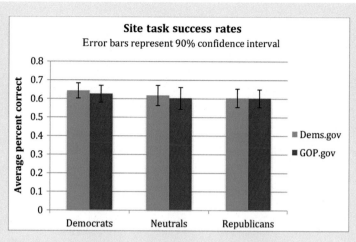

Figure 11.1 Average task success by Web site and participant group.

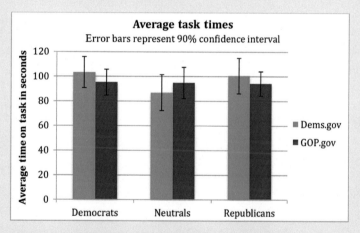

Figure 11.2 Average task completion times by Web site and participant group.

## Conclusions

The results of this study clearly demonstrate some of the methodological and recruiting issues that can undermine research efforts. While our study did not succeed in the way we hoped, we still believe that research in this

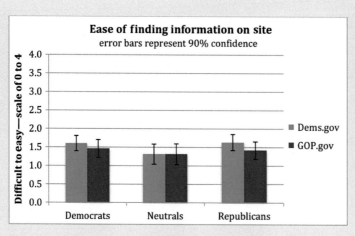

Figure 11.3 Ease of finding information ratings by Web site and participant group.

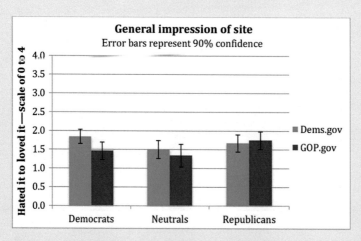

Figure 11.4 General impression of site by Web site and participant group.

area could provide important data to inform the results of usability studies where participant bias may be operating.

In future research, we will continue to explore the question of whether usability study participants can successfully set aside their personal biases

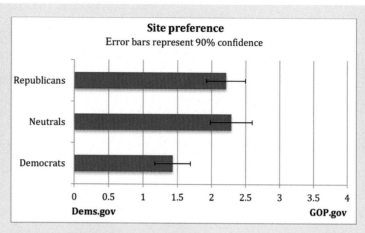

Figure 11.5 Site preference by participant group.

in completing their tasks. In order to be confident that our results really do answer this question, we will need to modify our procedures in the following ways:

- Expansion to other contexts—there are many known subjects that elicit strong emotional responses, such as allegiances to particular companies or products. Additionally, there is increasing interest in the area of health and wellness, a highly personal area in which socially desirable response bias is of particular concern.

- Recruitment strategies—it is essential to ensure testing on a sample that represents the expected user base. The number of participants must also be large enough to include adequate representation from each subgroup.

- Study design—while the within-subjects design meant that subjects acted as their own controls, it also made the comparative nature of the study apparent to the participants. Including a between-subjects component as well would enable us to evaluate the extent to which this aspect of the study design affects the results.

Whether the results of our future research support or refute the findings reported above, they will provide important data to usability professionals for interpreting the results of their own user studies and understanding the impact that user bias may have had on those results.

Information and Personal Beliefs

This case study points out the importance of the effect of personal beliefs on data collection. While the respondents were focusing on the performance of political Web sites, they could more objectively report reactions to usability and functionality of the site. However, this objectivity did not carry over to the preference ratings. The personal belief a participant had, did create a bias for them. This shows that there is more work to be done here. Questions regarding, for example, whether personal bias has an impact on the user experience could add a level of depth to the survey work being done in the field.

Getting information off the Internet is like taking a drink from a fire hydrant.

**Mitchell Kapor**

# Web Analytics and Social Media

Although many UX professionals know about the connection between data from social media and Web analytics (WA), very few make use of these data. In many development organizations the working groups are siloed so that a UX professional may not have access to the same WA that a Web site developer might have. Many people in the UX field do not know how to use the WA tools. Some UX professionals that already work on quantitative research use the WA tools to triangulate with more standard UX metrics, but they still have trouble making the UX a good one, despite the data. Part of the issue seems to be related to understanding how to use those data correctly. What is the right way to slice and then triangulate the data? Are the UX measures given more priority?

The answer lies in looking at the more holistic UX approach: the story behind the system, the persona, and use cases.

## Web Analytics: Telling the Story

- Who comes to your sites, what are they doing, how long do they stay, why do you think they leave?
- What does this information provide about the user?
- How can this information be applied to improving the UX?
- What about conversion rates?

Good data will tell you a story. Taking data from Web analytics can provide basic story pieces, such as Who, What, When, Where, and Why?

## Who Comes to Your Web Site?

The who of the story is the user persona, as discussed previously. WA can help understand more about this person by observing whether they visit a specific Web site, or whether they choose not to. This piece of data can tell us whether there are returning visitors or new visitors. High numbers of repeat visitors show that the users are generally satisfied with the site.

## What Is the User Doing on Your Web Site?

These could be thought of as the user tasks. This might involve the most straightforward of information, since the tasks help to provide the foundation for a use case. What are they doing on the site, are they able to carry out the tasks they want to? What is the order of steps they take to carry out their tasks?

## When Is the User Doing It?

Time information provides data about whether the assumptions about tasks and use cases are true. Are the users performing the tasks in the way the technology assumes they are, or are the users getting frustrated and creating a "work around" to solve a problem introduced by the design of the Web site.

## Where Is the User Doing It?

The answer to the question as to where the user is interacting with the Web site will tell us about the environment, which is helpful in understanding the limitations and capabilities of both the user and site. The where information can be helpful in terms of knowing: where the user comes from, where they go, and how they travel within the Web site.

## Why Is the User on the Web Site?

Users have specific goals when visiting a Web site, ranging from critical to casual Internet browsing. A person visiting a Web site that provides them with the ability to carry out financial transactions securely online could change their attitude to how they interact with their money. Web sites that deal with information that is critical to one's daily quality of life are judged more harshly if they don't work well. If you have trouble buying a book online, you can always go to a bricks and mortar store. If your financial institution has decided to put more of its operations online and is closing branch offices and adding more phone operators, it is possible that the phone operators could be overwhelmed with calls, especially if the Web site does not work well and the wait to talk to a live person is long. As a bank customer, it will be hard for you to do business if the Web site doesn't work and the nearest office is 45 min away. The most successful Web sites understand why the visitors are there and create the UX around the case study that answers the question of why.

Medicare.gov is an example of a Web site that is mission critical. The site services many types of users from: people on Medicare and Medicaid looking for health and drug plans; to patients and caretakers looking for doctors, nursing homes, and hospitals; to people just trying to understand the system. The following case study describes the work done on Medicare.gov as part of their UX strategy to incorporate Web analytics in an attempt to improve the UX. It is important because it is carried out on a government Web site that is complex with large data sets that included Web analytics. These data need to be available for the average person to use, as well as fit into the larger strategical goals of improving the quality of care and making nursing homes more accessible. The case study below illustrates the challenges faced in these complex types of systems.

## Nursing Home Compare Web Site Web Analytics

Tulsi Patel

### Background

The Centers for Medicare and Medicaid Services (CMS) created a Nursing Home Compare (NHC) Web site where users could get quality of care information while searching for nursing homes in their area. The NHC site used a 5 star rating system to rank nursing homes on various categories. The goal of the site was to help people find nursing homes while also educating them about nursing home quality. One overarching goal was to improve the overall quality of nursing home care. The target users of the site were:

- *Consumers*: family members or friends looking for information for a loved one;
- *Healthcare professionals*: doctors, nursing home advocates, and lawyers;
- *Nursing home providers*: administrators and managers working at nursing homes.

CMS hired our company to conduct ongoing user research on the site, from the prototype stage to updates to the live site. Our company worked on a variety of research methods during the multi-year commitment, including a competitive review, expert review, multiple usability studies, interviews, focus groups, survey, persona development, and Web metrics analysis. Multiple people worked on the research projects over several years, with one dedicated research manager driving the overall research strategy.

Each research project and the resulting findings were critical to help piece together a comprehensive strategic model for the site. The strategic model mapped out site goals, target users, user goals, and research methods to use, and provided an overall direction for future plans and updates.

The site was updated on an annual basis, and incorporated feedback from the research projects conducted in the previous year. In fall of 2012, CMS worked with a design firm to create prototypes for a Web and mobile experience. The goal was to implement a responsive site in the summer of 2013. CMS charged my team to conduct usability sessions on both versions of the prototype with consumers and healthcare professionals. I owned the mobile portion of the study, and found that participants had some interaction issues within the mobile prototype.

Around the same time, I was working on the focus group that was described in Chapter 10 in the case study entitled "Focus Groups with Nursing Home Providers" by Fiona Tranquada. The focus group was centered on nursing home providers. We had conducted previous research with consumers and professionals, but didn't have a lot of feedback from the professionals. The purpose of the focus groups was to learn about the providers' understanding of what the site did, how it impacted their facility, and to understand if the site rating data were useful, timely, and accurate.

Based on our findings from both of these projects, CMS continued to work on their annual update for summer 2013. However, CMS wanted to gauge the overall success of the site at that point. It was difficult to evaluate if the site was educating on and improving nursing home quality just from the usability study and focus group. We recommended reviewing the Web analytics of the live site to get a broader picture of what was happening, and find opportunities to increase new visitors to the site.

## Approach and Methodology

Our team decided to look at various data points to understand the overall process of using the site. We focused on site survey results, Web metrics, search engine optimization (SEO) data and potential social media referrers. Each of these data points would help piece together different steps in the overall process, and help create a big picture of what was happening on the site.

We first looked at results from a site-wide survey to better understand who was coming to the site, what their main purpose was, and what their overall satisfaction with the site was. We were able to segment the visitors and confirm that a majority of them fell into the main NHC target user groups, and had high satisfaction scores for the site.

We then analyzed Web reports to see trends in the following metrics, pre and post launch:

- **Unique visitors**: number of overall visitors to the site. A higher trend in visitors indicates more people are visiting the site. I noticed that while the number of unique visitors did double over the year, there were periods of fluctuations caused by specific promotions at certain times.
- **Bounce rate**: percentage of visitors who leave the site after only viewing one page. A higher bounce rate from main page indicates people might not be finding what they're looking for. The bounce rate increased by almost 10%, which is expected with double the amount of visitors, and seemed to be lowering toward the end of the year. However, I recommended that CMS continue to

monitor bounce rate over the year to see if it evened out as the number of visitors evened out.

- **Percentage of new visitors**: amount of specifically new visitors to the site. A higher trend in new visitors might indicate visitors are coming to the site from new promotions or sources. As the number of unique visitors doubled, the percentage of new visitors increased by 20%, with indications of leveling off.

- **Average page depth**: the number of pages viewed in a visit. The higher the page depth, the more pages a user is seeing in a visit, which is not necessarily a good thing. Pre-launch, users saw an average of 7 pages, while post launch saw 4. This decrease in page depth aligns with the strategic decision to cut the number of links and steps out of the search process.

- **Site referrers**: external sites linking to the NHC site. Site referrers can be unexpected sources of new traffic, including publication sites. We saw a spike in visits that lasted for about a month, which was attributed to an article featuring NHC.

We also focused on specifically on search data:

- **Search entry keywords**: words searched in Google to enter the NHC site. These keywords are important because they are the users own words. Looking at search entry keywords can show a disconnect in what people use to find your site versus what verbiage you use on the site. We found that people use the expected words "nursing homes" or "nursing home compare" to enter the site.

- **In site search keywords**: words searched on the NHC site. These keywords are important to look at because they might signify that users can't find specific content they need on the site. For example, users searched for "assisted living" on the NHC site. The NHC site doesn't incorporate assisted living centers, and explains this on the main page. However, since so many people were searching for it, I recommended that CMS better state the exclusion on the home page or provide a link to another page with more information.

- **Page rank**: how high in Google search results a site appears for a specific keyword. For example, the site appeared as the number one results when people searched for "nursing homes" or "nursing home compare."

- **Keyword analysis**: similar search terms based on top search entry keywords. We knew that many people searching for "nursing homes" or "nursing home compare" found the site. Through keyword analysis on "nursing homes," we found that many people searched for a variation of "nursing homes in" and a state or city, and didn't always enter the site. This indicates an opportunity for CMS to drive new visitors searching for "nursing homes in…" to the site.

We also looked at social media channels (YouTube, Facebook, Twitter, and Google +) to see what people were talking about regarding nursing homes. The above Web and search metrics provide a clear picture of what was happening on the site, but don't really give insight into why people were visiting or where they were coming from. We found many instances of people talking about and linking to the NHC site.

Our report for CMS contained a summary of what was going on with the site, with the above data grouped according to the following questions:

- Who is coming to the site?
    - From an on-site survey, we were able to confirm that over 50% of respondents that came to site were the main target user group, consumers. Through Web analytics, we learned that we had a 20% increase in new visitors to the site.
- Why do they come to the site?
    - Also from the on-site survey, we learned that a majority of respondents visited the site to research nursing homes for themselves or their family members, but did not choose one immediately.
- Where are they coming from?
    - SEO analysis showed that many visitors to the site came from search, and used keywords such as "nursing homes" or "nursing home compare." Common referrers to the site were other government sites such as healthcare.gov and cms.gov, and some publication sites.
- What do they do on the site?
    - We saw that after the launch, visits increased by 50%. Visitors spent less time on the site and on less pages than before, which aligned with CMS's goal of streamlining the search and compare process from before. We also saw some searches on the site for "assisted living" and "rehabilitation," things not included under the site.
- What do they do next?
    - We did see that the bounce rate increased slightly, which aligned with the great increase in unique visitors. The on-site survey results revealed that respondents would call or visit a particular nursing home next to get more information based on what they saw on the site.

As part of our recommendations, we provided a list of Web analytics reports to monitor on a monthly, quarterly, semi-annually and one off basis, including trends in page visits and bounce rates, site refers, goal funnels, and search keywords. We recommended pulling together the different data points to answer the above questions on a regular basis. This will allow CMS to continue to monitor the site experience and have a big picture for context. We also outlined a process to implement more social media activities on various CMS channels to promote new visitors to the site.

CMS appreciated seeing a comprehensive view of what was happening with the site, from where people were coming from to what they did next. They were able to make minor changes to the site based on our recommendations and to start discussing how they wanted to use social media to attract new visitors.

## Key Takeaways

Web analytics analysis is critical for understanding what exactly is happening on the site. However, it provides the "what" without the much needed "why." Pairing Web analytics data with some other voice of customer methods, such as interviews, surveys, or usability tests, provides a holistic view of what is happening on the site and why.

Our team was able to analyze the Web metrics of the site and better understand how many visitors came to site, where they went on the site, how many left the site, and where people were coming from. All of this information provided the "what" portion of the puzzle. We were able to pair this with all of the findings from our previous research methods to better understand the "why." We could better understand the entire experience knowing where people came from and what they searched to visit the site (based on metrics and SEO), who they were and why they came (based on site survey), what their major issues were on the site (based on usability studies), and where they went next (based on metrics and interviews).

Mapping together disparate pieces of data from different research methods (also known as triangulation) is important when trying to better understand the entire experience. Take a look at the research methods you've conducted for a product or experience and categorize what type of information you received from it. Did you hear more voice of customer feedback or "why" type information typically through interviews, focus groups, or usability studies? Or did you see hard facts and data about current behavior (not expected behavior) normally found through Web analytics or usability studies? Understand the type of findings you have and try to piece them together wherever they make sense. Take a look at the gaps of knowledge, which can help you identify future research projects. Who do you need to talk to and which method will you use to get that information?

## Social Media

Social media provides another touch point UXT for the user and your product or technology. It can be accessed using simple tactics such as posting links to information and media on key Web sites and encouraging user behavior by sending messages with direct calls to act, e.g., "Vote for me."

Social media is a wonderful source of information, similar to the water cooler experience in the workplace. Social media is the online chatter people share with others and can provide candid feedback from people interacting with the Web site or product.

Social media sites such as Facebook and Twitter create an online presence for a brand, product, technology, or group of people. These sites bring people together, often people who might not otherwise interact with one another. This creates a new environment within which users can interact and share.

# REFERENCES

Hertzum, M., Jacobsen, N.E., 2001. The evaluator effect: a chilling fact about usability evaluation methods. Int. J. Hum. Comput. Interact. 13 (4), 421–443. http://dx.doi.org/10.1207/S15327590IJHC1304_05.

Holbrook, A.L., Green, M.C., Krosnick, J.A., 2003. Telephone versus face-to-face interviewing of national probability samples with long questionnaires: comparisons of respondent satisfying and social desirability response bias. Public Opin. Q. 67 (1), 79–125.

Nancarrow, C., Brace, I., 2000. Saying the "right thing": coping with social desirability bias in marketing research. Bristol Bus. Sch. Teach. Res. Rev. 3(11)

Podsakoff, P.M., MacKenzie, S.B., Lee, J.-Y., Podsakoff, N.P., 2003. Common method biases in behavioral research: a critical review of the literature and recommended remedies. J. Appl. Psychol. 88 (5), 879–903. http://dx.doi.org/10.1037/0021-9010.88.5.879.

Sauro, J., 2012. 9 Biases in Usability Testing. Measuring Usability, Retrieved September 14, 2014 from: http://www.measuringusability.com/blog/ut-bias.php.

# BIBLIOGRAPHY

CIO Advice: Social Media Improves The User Experience. http://www.huffingtonpost.com/vala-afshar/cio-advice-social-media-i_b_4153460.html.

Collecting Survey Data. http://www.people-press.org/methodology/collecting-survey-data/.

Golbeck, J., 2013. Analyzing the Social Web. Morgan Kaufmann, Waltham, MA.

# Chapter 12

## SERVICE DESIGN

This chapter argues that service design is UX by bringing UX design principles to the field of service design. One case study describes service design for a design conference and one discusses voting systems in terms of service design.

# Chapter 12

The best customer service is if the customer doesn't need to call you, doesn't need to talk to you. It just works.

**Jeff Bezos**

## Service Design

Service design is an emerging field which began in the early 1990s, and shares many elements of UX. Service design is about creating a positive service experience for the person for whom the service is intended. It is similar to UX in many ways because it includes method and processes that will support the creation of positive service experiences.

In fact, many UX professionals include service design in their practice. The principles of both good design and good UX combine to build a framework for service design including:

- Design theory;
- Usability of system;
- Understanding the customer through research and best practice methodology;
- Customer journeys—how the customer moves through the system;
- Effective and efficient environment means that the physical environment that the person is interacting with should be designed with the person's needs at the center.

Service design brings together the body of knowledge that includes human behavior, marketing, UX, system design, and more. Service design is the process of planning and organizing the service so that it meets the needs of the person for whom it is intended.

*A business absolutely devoted to service will have only one worry about profits. They will be embarrassingly large.*

**Henry Ford**

# Service Design and the Role of UX

In designing the organization and infrastructure of services, focus needs to be on the interaction between the service provider and their customers. This means that the planning, organization, and complete customer journey must be designed with the person at the center. The same kinds of methodologies can be used to research, innovate, and iterate to create a successful user experience. When service design creates an easy and positive experience for the person, it creates a successful user experience.

## Touch Points in Service Design

There are many touch points for a person when interacting with a service, whether over the phone or on a Web site, some of these are as ubiquitous as opening a door and walking into a facility or through a long security line at an airport, where the door is a metal detector and the system includes many steps. These touch points include, but are not limited to:

- the case when a person searches for information, tickets or registration, schedules, and more. This can be done on a computer, or in a physical location, such as a ticket box office
- the experience of physically being in the system, standing in a line, sitting in a stadium seat or at a table in a restaurant. This experience can be augmented by a visit online to the venue Web site. The service design would have to incorporate the navigation through the service via phone menus or Web links and pages
- an interaction with the people providing a service, such as ticket takers, servers, and clerks.

## Same Principles, Different Domain

Many of the principles of UX can be applied to service design:

- Listen to the voice of the customer with techniques such as contextual inquiry to observe the person's environment:
  - Understand their goals within the context of that environment
  - Integrate the service to the physical environment to create a more positive experience
  - Connect the physical experience with their experience on a computer.
- Incorporate and coordinate the many touch points to create a seamless experience.
- Make it easy and obvious to the user how they are to move through the environment, incorporate clear and simple signage, and clear cues.
- Supply the information they need or want; help them with the decision points they encounter along the way.

In the following case study we can see how service design can be used when things are going well. A conference that is a huge success finds that success brings new issues to deal with. Good service design can be implemented using an iterative method to improve something that is experiencing growing pains due to its success. In the case that follows we can see how the iterative approach to service design greatly improves an already wonderful conference.

## Service Design at Big Design

Brian Sullivan

When you create a conference for designers and usability experts, you know the audience will analyze every part of the user experience. The schedule, registration, signage, music, t-shirts, apps, social media, the associated trade show, Web site, speakers, and pace of the conference offer multiple touch points for your customers. In many respects, a design conference is the ultimate service design project.

## Early Pains, Early Lessons

In 2008, the leaders of DFW-UXPA, IxDA Dallas, and Refresh Dallas started planning the Big Design Conference. In May 2009, the conference opened its doors to a crowd of 500 people. The problems we encountered the first year included:

- **Signage**. The conference was held at a local university which did not have the best signs to get our participants to the Student Union. Many people ended up running late. Luckily, we had volunteers with t-shirts to help guide attendees.
- **Registration**. As organizers, we were thrilled to have 500 people our first year. We did not plan on how to handle 25 + walk-ups. We were processing people in groups of three. It was too slow. We ended up handing out free badges to folks in the line that first year.
- **Trade Show**. The exhibitors were coming into the conference in the same line as attendees. In the first year, we ended up pulling the exhibitors from the line and assigning them volunteers to help them set up. We promised to do better in future years.
- **Schedule**. Three speakers backed out at the last-minute for different emergencies. The printed schedule was completely wrong. The Web site needed to be updated. We had back-up speakers. Two people asked for their money back.
- **Social Media**. The organizers were busy handling technical issues, deliveries, power problems, and so on. We did not have a dedicated person monitoring social media. As it turns out, some issues could have been handled through social media.
- **Environment**. We had the trade show in the middle of the conference, which was a huge hit with attendees, sponsors, and exhibitors. However, we ran out of table skirts, so some exhibitors looked messy, plus we had limited storage for giveaways.
- **Wi-Fi**. The student center was underground. Wi-Fi was spotty, which was our biggest complaint in the first year, with 500 people trying to get on Twitter and Facebook! The digital experience was disappointing in the first year. We uploaded pictures immediately to do damage control.

These issues were learning opportunities, which needed to be solved by thinking about service design at the Big Design Conference. The conference continues to grow at 10-15% annually. Almost 1000 people attended the Big Design Conference in its fifth year.

## Big Design's Service Design Strategy

We created a phased approach to implement a service design at the Big Design Conference. We started implementing some solutions in our second year, while other solutions took us 4 years to perfect. The basic strategy consisted of these three phases:

- **Phase One: Understanding the Users**. Speakers, volunteers, sponsors, attendees, exhibitors, VIPs, and organizers ended up being the main persona types at the conference.
- **Phase Two: Defining Customer Journey Maps**. Each persona type has different needs as they navigate the conference, so we developed customer journey maps to help spotlight areas we could improve.
- **Phase Three: Storyboarding Registration**. To perfect the registration process, we ended up storyboarding the experience to illustrate the flow, and train new volunteers.

As mentioned earlier, this phased approach took us several years to develop. Let's take a look at each phase and the artifacts that we developed.

## Phase One: Understanding the Users

After the first conference, we identified the various user types (attendees, speakers, sponsors, etc.). To better understand the different customers, we performed several surveys and followed up with phone interviews. We used some of the information from the survey in our sponsorship kit (Figure 12.1).

In addition, we developed personas for our attendees, speakers, and sponsors.

By sending out these surveys, we were better able to understand the service context for our users. Based on our research, we determined the primary

## Our Audience, Your Reach

We pride ourselves in having the best conference audience ever. Just look at our attendee breakdown and see how our audience speaks for itself.

### Attendee Breakdown

- More than 50% are under the age of 35
- More than 50% are decision makers
- They are a highly educated group of people:
  92% have a Bachelor's degree
  55% have a Master's degree
  10% have a PhD
- While technically Big Design is a local conference to Dallas/Fort Worth, 60% of our attendees travel from out of town to attend
- 56% of attendees are influencers at their work, while 31% are actual decision makers

### Spending Habits

Our audience is in love with technology and they aren't afraid to show it:

- Median salary: $84,000 USD
- Roughly 50% of our attendees earn $90,000+ annually and over $100,000 with 10 years' experience
- Nearly every attendee owns more than one type of electronic device including wireless home networks, tablets, smartphones, MP3 players, home theater systems, and portable computers

- Gaming: 64% own at least one game console while 21% own two or more game consoles
- Our attendees also are heavy users of smartphone games and apps
- Nearly 100% own a smartphone and nearly half of which are iPhones

### Social and Broadcast Media Behavior

Our attendees are heavily into social media and avid consumers of news and original content. For example, Twitter is Big Design's main back channel.

### Basic Twitter Details from 2013

- 2,697 Total Tweets
- 1,924 Original tweets
- 1,235 Tweets directed at speakers or the conference itself
- 773 Retweets

### Other Media Details

- 95% of our attendees watch videos from an online source like Netflix, Hulu, and Youtube
- 76% of attendees are also fans of traditional broadcast media like NBC, CBS, Fox, and ABC
- 50% of our attendees actively use DVRs

Figure 12.1 Audience and reach.

triggers to attend the conference were networking, learning, speaking, marketing, recruiting, and socializing. We built a Trigger Table to see how to map the triggers to each of the personas (Figure 12.2).

For the organizers, we were surprised to learn that networking and socializing with like-minded people were the two primary reasons to come to the conference. Plus, there was a very distinct difference between networking and socializing:

| Persona | Networking | Learning | Speaking | Marketing | Recruiting | Socializing |
|---------|------------|----------|----------|-----------|------------|-------------|
| Attendee | X | X | | | | X |
| Speaker | X | X | X | X | X | X |
| Sponsor | X | | X | X | X | X |
| Volunteer | X | X | | | | X |
| Exhibitor | X | | X | X | X | X |
| VIP | X | X | X | | X | X |
| Organizer | X | X | X | | | X |

Figure 12.2 Persona trigger table.

■ **Networking**: These meetings or encounters occur between individuals with the expressed interest of performing some kind of business activity, such as exchanging business information, forming a partnership, setting up training, and so on.

■ **Socializing**: These meetings or encounters occur between individuals with a shared interest. Networking conversations may occur, but they are limited. People want to connect on a different, more personal level.

As organizers, we knew that we had to develop networking and socializing opportunities at the conference. Excursions, tours, lunches, parties, casino night, movie night, and so on are now mainstays of the Big Design Conference.

## Phase Two: Customer Journey Maps

With collected information from our survey, we began to look at how we could better service our attendees to improve their experiences before, during, and after the conference. We built customer journey maps to showcase the online and offline activities. We developed more customer journey maps, but to simplify our discussion, we will focus on the attendees (Figure 12.3).

## Pre-Conference Activities

For any attendee, they must decide to come to the conference, buy a ticket, purchase a hotel room, review the schedule, engage us in social media, and more. For the most part, these activities occur online as part of the normal process for attending a conference. In many respects, the Big Design Conference has always done a great job with these pre-conference activities.

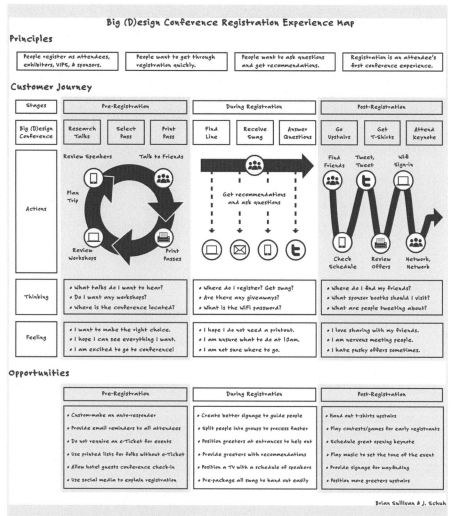

**Big (D)esign Conference Registration Experience Map**

**Principles**

| | | | |
|---|---|---|---|
| People register as attendees, exhibitors, VIPs, & sponsors. | People want to get through registration quickly. | People want to ask questions and get recommendations. | Registration is an attendee's first conference experience. |

**Customer Journey**

| Stages | Pre-Registration | | | During Registration | | | Post-Registration | | |
|---|---|---|---|---|---|---|---|---|---|
| Big (D)esign Conference | Research Talks | Select Pass | Print Pass | Find Line | Receive Swag | Answer Questions | Go Upstairs | Get T-Shirts | Attend Keynote |

Actions

Review Speakers · Talk to Friends · Plan Trip · Review Workshops · Print Passes

Get recommendations and ask questions

Find Friends · Tweet, Tweet · Wifi Sign-in · Check Schedule · Review Offers · Network, Network

| Thinking | • What talks do I want to hear?<br>• Do I want any workshops?<br>• Where is the conference located? | • Where do I register? Get swag?<br>• Are there any giveaways?<br>• What is the WiFi password? | • Where do I find my friends?<br>• What sponsor booths should I visit?<br>• What are people tweeting about? |
|---|---|---|---|
| Feeling | • I want to make the right choice.<br>• I hope I can see everything I want.<br>• I am excited to go to conference! | • I hope I do not need a printout.<br>• I am unsure what to do at 10am.<br>• I am not sure where to go. | • I love sharing with my friends.<br>• I am nervous meeting people.<br>• I hate pushy offers sometimes. |

**Opportunities**

| Pre-Registration | During Registration | Post-Registration |
|---|---|---|
| • Custom-make an auto-responder<br>• Provide email reminders to all attendees<br>• Do not require an e-Ticket for events<br>• Use printed lists for folks without e-Ticket<br>• Allow hotel guests conference check-in<br>• Use social media to explain registration | • Create better signage to guide people<br>• Split people into groups to process faster<br>• Position greeters at entrances to help out<br>• Provide greeters with recommendations<br>• Position a TV with a schedule of speakers<br>• Pre-package all swag to hand out easily | • Hand out t-shirts upstairs<br>• Play contests/games for early registrants<br>• Schedule great opening keynote<br>• Play music to set the tone of the event<br>• Provide signage for way-finding<br>• Position more greeters upstairs |

Brian Sullivan & J. Schuh

Figure 12.3 Journey map.

Our social media marketing was extremely poor in the first year. Luckily, for the second year Keith Anderson, a conference organizer, decided to use some social media automation tools to help us streamline many of our announcements and engage with our customers before the conference.

We developed a social media strategy. The Big Design Conference Linked-in group started with just three people. We tease news articles on Linked-in a few days before posting them on our site. After posting them on the conference Web site, the news articles are posted on Facebook. We use an Editorial Calendar to manage the content that we produce, too.

During the Conference Activities

For any conference to be successful, it must run on time. The customer journey maps revealed several unique opportunities to get our attendees to their sessions by engaging them both in-person and online.

From an in-person perspective, we developed a series of touch points to ensure the conference runs on time.

For example, each session has a track manager and a timekeeper with very specific duties:

- **Track Manager**: This person introduces each speaker, handles any equipment issues, and takes questions from the audience.
- **Timekeeper**: This person keeps track of the speaker's time. Plus, we provide them with an iPod filled with music to play between the sessions.

We pre-load the music with songs to represent either the speaker or the topic. For example, one talk was called "Touching the Future" and the songs all had the word "touch" in them. The music became a great way to get the crowd up and moving after each talk.

To improve the in-person experience throughout the day, we added lots of signage throughout the trade show. Between each talk, we have volunteers at specific stations to help guide people. All volunteers wear the same colored t-shirt to help guide attendees to their next talk. A paper schedule is handed out at registration to help people get to their next talk, too.

From an online perspective, we developed a special role called the Social Media Field General. This person monitors all social media channels to answer any incoming questions during the conference. The Social Media Field General pre-loads all of the conference tweets about the upcoming talks to go out via Twitter. Student volunteers take pictures to give additional content to Facebook and Instagram.

Post-Conference Activities

After the conference, we continued to engage with our attendees. We sent out a thank you email with a post-conference survey. The primary purpose of the survey was to collect information on how we can improve next year's conference. Some of the information goes into next year's sponsorship kit, too.

## Phase Three: Storyboarding Registration

At registration, the Big Design Conference must process between 800 and 1000 people in one hour. Most of the attendees will register between 8am and 9am on the first day. As mentioned earlier, registration was one of our earliest problems. We decided to storyboard registration to perfect it.

With so many people, we knew the registration would involve sorting people:

- 4 lines for attendees (A-G, H-N, O-S, T-Z);
- 1 line for walk-up registration (we had 30 walk-ups in the first year);
- 1 line for speakers;
- 1 line for sponsors, exhibitors, VIPs.

Any attendee staying at the hotel was automatically processed before the conference.

Ironically, we had too many attendees hanging out downstairs at registration. People were seeing old friends or being introduced to new ones. We needed people to go upstairs. Lara Becker, a co-founder of the conference, suggested that we give away a limited amount of t-shirts upstairs. We added music to draw people into the main room, where our opening keynote starts promptly at 9:00 am.

It worked perfectly.

## Final Thoughts on Service Design at Big Design

The conference continues to evolve. The service design strategy will continue to evolve, too. When we first put on the conference, our only thoughts were to have cool speakers talking in a crowded room. As we learned what else the users wanted, and what practical issues we were up against, we realized it was an opportunity for creative thinking through service design. Timekeepers, music, signage, t-shirts, parties, social media channels, and more had simply not been on our initial radar.

It is the Service Design at Big Design, which makes it special.

# Serving the People

The key to all good service design is understanding the people using the service. Who are these people and what do they need to do. Those are the basic questions that form the plans.

Service design can touch our lives in many ways, from the mundane, such as standing in line at Walt Disney World, to the very critical such as entering a hospital or using a voting system.

Examples of good service design, such as waiting in line at Walt Disney World, can help improve the UX of the whole place. The lines have entertainment built in, sometimes in the form of exhibits or videos people can watch while they wait. Walt Disney World also manages to disguise how long the line really is. I distinctly remember taking my kids on trip and waiting in very long lines. The kids would get impatient, but the line never really looked too long because it was always twisting and turning; we could never see all the way to the end, so we always felt like we were making progress. Sometimes, the lines for the younger kids' rides would have activities and entertainment so the kids had something to keep them occupied while they waited. Walt Disney World analyzed the issues related to waiting in lines and figured out how to fix them. For the places in line that are still unmanageably slow, they provide video games and other distractions to ease the wait (Figure 12.4).

Hotel signage is another example of an area where service design makes a huge difference. Hotel guests often arrive tired after a long journey, dragging their

Figure 12.4 Confusing hotel signs.

Figure 12.5 Similarly confusing signs in another hallway in the hotel.

luggage, and want to find their room quickly. One hotel I stayed at had many wings, hallways, and intersections within those hallways. All the hallways looked the same so the hotel was making a great attempt to help guests by posting many signs. However, the signs were hard to read, and provide arrows that ended up being very confusing. I could tell who had just checked in because they were the ones wandering the halls, wondering where their room was; occasionally walking in circles before figuring it out (Figures 12.5 and 12.6).

## Service Design That Impacts Our Lives: Voting Systems

Voting is an example of a critical service provided by a government to its citizens to maintain democracy. There are several steps, or user touch points, in the process that include:

Figure 12.6 More confusing hotel signs.

- Voter registration;
- The physical experience at the polling place;
- The machines that allow a user to cast a vote.

The user's journey through voting ends with the vote being cast. However, the process itself does not end there. The votes are counted at the local polling place and then sent up to the central Election Commission for a final tally.

There are many layers of interaction between the person who is casting a vote, and the actual vote that is counted. Many things can go wrong along the way, which can produce quite serious consequences.

The Presidential election in 2000 was a close one where every vote made a difference, with the final outcome hanging on Florida's election results.

The race was a close one and every vote made a difference. The complexity of the voting systems in America became clear during that 2000 USA Presidential election in which the outcome and final decision was delayed by months while the election officials tried to count the votes and struggled with the technology in order to understand the voter's intention. The crisis was highlighted when it was reported in the media (though of course, all the users already knew!) that the design of the voting machine and ballot format was very confusing to many voters, causing their votes to be invalidated when they tried to correct their ballots.

During the 2000 election, though many states called in close election results, the focus was on Florida which used a punch-card voting systems. The punch cards produce small paper rectangles called "chads" when a voter punches out certain positions on their ballot. The problem occurred when a voter did not fully punch out the chad, creating "pregnant," "dimpled," "hanging," and "flapping" chads. Since a mistake made by a voter on this type of voting technology could result in what looked like two votes for a President, those votes were considered spoiled and not counted. In order to get the numbers right, these votes had to be counted and recounted for several months while the country waited to find out who their next president would be.

Many research studies tried to identify what went wrong.

A review by an independent consortium, looking at the broader group of rejected ballots, found that Mr. Gore might have won if the courts had ordered a statewide recount of all the rejected ballots

In addition, the review found statistical support for the complaints of many voters, particularly elderly Democrats in Palm Beach

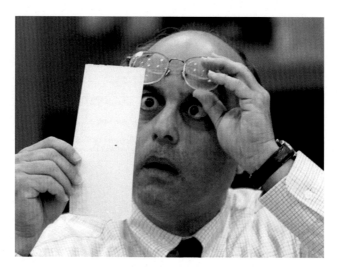

Figure 12.7 Ballots being examined.

County, who said in interviews at the election that confusing
ballot designs may have led them to split their ballots by
voting for more than one candidate.

The impact of bad design on voting is to put citizens' rights in jeopardy. If the
information and instructions are confusing, some votes may not being counted
(Figure 12.7).

## Help America Vote Act 2002 (HAVA)

After time had passed and research showed that the technology was partly to
blame, Congress passed the Help America Vote Act in 2002. HAVA explicitly
stated that the punch card technology was no longer going to be used. It also

H. R. 3295

**One Hundred Seventh Congress**
**of the**
**United States of America**

**AT THE SECOND SESSION**

***Begun and held at the City of Washington on Wednesday, the twenty-third day of January, two thousand and two***

**An Act**

To establish a program to provide funds to States to replace punch card voting systems, to establish the Election Assistance Commission to assist in the administration of Federal elections and to otherwise provide assistance with the administration of certain Federal election laws and programs, to establish minimum election administration standards for States and units of local government with responsibility for the administration of Federal elections, and for other purposes.

*Be it enacted by the Senate and House of Representatives of the United States of America in Congress assembled,*

**SECTION 1. SHORT TITLE; TABLE OF CONTENTS.**

(a) SHORT TITLE.—This Act may be cited as the "Help America Vote Act of 2002".

Figure 12.8 HAVA.

included the need for assistive technology for individuals with disabilities (physical, learning, and other).

HAVA further stipulated that voting technology would be developed with best practices in human factors in the design. This provided the opportunity for research and centers of excellence to develop throughout the country, including the AIGA Design for Democracy and the MIT-Caltech Voting Technologies Program (Figure 12.8).

The positive outcome of HAVA, for the American public, was the recognition of the role that good design plays, both in helping people vote for the person that they choose, and in making sure that their vote is counted (Figure 12.9).

under subchapter I of chapter 57 of title 5, United States Code, while away from their homes or regular places of business in the performance of services for the Development Committee.

(e) TECHNICAL SUPPORT FROM NATIONAL INSTITUTE OF STANDARDS AND TECHNOLOGY.—

(1) IN GENERAL.—At the request of the Development Committee, the Director of the National Institute of Standards and Technology shall provide the Development Committee with technical support necessary for the Development Committee to carry out its duties under this subtitle.

(2) TECHNICAL SUPPORT.—The technical support provided under paragraph (1) shall include intramural research and development in areas to support the development of the voluntary voting system guidelines under this part, including—

(A) the security of computers, computer networks, and computer data storage used in voting systems, including the computerized list required under section 303(a);

(B) methods to detect and prevent fraud;

(C) the protection of voter privacy;

(D) the role of human factors in the design and application of voting systems, including assistive technologies for individuals with disabilities (including blindness) and varying levels of literacy; and

(E) remote access voting, including voting through the Internet.

(3) NO PRIVATE SECTOR INTELLECTUAL PROPERTY RIGHTS IN GUIDELINES.—No private sector individual or entity shall obtain any intellectual property rights to any guideline or the contents of any guideline (or any modification to any guideline) adopted by the Commission under this Act.

(f) PUBLICATION OF RECOMMENDATIONS IN FEDERAL REGISTER.— At the time the Commission adopts any voluntary voting system guideline pursuant to section 222, the Development Committee shall cause to have published in the Federal Register the recommendations it provided under this section to the Executive Director of the Commission concerning the guideline adopted.

Figure 12.9 HAVA text.

# Case Study: Arlington Voter Verification Study

Elizabeth Rosenzweig

This case study describes research that was run in the fall of 2005 by the MIT-Caltech Voting Technology Project (VTP) to examine voter verification auditing schemes. This research was built on previous VTP studies.

The project created the real-world scenario of a mock election, using genuine registered voters and the Arlington, Massachusetts, Town Hall, which is an actual venue that the town of Arlington uses for its elections. In service design, this provided a "real time" user walkthrough that can uncover many unknown problems.

In addition, real poll workers were used to further simulate this real-world scenario.

Four machines were used, in an A/B test design, to compare the four technologies being tested. Real candidates were used on the ballots, the hypothesis being that this would further simulate the real-world voting experience. The mock election process did provide a real-world context for the entire system and helped test user experience touch points, such as the process used by poll workers, and machine interactions.

## Four Technologies

The voting machines used in the study included the following:

1. A Diebold optical scanned paper ballot system, where voters write the vote on a paper ballot which is then scanned;
2. A voting simulator developed by MIT as part of VTP. This system has a Diebold-like ballot but also includes a Voter Verified Paper Audit Trail (VVPAT) which prints a paper trail of the vote after all the ballot selections have been made and the vote has been cast;
3. Another simulator developed by MIT, also part of VTP, with a VVPAT. However, the VVPAT prints the vote each time a selection is made (as opposed to when the voter has completed all the voting selections as in the second technology);
4. A third voting simulator, also with a Diebold-like ballot, had a Voter Verified Audio Audit Trail for voters with visual disabilities that would prevent them from being able to read either a paper ballot or a VVPAT. The audio system first reads the ballot and then the VVAAT affirms the votes by reading them back to the user once they have been cast.

To understand the voters' reactions to the four technologies, the study also asked specific questions about the voting machines such as: "Does paper or audio feedback help in knowing your vote is cast and in being confidant your vote will be counted correctly?"

### Issues with the Study

- Trying to test too many things at one time. While the mock election setup was helpful, it also provided too many variables. For example, using four machines provided more complexity that was necessary.

- Using prototypes of two of the machines in a real-world simulation. Prototypes present a possibility that a machine will break down, as it did, introducing more variables into the protocol.

- Using ballots with real candidates, and then asking people to vote a certain way. This did not always match the user's own personal bias, and a truer interaction with the process was lost.

### Takeaways

- A real-world simulation must focus on creating that believable real-world context, and not use prototypes.

- Prototypes are wonderful for testing functions such as verifiable audit trails, but this should be done as a separate piece of research.

- When testing ballot designs, issues of confidence in test results can be mitigated by using candidates that are not found in the real world. Instead consider using ballot choices that might be fictional characters, or better yet, items that are recognizable such as colors, flavors, or simple shapes.

# Successful Service Design

It is easy to see the impact of service design in everyday scenarios, but what really brings home the importance of good design are the scenarios where the experience the person has is critical to the success of the service. The more critical the service, such as voting, the more critical is a good design. In the case of voting, if voters have trouble voting, they might not come back to vote again. Add to that, if the votes are not being counted, the citizen's democratic rights are being taken away; technology then gets in the way of democracy. Service design impacts lives.

# BIBLIOGRAPHY

Center for Civic Design. http://centerforcivicdesign.org/.

Designing Waits that Work. http://designforservice.wordpress.com/2009/08/02/designing-waits-that-work/.

Disney Tackles Major Theme Park Problem: Lines. http://www.nytimes.com/2010/12/28/business/media/28disney.html?_r=0.

Fessenden, F., Broder, J.M., November 12, 2001. Study of disputed Florida ballots finds justices did not cast the deciding vote. New York Times.

Help America Vote Act, 2002. United States Election Commission, United States Congress, USA. http://www.eac.gov/about_the_eac/help_america_vote_act.aspx.

Holmlid, S., 2007. Interaction Design and Service Design: Expanding a Comparison of Design Disciplines. Design Inquiries. Human-Centered Systems, Linköpings Universitet, Linköping, Sweden, Stockholm www.nordes.org.

Queues at Walt Disney World. http://designforservice.wordpress.com/2011/01/01/queues-at-walt-disney-world/.

Ramaswamy, R., 1996. Design and Management of Service Processes. Addison-Wesley Pub. Co., Reading, MA.

Selker, T., Rosenzweig, E., Pandolfo, A., 2006. A methodology for testing voting system. J. Usability Stud, 2 (1), 7–21.

Shostack, G.L., 1982. How to design a service. Eur. J. Mark. 16 (1), 49–63.

Shostack, G.L., 1984. Design services that deliver. Harv. Bus. Rev. (84115), 133–139.

Study of Disputed Florida Ballots Finds Justices Did Not Cast the Deciding Vote. http://www.nytimes.com/2001/11/12/politics/12VOTE.html.

What is Service Design? http://www.service-design-network.org/intro/.

# Chapter 13

## GETTING BUY IN

This chapter addresses issues that arise during teamwork, and getting buy in from stakeholders. Two case studies illustrate different strategies for getting buy in one from financial services and one from Medicare.gov.

# Chapter 13

The keystone of successful business is cooperation. Friction retards progress.

**James Cash Penney**

## Getting Buy In

Integrating all team members in the UX process has and will continue to be a helpful method to get stakeholders to buy in and understand the value of a good user experience.

The methods for sharing these user experiences with developers and product stakeholders usually included focus groups and customer interviews, with an occasional field visit to potential user sites to assess their needs for future products. That last part was often an activity that was driven by marketing requirements, with market researchers doing the data collection.

Good design is invisible, and that makes it even harder to get people to recognize the value of a well-designed product or service.

In the late 1980s, companies who knew enough about innovation understood that they needed to listen to their own customers if they wanted to invent new and helpful solutions. In the 1980s companies only had positions for Graphic Arts Specialists, User Interface Designers, Technical Writers, and Quality Assurance Engineers. Throughout these disciplines, those professionals who cared about the user tried to informally coordinate a strategy to make products that worked for the people using them. For the next 10 years, this goal had a place in the product and service development cycle, but no one thought of coordinating these activities.

Much has been written about how to get stakeholders and project managers (PJM) to buy in to the UX process. Sometimes Lean UX is prescribed; sometimes doing a Return on Investment (ROI) analysis helps. I think the most important thing in getting buy in is to apply the UX process to the project itself. For example, you can think of the stakeholders as the "user" and you can study them:

- **What is their pain point?** Does the stakeholder or PM have a tight or even unrealistic schedule? Is their budget too tight? Do they have an external pressure? Maybe someone in his or her family is sick?
- **What do they need to get a win?** How can you make them successful? How is success measured?
- **How to communicate effectively**: maybe you can get more information by having a direct conversation.

## Dealing with Resistance

There are many reasons not consider UX. It is helpful to think of discussions with resistant stakeholders as just another user study. What are these stakeholders resisting? What is their agenda? Pay attention to their concerns and a stronger relationship will develop. It is through this stronger relationship that you will win them over. Furthermore, getting people involved in the process is a good way to get buy in, since they become more invested in the outcome if they are involved in the process.

Although UX professionals have made great progress in gaining a real place on development teams, there is still work to be done. Often the usability of a product is not seen as a high priority, for many reasons. Some companies and research institutions state that they don't want to listen to users, since the users are too uneducated about technology; they don't understand how to make it work. Therefore, why listen to someone who does not know what he or she is talking about? Some developers are afraid that listening to users will get in the way of their schedule, some marketing managers are afraid that the more usable solutions might lead the customers to buy less expensive versions (and jeopardize the marketing people's bonuses).

When times are tough, constant conflict may be good politics but in the real world, cooperation works better. After all, nobody's right all the time, and a broken clock is right twice a day.

**William J. Clinton**

## Resistance to Listen to Users During Innovation

**Too early in the process and users can't tell us what they want if they don't understand the technology**. Many developers feel that it is not helpful to get the voice of the customer in the early part of the development process, since users don't know what they want. Users don't understand how technology works or how to solve complicated problems (even though it is the users' own problems). Users don't understand the issues of development and get in our way.

**We can't have the users tell us how to develop/invent**. Any company that wants to be seen as innovative does not want to be seen as not knowing about technology, innovation, or design. This is sometimes interpreted as, "We don't want the market to think we don't know what we are doing and have to ask our customers for advice."

**We are the experts, not the users**. There is a reason we are professionals, we are trained in the field, we know what we are doing. Developers and marketing professionals are highly trained and, as such, often think of themselves as the experts.

**Isn't that what the requirements are for?** A good development plan will include requirements. Sometimes they don't. Although developers and marketing team members look to requirements in order to know what to build and what to sell, these requirements are often not user requirements. There is a big difference between functional requirements, which focus on specific functions, and the performance of the system. User requirements are different in that they focus on the users, what affordances are provided, what standards are applied and what design is best for the persona and use case that are involved.

## Users Get in the Critical Path

**Rush to get out the door.** Development teams often feel under pressure to get the next release out. Even some companies that have adopted Agile and Lean UX processes sometimes think they don't have time to get user input and that it will slow them down. Although this does happen, that getting user input takes time that a team might feel they do not have, I have found that there is usually enough time for an interview or two, or at least an informal evaluation or perhaps a survey. Fitting in even a small piece of user research will benefit the product in many ways. There are so many tools and methodologies now that the field has evolved and there is usually a UX solution that can fit into every development process.

**Developers already know all they need to know.** As I stated previously, developers are highly trained and intelligent. They are used to finding solutions to problems and puzzles; that is part of the process of developing products and services—figuring out how things get built and then building it. Many developers feel that they know how to build things and that there is no need to ask for more input from users, since that would result in too much information. While it is often hard to persuade people who feel strongly about something, there are ways this can be achieved. Particularly in the field of UX, the idea of backing up an assertion with data helps. For example, if a developer thinks the shopping cart he created on an ecommerce site is working, he or she would not be inclined to change it. If customer support data showed that people were having trouble checking out of the cart more often than not, the developer might be more inclined to fix the problem. The UX field incorporates many methods for collecting data that should be used to show the value of applying UX to build a better product.

**Isn't that what QA is for?** Developers in particular see that the QA team spends time evaluating products during the development process and don't see a need for further work. In these cases, it is important to educate the developers as to the difference between QA and UX.

## Limitations of Commercialization Schedules

**Too late.** It is never too late. There is always some room for improvement. Even if your work is not able to be integrated into the current release, you can aim to get it included in the next release. I find that sticking to the goal of getting UX into the process, is a goal for the good, and it is never too late to do some good.

**We are doing bug fixes.** Oftentimes, a UX problem can be seen as a bug and that should be filed away for the developers. I challenge the assertion that usability problems are a form of software bug, if it doesn't get fixed it will slow down the user, create performance problems, and create errors. This is the same effect as a software bug.

> The most important single ingredient in the formula of success is in knowing how to get along with people.

**Theodore Roosevelt**

# Solution to Resistance: Remember the Iterative Approach

While many UX professionals have psychology training, and use those skills directly when interviewing and observing users , these very same professionals forget to employ these basic psychological skills when working with their team members:

- Practice Active listening BE EMPATHIC;
- Project Managers and Developers are people too! Respect their concerns;
- Pay attention to differing perspectives resulting from differing roles as well as to turf battles and personal needs.

Many factors come into play in creating successful well-designed products. It is often the combination of things, such as sizing up the team's needs (applying UX principles to the team work), using the right tool at the right time, and creating a manageable schedule.

The UX Medicare.gov project strategy started with a single project, walking through the different steps one at a time. The team did not get a whole strategic modeling project from the beginning. The methods were broken down into sections, first an expert review and then the team created a clickable prototype to test the design ideas. This worked well and the next step was the usability test. The step-by-step projects worked well. The team at CMS needed time to develop trust with the UX team. In fact, they had to get buy in from the General Accounting Office of the US Government, so it was not going to be a fast process, but starting by building credibility through working in small steps really paid off.

The following case study illustrates these principles.

## You Can Build a Successful UX Strategy, But Not in One Day

Bob Thomas

As a user experience research professional, I have worked for big and small companies, mainly in the technology and insurance industries. At the time of writing, I am the Director of User Experience Research at Liberty Mutual, a Fortune 100 Company with over 50,000 employees worldwide. Offering auto, property, life, and other insurance products for consumers and businesses worldwide, Liberty Mutual has to focus on statistics and underwriting—in other words, quantitative data—to keep the company profitable. But it also has to understand its customers' needs and be empathetic, because it can be argued an insurance company's most important service is its response to customers when disasters strike. This combination of hard data and soft skills applies to our team, too.

Our UX Research team is in the Personal Insurance Small Business Unit (SBU) of Liberty Mutual (other SBUs are Commercial, Global Specialty, and Liberty International). This means we work in the consumer-facing arm of the company. Our UX research team is responsible for our public sites, www. libertymutual.com and mobile.libertymutual.com. We are also responsible for eService, where current customers can log in and manage their policies online. But our most important focus is on the online quoting process, where prospective customers can complete online forms to get an auto, property, or life insurance quote, and then buy that policy online.

This latter responsibility is the most important for the company, because it is where we as a business generate leads and sales. And it is most important for the UX team, because it's where we need to engage customers, who often equate insurance sales people with used car salesmen. To overcome this, we need to understand our potential customers' mental models and points of view. Understanding insurance is on a par with understanding taxes; people deal with it infrequently enough to be overwhelmed by it. Potential customers want to know, Will the insurance company make itself understandable, or will it resort to insurance jargon and obscure terminology? Will the company be able to cover me and my family at a price I can afford? Will they provide instant customer service if I get into an auto accident or if my basement gets flooded?

Understanding users involves empathizing with their concerns by understanding their motivations and gaining their trust.

A successful UX strategy can help you build your UX brand. Based on my experience as a Research and Design Associate, Product Manager, Usability Manager, and Director of User Experience, I've come up with six rules of a UX strategy that have worked for me over the last 20 years. I'll explain each rule as we go along. Let's start with my first rule.

## Rule #1: A Two-Pronged UX Strategy Works Best: One That Supports the Business, and One That Supports the UX Team

For a UX strategy to succeed, it must be aligned with the overall business strategy of the organization. But you can also have a secondary UX strategy that promotes user experience research and design within the organization. I'll explain more about this later.

Our UX strategy has been built around designing a consultative, engaging experience to overcome issues with users' motivation and trust (see Figure 13.1). On the Internet, you need to be transparent. This is true of online insurance forms, which our prospective customers can complete to get an online insurance quote. If users don't understand why they are being asked certain questions (date of birth, address, Social Security Number)— who is interviewing whom, here?—they start distrusting you. If they start distrusting you, they start totting up in their heads the questions that make sense and don't make sense to them. Then they look at how long the online process is going to take. And at some tipping point, they may become unmotivated to continue. It is at this point that you have lost any chance at gaining their trust and empathizing with their concerns.

Figure 13.1 Liberty Mutual Consultative/Engagement Tools, Auto Insurance Quote Summary Page (2012).

So this leads to my second rule of a successful UX strategy.

## Rule #2: Understand the Business Objectives of Your Stakeholders

Liberty Mutual is a data-driven company. We are all about improving numbers, year over year. We use acronyms all the time, for example, QSR, or Quote Start Rate, the number of unique users who start an insurance quote on our site, as measured from arrival at the first page of the insurance quote form. If the QSR for 2013 is 1.1 million unique users, then it better be at least x% above that in 2014. And if it isn't, you are held responsible for it on your performance review. And this applies not only to the product owners, but also everyone on the eCommerce team: senior vice-presidents, sales directors, product managers, business analysts, Web site analytics leads, designers, information architects, content strategists, and UX researchers. In this sense everyone is judged on the same business-driven criteria that derive from the same business objectives: improve the QSR. What does this mean? It means we all have to work together.

Frequently, our business owners will come to us with specific issues. For example, they will tell us that based on our Web analytics (we use Adobe Omniture) from the last 3 months, x% fewer users move forward from our home page to the quote start page. In other words, visitors to our site were not engaging with the highlighted "Get a Froc Quote" call-to-action box our home page (see Figures 13.2 and 13.3). Our business owners may also tell us, again based on our Web analytics, that x% more users are dropping off from page 1 to page 2 of the auto insurance quote process. They present business problems to us, and we as UX researchers have to solve them.

This leads me to my third rule of a successful UX strategy.

## Rule #3: Build Your UX Strategy to Meet the Needs of the Business

We make a point of meeting with stakeholders annually, quarterly, and on a project-by-project basis, to understand what the high-level goals and business objectives of each project are. If we understand the business owners' strategy, then we can build a UX strategy around it. By identifying the problem areas and issues, we can move forward with the right UX methodology.

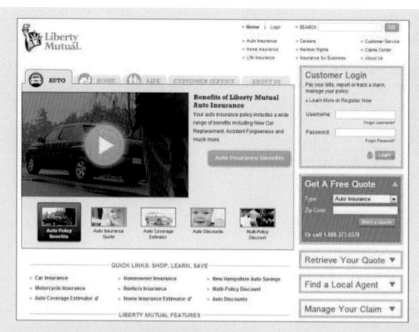

Figure 13.2 Liberty Mutual Home Page (2010).

Our UX research team has been successful by working shoulder to shoulder with our stakeholders. To build a UX strategy that meets the needs of the business, you need to involve the business team in the UX process. For us UX researchers, this means collaborating with them on the UX methodology chosen, the participant recruiting screener, and the usability test plan. In some cases, we'll do practice runs of a usability session and involve the business as participants or observers. The business is involved in the UX process from the start. Few surprises come out of such collaborations.

In the first example explained previously, we knew we had to move users from our home page to the first quote page. In the second example, we knew we had to improve the drop-off rate for users moving from

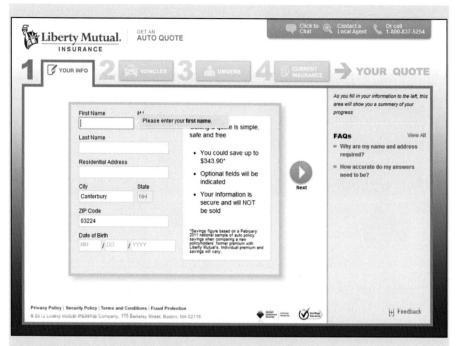

Figure 13.3 Liberty Mutual, Quote Start Page, Auto Insurance Quote (2012).

page 1 to page 2 of our online auto insurance form. So we have the quantitative data, but what about the qualitative? The quantitative data told us what was happening and where; we just didn't understand why.

In running our usability tests to get at the nugget of these issues, we used think-aloud protocols, and we recruited participants who met our demographic, motivational, and behavioral criteria for one-on-one sessions led by a moderator, who was a member of the UX research team. We asked our participants to complete task-based scenarios, such as, "You have just purchased a car and are interested in insuring it. Starting from this page, please show me what you would do."

Our participants' qualitative comments would help us to understand why users weren't clicking to get a free quote from our home page, and why, once they arrived on the quote start page, they were not advancing to the second page of quote.

What we found out from our usability tests was instrumental in redesigning solutions:

- On the home page, our participants didn't see the Get a Free Quote call-to-action area right away, as it was on the right side of the page and not a principal point of focus (see Figure 13.4)
- On the first page of our online insurance form, our participants did not know why they were being asked for their personal information (first and last name,

Figure 13.4 Liberty Mutual Home Page (2010).

residential address, date of birth). More importantly, they didn't want to give that information up so quickly. They wanted to be anonymous. They questioned who was interviewing whom. They did not want to give up personal information without getting back some benefit in return. Can you imagine someone expressing interest in your product at a trade show, and you snapping back: "Nice to meet you! What's your name? Where do you live? When were you born?" That's what the experience felt like to our users. Our conceptual model didn't match our users' mental models; our users simply wanted to enter vehicle information, which seemed relevant to them for a car insurance quote.

From this and subsequent usability tests, we have been able to design more straightforward solutions to enable people to move from our home page (see Figure 13.5) to the first page of quote. And we have been able to provide context and consultation to explain, on the first page of quote, how long the process should take, and why we're asking them for name, address, and date of birth. The business owners are happy because we've been able to increase the quote start rate and decrease the page one drop-off rate over time.

Positive changes in business results at our company have proven the value of user experience research. However, we still have to constantly substantiate our findings and actionable recommendations for executives in a data-driven company such as ours. For Liberty Mutual, this involves our vice presidents, and we have a lot of them, from associate vice-president up through senior vice-president in four SBUs. Executives have questioned the validity of UX sessions when only 10-12 participants are involved. Note that, although Nielsen states you can find 85% of usability problems with 5-8 users (Nielsen, 2000), and Krug states that testing 3 users once a month is enough to effect change (Krug, 2010), our company rests easier knowing we're in double digit numbers when it comes to the number of participants in our usability tests. Although this requires more work on everyone's part, it's

Figure 13.5 Liberty Mutual Home Page (2014).

a concession that has worked out well without too much fuss. Although it means more work for our UX research team, we have more qualitative data to back up our findings.

Testing with 10-12 participants leads to rich qualitative results. But sometimes the business wants more. This leads to my fourth rule of a successful UX strategy.

## Rule #4: Don't Fear the Data. Supplement the Qualitative with the Quantitative

After 3 years of relying mostly on qualitative findings, but also including some quantitative data such as task pass/fail ratings, Likert scales, time on task, and surveys, we began designing large-scale, remote, unmoderated usability studies with UserZoom to generate quantitative results.

With UserZoom, we can create surveys, five-second tests, prototype comparisons, task-based studies with actual sites or with interactive prototypes, and so on. We can set up our studies so that our participants can run them from laptops, tablets, or smart phones. We can recruit hundreds of participants for between- or within-study designs.

What compelled us to do this? In our data-driven company, our stakeholders always want to slice data by use case or customer segment. For example, they might ask, "Bob, in this study, how many current Liberty Mutual customers between the ages of 30 and 34 completed each task successfully?" To which I usually say something like, "That segment represents 3 of our 12 participants. You want a breakdown of that segment, task by task? Why don't we take a look at that in a quantitative test."

The quantitative data reassures our data-driven stakeholders. It also helps to demonstrate our value, to show the ROI (return on investment) of UX. Quantitative data shows us *what* happened, but not *why* it happened. In this respect, we use the quantitative data to back up the most important qualitative findings, because the quantitative validates the qualitative in most cases. We can also start with a remote, unmoderated quantitative-driven usability study, analyze the data to determine what tasks and designs fare more poorly than others, and then run an in-person qualitative study to discover the "why" behind the "what" for those tasks and designs that lagged behind others in usability testing. In our usability readouts, we always lead with the qualitative findings and follow-up with the quantitative results to back them up. That, in my mind, is the way it should be, because the quantitative data (the what) substantiates the qualitative comments (the why).

Our UX strategy has been largely successful because it has been aligned with the business strategy of the company. But that's not the whole story. There is another component to our success. We would not have been as successful if we had not increased our overall exposure within the organization. People are interested in or curious about our services—or even what UX is—because they hear about what we do from their co-workers. Never underestimate the power of word-of-mouth recommendations.

This leads me to my fifth rule of a successful UX strategy.

## Rule #5: Build Your UX Brand

Our Digital Experience and eCommerce teams have grown since I first started working at Liberty Mutual in 2008. When I was hired, my job title was

"Principal Systems Analyst" and I worked for IT. I started at UX zero. Not only did our Fortune 100 Company not have a job title for UX hires, but it did not have a dedicated UX team to put them in. We had no other UX researchers. We had no in-house information architects. We had one technical writer and one designer, who were both contractors.

One thing that I value most about my current company is the fact that I haven't had to explain the benefits of usability research to the executives. They believe in putting products in front of users. Having an executive champion or executive-level buy in is important for UX to succeed in any organization.

I learned this valuable lesson a while back, when I was working as a product manager for a different company. I was trying to incorporate usability testing into the product-development cycle through a series of small steps: getting buy in from my boss, who was head of engineering, to do an expert review; doing paper prototyping; and running usability tests with a small number of internal employees and reporting back to the team on the issues we found.

The product eventually went on to win an award, but before it did I got called into the president's office. The president told me, "We don't need usability here. Go help the sales people sell our product." I was dumbstruck, and maybe a little **naïve**. I learned two lessons from this. The first was, if management doesn't support UX within the company, then get out. The second was that in some organizations it does help, in terms of UX, to start small and keep building—running qualitative think-aloud protocols with 10-12 participants for the most part, but also writing expert reviews, and running in-house test with employees—because you can build on small wins at each stage, publicize your findings, effect positive change and a return on investment, and increase your budget and scope with each win.

As I mentioned, I started at Liberty Mutual as a usability department of one, but have been able to hire other UX research professionals each year by making a case for usability. I'm now responsible for creating, proposing, and keeping to an annual UX research budget.

I've been able to promote usability research in different ways, such as running lunch-and-learn presentations, conducting practice focus groups or usability tests with stakeholders, and presenting UX research standards to executives to be adopted as governing standards.

We have built up a usability wiki on SharePoint, where anyone on our eCommerce team can review readouts and presentations from usability tests going back to 2008 (see Figure 13.6). In this way, our work—qualitative and quantitative findings, actionable recommendations—is completely transparent.

All of the above increases the visibility of UX and establishes a UX brand. (I even have a boring nickname, "Usability Bob," which my boss gave me my second week on the job. For better or worse, it's a nickname that has stuck because it has differentiated me.) The point here is that if people in an organization *believe* that a UX brand or strategy exists, then it does exist.

## Conclusion

Let's review my five rules again:

- Rule #1: A two-pronged UX strategy works best: one that supports the business, and one the supports the UX team.
- Rule #2: Understand the business objectives of your stakeholders.
- Rule #3: Build your UX strategy to meet the needs of the business.
- Rule #4: Don't fear the data. Supplement the qualitative with the quantitative.
- Rule #5: Build your UX brand.

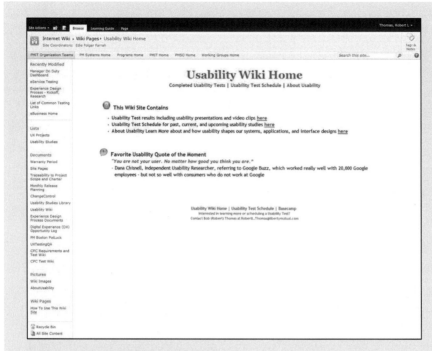

Figure 13.6  Usability Wiki, SharePoint Site (2014).

Product owners and product managers often argue from the point of view of the business. UX researchers, designers, information architects, and content strategists often argue from the point of view of the user. Ultimately, the point of having a business strategy and a UX strategy is that two groups within an organization can work together to design products that work from the business's perspective for the user. Who can argue with that?

This leads me to my sixth and final rule of UX strategy:

- ■ Rule #6: Demonstrate UX success to management, and then you can work together to establish a UX strategy for the company.

The conundrum we face as UX leaders is that to get more staff hired to our UX teams, we need to demonstrate UX success. To continue to demonstrate UX success in more projects, we need to hire more UX staff. How do we demonstrate that success? One way is to show the executive team that there is demand for our services, which we can't meet with the current staff we have. A second way is to show the ROI of UX, by demonstrating how UX has contributed to the success of the business and its bottom line; and then increase that success and bottom line year after year.

At Liberty Mutual, I have been able to add one new hire a year because of a demand for usability research in the organization. I have created UX research standards and vetted them out with executives, so that they are now part of our governing committee guidelines. At the time of writing, I am building a new UX lab. I am demonstrating the ROI of UX so that we can tie business gains directly to UX research. These initiatives have come about through years of hard work, which I owe in large part to my team and my colleagues in the business unit where I work. And it is only right now, at this moment in time, that I'm confident I've established a UX strategy that resonates with management, one they take notice of and continue to fund.

## Takeaway for Getting Buy In

- UX strategy must include the stakeholder of the project, think of them as the users of the UX processes and methods. The stakeholders need to be included so that they will be more inclined to buy in to the process.
- Understand the project issues and constraints and be sensitive to them: take budget and schedule into account when planning UX strategy.
- Use the data to support your case. Work through the issues through data analysis, share what you learn, and be on the lookout for places where it will shed light on a problem.

# REFERENCES

Krug, S., 2010. Rocket Surgery Made Easy: The Do-It-Yourself Guide to Finding and Fixing Usability Problems. New Riders, Berkeley, CA.

Nielsen J., 2000. Why You Only Need to Test with 5 Users. http://www.nngroup.com/articles/why-you-only-need-to-test-with-5-users/.

# Chapter 14

## SUCCESS STORIES

This chapter focuses on what makes successful UX work through goal setting and aligning priorities with the team. There are two case studies that demonstrate successful approaches to goal setting and clear tactics.

# Chapter 14

No matter what people tell you, words and ideas can change the world.

**Robin Williams**

This book is about getting it right, in all aspects of design, usability, performance, and technology. A good user experience is one that understands the user's mental model and provides the right solution: it gets it right.

The field of UX and our understanding of usability are evolving. We are learning more about how to combine cognitive science, design thinking, UX design principles, and usability evaluation methods to create reliable processes that put the person at the center. These processes help to create improved products and technology that makes our world better.

The next two case studies have a common approach in developing and implementing strategies for their work. They involve setting goals and aligning those goals with the UX work. Each author created her own version of a strategy and each one worked. There are several ways to implement a good strategy; the important thing is to choose an approach that works for you. Put together the right set of tools that fit for the specific personas, use cases, and development team timeline and budget. Remember, you will have to sell the work, so you have to stand by it. Educate yourself and find the method you know is right for the project at hand.

# Creating a UX Strategy That Aligns to the Business

Janice James

*Note*: The company names, towns, and regions have all been anonymized.

## Introduction

In Canada, a "region" is similar to a U.S. "county." Canadian regions often consist of multiple local municipalities comprising smaller rural areas, as well as more densely populated urban areas. Regional municipalities provide core services such as water, waste management, police, and emergency services to residences and businesses within the region.

In the region of Dunright in British Columbia, Canada solicited Accent is a technology and management consulting firm that provides its citizens and employees with enhanced electronic services. Dunright envisioned a portal technology solution that included two portal applications: one that could be shared initially by the residents and businesses of the town of Taylor, one of the local municipalities in the region, and another internal application for the employees of the region of Dunright. The intent was that other local municipalities within the region could leverage the new portal solutions in the future.

The region of Dunright did not have an in-house user experience team. In terms of a UX Maturity Model,[1] the region would be considered to be in the lowest level stages: unenlightened or unimportant. Web developers relied on their own intuition about users and their needs. They apparently completed "design" tasks on an operational level simply when they were needed and only for a very specific purpose. As might be expected, since individual team efforts concentrated only on specific areas of responsibility, the existing site and micro-sites had grown organically out of control. No one was really focused on the global growth of the site overall.

The following case study focuses only on the portal solution Accent created for the town of Taylor in the region of Dunright. The UX team employed a UX strategy for the region's employee portal very similar to that created for the town of Taylor.

## Requirements Gathering and a Roadmap

Prior to Accent's engagement with the town of Taylor, ARC, a large business consulting firm, had worked with the town and region to gather, validate, and prioritize high-level requirements. Although it was helpful to have the requirements as a starting point, they were rather broadly defined and it was necessary to collect some additional details to ensure we accurately understood the original requirements.

Based on the collected requirements and priorities, ARC also developed portal infrastructure, hardware, and software implementation roadmaps. Although they didn't define a separate user experience "roadmap," ARC identified in which phase of the implementation each of the UX requirements should be addressed. For Phase 1, ARC defined the new user experience requirements as follows:

- A new user experience designed to address accessibility standards;
- Revised content included within seven micro sites;
- Enhanced search capabilities;

- Event calendars for multiple areas;
- Improved search capabilities;
- Limited rollout of social media capabilities;
- New content management tool;
- A new repository to store council documents.

Although ARC defined the requirements above as "user requirements," they also seemed to include what appeared to us at Accent as more "functional" requirements (i.e., event calendars).

## Understanding the Business Strategy: The First Step in Creating a UX Strategy

Before we could align a well-developed UX strategy to the region of Dunright's business strategy, we first needed to understand its major components:

- **Vision and Goals;**
- Branding Strategy;
- **User Experience Requirements;**
- End Users and Prioritization;
- **Functional Requirements;**
- **Content Requirements;**
- **Budget.**

We outlined a plan that defined the methods we would use to collect and analyze the business strategy information. This became part of our *Discovery* phase. The items in bold above identify those areas that ARC had previously defined and documented. Of course our first step was to review the existing documentation. During our review, we identified gaps and determined where we needed to (a) validate the documented information with stakeholders and/or (b) request additional business documents and/or plan to collect missing information from stakeholders, or (c) determine that the documents provided adequate information.

We had to be sensitive to the fact that ARC had already spent a good deal of time (and money) with most of the stakeholders gathering requirements to create their roadmaps. The town of Taylor made it clear they did not want us to "waste" time repeating the same processes carried out by our predecessor. However, our team felt we needed to hear first-hand from the stakeholders what they felt were the vision and goals of a successful new portal. Wherever possible, we streamlined our data collection by focusing only on validating what had been previously documented.

## Stakeholder Workshops

Stakeholder workshops were our primary means of collecting information and understanding the pieces of the business strategy that had not clearly or precisely been documented. During the workshops, we concentrated on areas that needed vetting, such as the business vision and goals, branding strategy, users and prioritization, user requirements and, to a lesser degree, functional requirements.

We defined "stakeholders" as those who could **express** and **set priorities** for their business units and who had a vested interest in the success of the overall redesign efforts. We attempted to identify stakeholders for each "department" represented in the current Web site with the understanding that there may be some overlap between departments. We identified 40 different departments for which there could potentially be representative stakeholders, but the town of Taylor provided us with the names of only 27 stakeholders.

This meant that some of the areas of the current Web site would not have a direct stakeholder representative, if there was no overlap of responsibility.

Our UX team conducted a series of stakeholder workshops (qualitative interviews), first with all stakeholders and then individually with the stakeholder(s) for each department.

To facilitate collection of information, we distributed our interview questions to the stakeholders prior to the workshops. As always, their time was more precious than ours, so we did what we could to help them prepare for the workshops. We did not ask them to fill in the answers to our questions (although some did); we just asked that they at least think about the questions and come prepared to contribute their input.

The purpose for the group and individual workshops was that we believed we could collect different pieces of information from the group as a whole vs. from the individual departmental stakeholders. And, our assumptions were correct. We collected information during the department-specific meetings that did not surface during the group meetings. For example, some department stakeholders had concerns about how prominent and easily accessible information about their department would be displayed on the new Web site, but they didn't express this during the group meetings. Again, this didn't surprise us. We interpreted this behavior as a natural willingness to be more open and outspoken about individual areas of responsibility in a more private or "safe" environment.

During the first workshop with all stakeholders together, we focused on high-level questions that would allow us to gain an understanding of their vision and goals, and whether the stakeholders were all on the same page or whether they had varied opinions. Again, we made sure that we communicated that we had read all of the documentation shared with us, but that we just wanted to confirm our assumptions during the workshops. We asked questions, such as the examples below, that uncovered details in the following main areas:

- Purpose/vision/goals of the new portal: What do they see as the major impetus for the project? What are the business goals? How do they expect to measure success of the redesigned site?
- Users of the sites: Who are the primary, secondary, tertiary users of the site? Who are the new targeted users?
- Tasks/usage: What are the primary scenarios in which different user types will use the site?
- Browser and Web standards: How will users access the site? What will the browser standards be? Will there be language and internationalization standards?
- Accessibility requirements: What level of accessibility standards should be adhered to? Has there been any previous accessibility testing?
- Branding requirements: How would they like the town to be visually represented?
- Interactive design requirements: What are their plans for integrating video, audio, and other multimedia content? Are there existing design, style, or writing style guidelines?
- Marketing: What marketing programs run in tandem with what's represented on the Web site?
- Differentiation: How did they want to differentiate the online presence of their town from others?

The follow-up workshops with individual department stakeholders allowed us to ask more detailed, but similar questions related to their specific areas of the site. We also asked individual stakeholders to define issues they saw for their specific areas of the current Web site and their plans for adding new or eliminating old content. One of the interesting and repeated themes we heard was that the departments didn't want to lose their identity in the redesign. They wanted to be autonomous and not "mixed in with the rest of the town of Taylor." Of course, this could have gone against the overall goal of producing a look and feel of consistency, but it was an important piece of information for us and affected the UX strategy we later employed. We also learned during these individual sessions the tone or flavor that the departments wanted for their specific areas, whether it was to be a more "promotional" flavor, purely informative, kid-friendly, professional, etc.

The information we collected from the series of group and department stakeholder workshops and from the additional documents that department stakeholders shared with us was invaluable. The details we collected from the stakeholders to clarify the original rather broadly outlined user requirements defined by ARC, allowed us to create an interface closely aligned to the overall business and individual stakeholder needs.

## Creating a UX Strategy

With a wealth of information behind us and a greatly improved understanding of the overall business strategy, we still suspected that there might be some pieces missing. However, as with many projects, we were out of time and budget dollars, so we settled for what we had. We created a UX strategy that would align to the business strategy and one that would attempt to surface answers to the most important of the outstanding issues and questions, such as:

- How to provide a clear brand message definition.
- What type of site organization would be most meaningful and efficient for users?
- What were the departmental stakeholders' plans for new content? What content would be retired?
- What are the primary scenarios that drive users to come and rely on the site?
- What tools and functionality would drive more users to the site?

At the time, we did not think to document a one-to-one map of business goals/values to UX activities that we would employ during Phase 1 of the project. It would have been a good deliverable to provide the client with, but we simply had not included it in our Statement of Work. We did, however, reflect and carefully consider everything we had learned and stored this information in our heads, collectively, as we began to create the UX strategy.

Now, after the fact, using a concept similar to what Lis Hubert and Paul McAleer developed for their Mapping Business Value to UX Workshop, the graph below illustrates the town of Taylor business values and goals mapped to UX activities in our UX strategy. The graph also illustrates gaps where we were unable to include UX activities due to time and/or budget constraints (Figure 14.1)

## Our UX Strategy

- **User Profiles:** We created user profiles to identify the demographic and psychographic characteristics of all user types across the residents, business, and partner customer segments. Not only did we uncover the number of languages spoken by the users of the site, but also we learned that users generally had "little knowledge of internal workings of the town." We used plain language in our wireframes and prototypes and paid special attention during usability testing to determine if users had difficulties understanding any of the language. Of course we were not responsible for rewriting any of the content, but we interfaced closely with the content management team to ensure they understood the importance of this goal.

- **Personas and Contextual Inquiry:** Unfortunately, time and budget constraints prevented us from creating personas or conducting contextual inquiry studies. We felt both of these activities would have provided the UX team a broader and more in-depth understanding of the different user types within the customer segments. More importantly, data collected during a contextual inquiry study would have allowed the UX team to create personas that

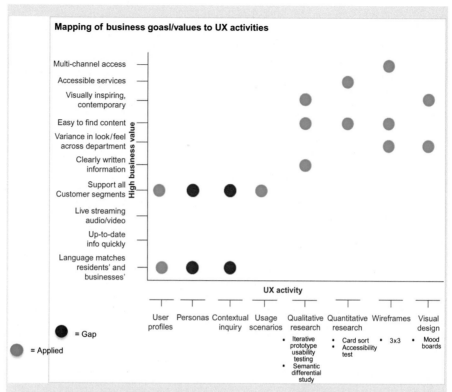

Figure 14.1 Mapping of UX strategy.

would become an excellent reference source for stakeholders as they continued forward in future phases of the project.

■ **Usage Scenarios:** Although worked with stakeholders to create usage scenarios, and others already existed in the documentation with which we were provided, the only opportunity we had to work directly with residents, businesses, and partners was during the iterative prototyping tests. We were very careful to recruit participants who represented the different customer segments. During the tests, we strove to understand the users' needs and the different types of situations that would drive them to the site.

■ **Qualitative Research:** During iterative prototyping testing, we tested the new information architecture that was derived from the card sorting study, focusing on the overall organization and sample areas within lower level areas of the site. We also conducted a semantic differential study of three sets of mood boards that represented three different themes, all supportive of the town's brand messaging. The user feedback gave us a clear indication of which theme best represented the town's values and brand.

- **Quantitative Research:** Preparation for a card sorting study gave us the opportunity to work with stakeholders to do an inventory of their content. This exercise revealed the amount of redundancy in content across the seven microsites and forced the stakeholders to take a hard look at the validity and relevance of the content. The card sorting data and resulting information architecture moved our UX team one step closer to meeting the goal of users easily finding what they needed on the site. The UX team also conducted accessibility testing of the out-of-box portal solution the town had selected to use for the new redesign. We needed to ensure that all services to be provided by the site would be accessible and 508 compliant.

- **Wireframes:** We began our "3 × 3" usability testing with three different sets of wireframes. Each set of wireframes was three levels deep (landing page, 2nd and 3rd level pages), each representing the same areas of the site, but with different navigational and layout design schemes. Each user completed a series of tasks using each set of wireframes, one at a time. The wireframes were counterbalanced between users.

At the end of day one, based on the user data collected that day, we modified the wireframes and began the 2nd day of testing with two new sets of wireframes, again representing the same areas of the site. We repeated the same testing process on the 2nd day, made modifications based on user feedback and began the 3rd day of testing with one new set of wireframes. At the end of the 3rd day of testing, we analyzed the data we had collected during the day and over the week to then create a new set of wireframes representative of our recommended navigational structure and page layouts, based on user feedback and input.

- **Visual Designs:** As mentioned previously, the visual designers on the UX team created three "mood" boards, each reflective of the town and brand messaging. The mood boards illustrated the individual components, such as typography, tables, photos, graphs, and a color scheme, that would be used on the site. We used the mood boards to conduct a semantic differential study to measure the users' attitudes toward the mood boards.

Users rated the designs against a scale of polar adjectives placed at each end of the 5-point scale (Figure 14.2).

**This visual design is:**

| | | | | | | |
|---|---|---|---|---|---|---|
| Inconsistent | ☐ | ☐ | ☐ | ☐ | ☐ | Consistent |
| Outdated | ☐ | ☐ | ☐ | ☐ | ☐ | Relevant |
| Confusing | ☐ | ☐ | ☐ | ☐ | ☐ | Understandable |
| Exclusive | ☐ | ☐ | ☐ | ☐ | ☐ | Inclusive |
| Hard-to-Use | ☐ | ☐ | ☐ | ☐ | ☐ | Easy-to-Use |
| Amateurish | ☐ | ☐ | ☐ | ☐ | ☐ | Professional |
| Traditional | ☐ | ☐ | ☐ | ☐ | ☐ | Innovative |
| Conforming | ☐ | ☐ | ☐ | ☐ | ☐ | Diverse |
| Plain | ☐ | ☐ | ☐ | ☐ | ☐ | Visionary |
| Disparate | ☐ | ☐ | ☐ | ☐ | ☐ | Conglomerate |

**This visual design captures these qualities:**

| | | | | | | |
|---|---|---|---|---|---|---|
| Corruption | ☐ | ☐ | ☐ | ☐ | ☐ | Integrity |
| Complacent | ☐ | ☐ | ☐ | ☐ | ☐ | Commitment |
| Irresponsible | ☐ | ☐ | ☐ | ☐ | ☐ | Accountability |
| Condescending | ☐ | ☐ | ☐ | ☐ | ☐ | Respect |
| Imperfection | ☐ | ☐ | ☐ | ☐ | ☐ | Excellence |

Figure 14.2 Semantic differential example.

---

[1]A User Experience Maturity Model defines the sequence of stages through which a corporation progresses as their user experience processes evolve and mature. Several usability or UX maturity models have been published, including J. Nielsen's Corporate Usability Maturity Model (2006), S. Van Tyne's Corporate UX Maturity model (2007), T. Jokela's Usability Maturity Models (2010), and J. Ashley and K. Desmond's Enterprise Usability Maturity (2010).

If everyone is moving forward together, then success takes care of itself.

**Henry Ford**

It is important to listen to all the members of a team. I know it is not realistic to be able to meet everyone's needs, pay attention to all the issues raised and still stay on schedule, but in order for a project to be successful the team needs to meet a goal, together.

## Setting Goals

Sarah Bloomer

In my UX design practice, I've found it essential to establish user experience goals. UX goals embody your design strategy, align with your brand experience and, above all, drive design decisions. UX goals are not the same as design principles. Design principles are universal (Keep it simple), whereas UX goals are specific to a product or set of products. A principle is "a fundamental truth or proposition" while a goal is "a desired result."

Effective UX goals describe the experience you aim to deliver. I like to think of them as the way you *want* your customers to describe their experience after they use your product. A UX goal distinguishes your product or products from your competitors. Ideally they are:

1. aligned with your unique value proposition and brand experience to differentiate your products;
2. applicable to multiple products to create a common, shared experience;
3. broad enough to apply to different products and allow a more specific definition, e.g., what is "speedy" on a desktop app vs. a mobile app?
4. the words your customers will use to describe their experience;
5. guides design decisions.

UX goals provide a powerful way to focus design especially when deadlines are tight or you have a disparate team.

We developed a set of UX goals with Balihoo-, a Boise-based marketing automation software company. Balihoo were adding a new product to their existing suite of products. As part of our design research, we worked with them to develop a set of UX goals. They renamed these "design tenets."

UX goals must be derived from design research as well as the company brand. Design research gave us the customer view while brand research gave us the unique attributes of working with Balihoo products. After field research and persona development, we held a UX goal workshop with key stakeholders. Having the right people at the workshop is critical to establishing representative goals and getting buy in. Our workshop included 5 people who attended the client interviews including the UX designer, product manager, plus the visual designer, VP of engineering, VP of marketing, and CEO.

We opened our workshop by presenting our key findings about the context of use, the personas, and issues they face. The group then broke into 3 teams, each instructed to come up with 5 goals. We constrain the number to 5 to keep the goals to a manageable number. I like to be able to rattle them off, one to each finger. Each group presented their 5 goals back to the whole team, and together we identified and refined the common goals for further discussion.

The goals were refined until they were short and clear. At the workshop, for example, one goal was:

Powerful enough to do more
Execute more sophisticated campaigns with greater precision; I can do more with less; a
    more technical marketing person can "get under the hood."

This goal was refined to:

Power through precision
- Enables sophisticated local campaigns that are scalable
- Allows marketers to do more with less.

Another rough version of a goal:

Up-to-date, clean and consistent look and feel
Visually appealing; professional looking, without being stodgy; pleasing to marketing people.

Became:

Clean Experience
- Modern, professional look, and feel
- Uncluttered, fast, and responsive.

Socializing the goals helps this product vision gain traction. Scott Baird, Balihoo's UX Designer, posted the goals around the development area. Balihoo also had a champion in their CEO, Pete Gombert. He launched the goals at an all-hands company meeting to describe the direction of the product.

The goals are used to think through design decisions. For example, if there are competing ideas for how a feature should be designed, the team uses the goals to find the best solution. When UX goals are applied in this way, there's a better chance at achieving a coherent, seamless experience.

Scott describes how he applied the goals:

I've been referring to the UX Goals frequently to guide design choices with Product and our developers, and in three or four instances Pete and Paul (CEO and Engineering VP) referred to them as well, to weigh in a technical decision or to validate a position they held on how the product should work.

The goals have also influenced Balihoo's choice of platform, development framework, and Web design. Scott reports that the goal "Intuitive Design: 'I know what to do', easy to learn; don't need a manual" has driven him to design a powerful tool that includes concepts new to the marketing world. That's a real challenge with a product as complex as Balihoo's and the goals served the purpose of keeping the team focused.

After evaluating each of the three mood boards, users then selected their preferred design, indicating why they chose the design, what they liked most about it, what could be done to improve it, and what aspects they also liked of the other two unselected designs. Based on the users' ratings and final preferences, the visual designer created a final recommended mood board. Our goal was to create a design that met the goal of a visually appealing and contemporary design. Of course stakeholders had the final review and say, but they were greatly influenced by the users' feedback. Once the final visual design was agreed upon, the visual designer created themes and skins based on the final design to support the stakeholders' desire to retain the variance in look across departments.

As Figure 14.3 illustrates, we did not implement UX activities that directly supported the two business values of: Live/streaming video or up-to-date information. However, during the iterative prototyping and usability test sessions, we collected input from the users about these two characteristics of the new site that stakeholders had assigned a high business value. We found that users considered live streaming video as a "nice-to-have," but up-to-date information in a timely manner was very important to them.

Take Away

All in all, given the constraints of budget and time, we ensured that our UX strategy supported and aligned with the town's business strategy. The up-front time to meet

Figure 14.3 Collaboration with mood boards.

with and closely listen to the stakeholders, both as a group and individually, better prepared us to create a UX strategy we were confident that would meet their high value business goals. The one piece we felt was somewhat deficient in the strategy was more one-on-one time with the users. Although users participated in the card sorting exercise and in the iterative prototype usability studies, we would've liked to have had more individual time with more users across the three different customer types. We didn't have a high confidence level that we thoroughly understood their similarities, differences and priorities. But, isn't that the nature of UX work? We always wish we had just a little more time with the users!

Always be yourself, express yourself, have faith in yourself, do not go out and look for a successful personality and duplicate it.

**Bruce Lee**

# How Do We Define Success

Each one of us knows what it feels like to succeed. We can recognize when things work well and when they don't. The field of UX is evolving and there are many different methods to create successful experiences for people. We know that it is important to put the person first, to create personas, use cases, workflows, and maps, and that there are many methods for testing those assumptions on prototypes that can be quickly created. If you are working in the field of UX, you should know that trusting yourself is one of the most important things you can do. If you are in the field, the odds are you are an observant person, who knows when something is working easily and when it is not right. Trust yourself when you are in a room with stakeholders or developers who disagree. You know that the most important key to a successful UX is to keep the person at the heart of it all.

The produce a good user experience a team must to create a balance between resources, technology, and the users' needs. A successful UX puts the user needs first, as the foundation for development and then builds the product or service from that ground truth: the user. Sometimes these successes come over time: weeks, months, and sometimes years. Sometimes success comes in a single moment, when the elements come together, facts speak for themselves, and product teams find that place of balance.

I found that a great way to start a project is to define what that project's success looks like. How will the team know the project was successful? Those goals are the first step in creating a successful strategy and a wonderful way to get a group of people to work together. Everyone on the team needs to buy in to the goal, or it won't work. It is up to the team to come together and make it work. There is always a balance, a creative tension between the users' needs, the project budget, and the timeline. The balance can be achieved with clear goals, which provide metrics that help us know when we have made progress.

# REFERENCE

Hubert, L., McAleer, P., December 9, 2013. Mapping business value to UX, part 3. UX Matters, Retrieved February 22, 2014 from: http://www.uxmatters.com/mt/archives/2013/12/mapping-business-value-to-ux-part-3.php.

# Chapter 15

## A FEW WORDS ABOUT FAILURE: TURNING IT INTO SUCCESS

This chapter discusses the value of failure, especially how to use it as an opportunity to improve.

# Chapter 15

Success is a lousy teacher. It seduces smart people into thinking they can't lose.

**Bill Gates**

## Failure as Success

It would be incomplete, in a book about successful user experience, not to mention failure, which is arguably a key element to success. Many people don't feel comfortable admitting failure; it seems we openly place more value on success. That is misplaced, since failure is the balance to success. How can we know success if we don't also recognize failure?

There is no shame in failing at something. It means that you tried. Perhaps a person tried something in a new way. Trying something new is brave and being brave is admirable. The value of our failures is in what they can teach us. What happened during the experience that you can learn from? Failure provides data, which you can look at to improve the situation the next time. Much has been written about the benefits of failure, as a way to learn from the mistake in order not to repeat it in the future. This learning requires of a person a degree of introspection. To turn failure to success a person must withstand the emotions that come unbidden with failure and simply use the experience as an opportunity to improve.

Thomas Edison invented the light bulb. Edison understood the importance of iterative design and built over ten thousand prototypes before he made a light bulb that successfully produced light for a continuous period and became useful. A famous Thomas Edison quote refers to the light bulb invention, "I have not failed

10,000 times. I have not failed once. I have succeeded in proving that those 10,000 ways will not work. When I have eliminated the ways that will not work, I will find the way that will work."

If we consider the iterative approach that one learns from failure, integrating it into the next success, then we can see how important it is to fail. How else will we learn? Experience is one of the best teachers.

People might feel that they failed because they did not control a situation properly. If only they had maintained control they would have succeeded. That belief is misleading, because it assumes that you can control everything. While we need to control our testing scenarios and stay focused on user personas, we might not always be able to control how the user research will play out. Maybe something that seemed like a failure will allow us to discover something new. We can succeed more often if we allow ourselves flexibility in how we respond to the situation. We can learn from our mistakes and take that experience with us, informing our next situation, and so on. In short, failure teaches us to iterate on our own experience.

I cannot prevent the wind from blowing, but I can adjust my sails to make it work for me.

## Code of the Order of Isshinryu

What Does It Really Mean to Fail?

Failing can be seen as an opportunity, not a disaster. Once we are in the habit of observation, we can more easily learn from our mistakes. Sometimes we can even see a failure coming. It is at those moments that our experiences can guide us to make course corrections and make use of teachings from past experiences. While we would like to think we could control a situation, and other people, in reality we can only control our response to what is happening around us. No matter what we do, their behavior does not change, so we must change our own tactics. One of the ways that we can control our responses is to choose our battles, and be strategic with our actions, keeping our goals clear.

The following case study illustrates the wisdom of spending time in getting a good understanding of what is happening around you, and then choosing your battles.

## But Thank You...

Scott Williams

Context and intent are the dual anchors of my thinking as I engage in a project. What are the conditions of a user's environment and what are they trying to accomplish? By looking at a case from the outside in, I strive to find the points where we can adjust and improve the experience and, hopefully, allow the user a moment of greater satisfaction. However, my context and intent are not always in accord with the client's, and occasionally the outcome is less than fully satisfying.

I had been engaged by an American regional financial institution (FI) to perform an expert review of an online payment portal—while entry rates to the site were good, completion rates were less than outstanding, and naturally this was of considerable concern to the FI. Not only were business opportunities being missed (and revenue left on the table), but also other concerns arose. If we consider that the workflow consisted of seven steps, then at the fourth step roughly forty percent of users were abandoning the process, a four in ten indictment of what should be considered a standard exchange. As a part of the overall engagement I was charged to perform a review, which would indicate where the biggest challenges were in keeping users from completing the task.

This particular portal served to allow people to make a payment to public entities (e.g., town assessor, state tax board). The processes began on the FI's site, where the user could select the destination entity and then enter salient payment information, and after a review sheet, the user would be passed along to the public entity's site.

The review was fairly straightforward, revealing some information architecture (IA) issues and organizational issues on the FI site proper. However, the process of transitioning from the FI's portion of the workflow to the public entities' portion—after entering a significant amount of personal information—was not smooth at all. IA and design elements abruptly shifted and the user would land on the destination site without notice, changing the established cues and markers of a trusted experience and replacing them with unknowns. One could certainly understand—in this day and age of phishing and identity theft—why such a shift could lead a user to develop second thoughts and abandon the online execution of the task and then seek another solution. Along with my notes concerning the IA, I compiled my thoughts and some research highlighting the challenges of transitioning a user in a payments workflow from a "trusted" location to an uncertain location.

As I presented my findings, the client acknowledged the abruptness of the transition, but considered it to be the public entities' problem. As for the IA and design issues, the client showed me a staging site where a redesign was being hosted.

Me: Interesting. This redesign uses the same IA and organization of on-screen elements, only in a different color and with some different icons. Also, it seems to have more advertising.

Client: We felt that our branding wasn't fully on-point.

Me: And as I've only just now presented my findings, this redesign in fact takes none of the research into account.

Client: We felt that we had a good sense of direction on this after all. Thank you, though, for your hard work.

Me: You're welcome. May I just say that redesign or no, the major issue with completion rates stems from a lack of instruction and expectation setting? You aren't telling your users that they will be moved from your site to the public entities' sites. Nothing has changed.

Client: We believe that a firmer branding message will help.

Me: ...

Client: But thank you for your hard work.

I could have, I suppose, gone on to speak of the differences between marketing and user experience research, could have gone further to speak about how the two aren't in competition but rather two of many tools to use in concert, but... context and intent. There are many points of contact and inflection in a working relationship, and they cannot be considered as discrete. Some moments are for taking a stand, some for pausing and observing. This moment was not the moment to fight a battle. Part of being a UX practitioner is understanding that not everyone knows about UX, and that a longer, gentler approach and engagement may provide greater opportunity for the endgame of user satisfaction.

My outside-in approach did provide worthwhile information: navigation links were hidden, in-line and contextual help was lacking, and interaction patterns were inconsistent. On the other hand, the client's inside-out approach was undoubtedly satisfying other metrics of which I was unaware. Fortunately the engagement continues, and as time progresses I will try to blend the viewpoints to help the end-user achieve informed, confident, task completion.

## Learn from Failure

An essential aspect of creativity is not being afraid to fail.

**Edwin Land**

Sometimes a project fails and it takes a while to understand why. First answer the questions, "What does success on this project look like? How will we know it was successful?" Get stakeholders to answer the questions at the beginning of the project.

If stakeholders answer the questions differently, their goals differ. If that is true (and sometimes there are other reasons for people having different answers to the same questions, such as competing agendas) then the stakeholders need help coming together. Try to find out the source of the conflict. What is keeping the stakeholders from agreeing on their key goals? Getting the answer to that question might be the first piece of work for the UX professional, to bring the team together with a single vision of what it means to succeed:

- Take what you can learn from the situation and use it as a learning opportunity, then iterate.
- If you don't fail ever, then you are not trying hard enough. Failure can be a sign of admirable effort and determination not to quit.

The next case study is a project I worked on as a consultant. From the point of view of UX the project was not a failure, since we learned a lot about the user base, better understood some issues they were having, and were able to make some correlations with user and business goals and provide data to help make incremental improvements. The project was a failure in the eyes of the client, because it returned results that were far from what they expected and they were not prepared to deal with the result.

# That is Not What We Expected

Elizabeth Rosenzweig

A Calling Product Company (CPC) company hired Bubble Mountain Consulting to put together a survey for a PhoneCard offered by CPC. The product was a service of a much larger carrier of international telephone services.

PhoneCard offered great rates for international calls. CPC is a subsidiary of a much larger company that owns and operates hundreds of telephone carriers from around the world, who claim to send millions of calls through its networks daily.

PhoneCard was operated out of an office in Northeastern United States. For the first few years of business, the PhoneCard team had not done any UX work on its products. In addition, it had not done any market research or surveys of customers. The PhoneCard team had informally talked to a few customers in various parts of the world and the team felt they had a pretty good idea of who was using their service, and what the customers liked and did not like. The team wanted to validate their assumptions with the survey, fully expecting the data to support its direction.

PhoneCard was marketing the product as being easy to use, and having clear terms, no tricky hidden fees, and the ability to allow access to 30 countries.

## Project Goal

The goal of the project was to research the questions of who was using the phone card, what they were using it for and how satisfied they were. Bubble Mountain Consulting conducted a Web-based survey to determine the usage and overall level of satisfaction of active CPC customers. The survey probed issues such as brand recognition, product, and Web site ease of use in an attempt to identify issues such as what is compelling and what is difficult about using PhoneCard.

## Methodology of Work

Bubble Mountain Consulting conducted the survey using standard online tools. The data were compiled and analyzed using a combination of online automatic analysis tools and the traditional method of one-to-one analysis. The latter approach entails examining data sets in different combinations that led to finding trends and connections to help draw empirical conclusions.

Bubble Mountain worked with the PhoneCard team leaders to design the survey and to counterbalance the questions to ensure the data were valid. Bubble Mountain was given access to CPC's entire customer base of 28,497, which included both active and dormant users. The survey launched through surveymonkey and the link was sent to all 28,497 users of PhoneCard. After 2 weeks, 2639 people had responded.

The overall response rate was 9%, which can be further broken into:

- current customers, who responded at roughly 10%
- dormant customers, who responded at 4%.

Dormant customers were defined as not having used PhoneCard for the last three months. 3.1% of these customers reported that they had actually used

PhoneCard the same day that they filled out the survey. This could be the result of the fact that they were reminded of their PhoneCard when they received the survey invitation.

## High Level Results

Customers seem generally satisfied with PhoneCard, with the good value and ease-of-use getting the highest ratings.

The data indicated that most people used PhoneCard for personal calls to friends and family overseas. They were not using PhoneCard for business calls. The reasons for this pattern of usage were that users' workplaces do not have overseas calling plans or users had time for overseas calls only when they were at home.

## Findings and Recommendations

The data analysis was conducted in several rounds, which was necessary given that the two customer databases were examined from two perspectives. The first round looked at each customer database as a separate set. This analysis included a knowledge set that the dormant customers were reported as having let their service lapse. At the same time, the current customers were often loyal customers, who had some positive reasons for continuing to use PhoneCard. The steps for this process included comparing the results of the two groups against each other. In many cases the results were very similar, with the largest difference being only .05% point. Regarding only one question, How did you learn about PhoneCard? were the results quite different.

The second round of analysis was done looking at the complete data set, combining both current and dormant customer groups into a single group. The results closely matched those of the first-round.

Since the results were approximately the same in both rounds, the results and conclusions shown are those for current customers, except in regard to one question, where there was a difference.

Subsequent rounds of analysis included deep investigation into each question and correlated questions, such as regarding the low representation of the demographic group aged 40-44 and the low representation of business customers. Data were sliced and correlated with results from specific inquiries from key stakeholders and produced key findings.

Clearly the low per minute rates were the primary reason for using PhoneCard for international calls with 55.7% of total respondents. This shows that the consumer sees value in PhoneCard:

- Comments ranged from positive to negative. The positive comments, which were in the majority by a slight margin, underlined the great value and ease of use. Customer service appeared to be spotty, sometimes reported as good, but more often reported as negative. The second most common negative comment made by respondents who provided text data regarded line quality.

## What Happened?

The data point to the fact that most people using PhoneCard use it for personal calls to friends and family overseas. They were not using PhoneCard for business calls, as the company has assumed. There could be several reasons for this, either the user has a job where they can't make overseas calls, or they only have time to call friends and family overseas when they are at home.

If PhoneCard wanted to attract a new target market, international business calls would be a promising area to investigate. The question of security was the only issue that was raised and could be addressed through several possible solutions.

The data showed that many of the company's assumptions about the market and how customers were using their product were challenged. The PhoneCard client challenged the research executed by Bubble Mountain and the data, thinking the problem would lie with the research and not the conclusions. Bubble Mountain anticipated this reaction and included much of the data analysis in the report. While this helped prove the validity of the conclusions, the client was still not happy with the results.

Takeaway

The client did eventually make the necessary changes to the product, listening to the user to improve the UX. I learned that there are many ways to deliver bad news. In the future, I would always make sure to deliver positive news first, even if I had to search hard to provide it. The positive first approach helped me deliver bad news; perhaps it softened the blow and made the client more receptive.

Sometimes when you innovate, you make mistakes. It is best to admit them quickly, and get on with improving your other innovations.

**Steve Jobs**

# A Few Words on Failure

In June 2005, Steve Jobs, CEO of Apple Computer, gave a commencement address at Stanford University in California. Jobs spoke about the time that he was fired from the company he started, Apple computer. By all accounts, that looked like a failure, and a very public one. But, after picking himself up, he stayed in the field and found a way to start over. He felt, over time, that what looked like a failure was actually liberating. Jobs speaks about the period of time being one of great creativity, when he started two companies, got married and ended up back at Apple. One of the companies he started during this period was Pixar, which went on to become an award -winning computer animation company producing full length feature movies that are well received around the world. Jobs ended up back at Apple introducing new products such as the iPod, iPhone, and iPad. Jobs legacy was that he brought Apple back from possible failure to success.

Instead of running away from failure, we should be thinking about it as a way to learn. What went wrong? How can we change it for the future? What would we do differently the next time?

Failure gives us information that we can use to help us improve and iterate. It is often a primary ingredient in any successful activity. Don't be afraid to fail.

## BIBLIOGRAPHY

Dalcher, D., Drevin, L., 2003. Learning from information systems failures by using narrative and antenarrative methods. In: SAICSIT '03 Proceedings of the 2003 Annual Research Conference of the South African Institute of Computer Scientists and Information Technologists on Enablement Through Technology. Middlesex University/Potchefstroom University, London/South Africa, pp. 137–142.

Hendry, E.R., November 20, 2013. 7 Epic Fails Brought to You By the Genius Mind of Thomas Edison. smithsonian.com.

Jobs, S., June 12, 2005. Commencement Speech at Stanford Graduation. Stanford Report, USA. http://news.stanford.edu/news/2005/june15/jobs-061505.html

Shepherd, D.A., 2009. From Lemons to Lemonade: Squeeze Every Last Drop of Success Out of Your Mistakes, first ed. Pearson, Upper Saddle River, NJ.

Success Magazine. http://www.success.com/article/why-failure-is-good-for-success.

Why Success Always Starts With Failure. http://99u.com/articles/7072/why-success-always-starts-with-failure.

Why Failure Is Good for Success. http://www.success.com/article/why-failure-is-good-for-success.

# Chapter 16

## BIG PICTURE TAKEAWAYS

This chapter presents examples of tools used in the methodologies described in the previous chapters.

# Chapter 16

A good user experience helps a person get the most out of their product or service. A person shouldn't feel intimidated by a piece of technology. A product should not make a person feel inadequate if they can't figure it out.

The first step in creating better relationships between people and their technology is to create better products that don't require a person to learn a new way of thinking.

It is understandable that if a product is of high functionality, it has a lot of necessary features (an airplane dashboard); however, it can and should be built to fit how a person thinks. How an expert in the field (the pilot) would think. Anyone who mastered a domain such as aviation should not then have to master an overly complex interface to a systems.

# Usability Test Checklist

- Before the kickoff meeting:
    - Prepare materials such as slide deck, handouts of schedule, and deliverables
    - Set the meeting time
- Set benchmarks and deliverables schedule
- User persona identified:
    - Collect as much information as possible, including marketing materials as well as user persona material if that is available;
- Use case identified;
- Recruiting screener, reviewed and finalized;
- Test plan, reviewed and finalized;
- Test prototype, Web site, application, or low-fidelity prototype:
    - Ideally have plenty of time to become comfortable with it before the test;
- Task list for users;
- Moderator's guide:
    - Include introduction preamble
    - Pre-test questions
    - Scenarios for tasks
    - Time for each task
    - Post-test questions;
- Notes grid or template to record findings;
- Data analysis plan;
- Final report.

# Expert Review Checklist

Spend time planning ahead. Make sure you identify the user persona and use case, as well as heuristics before you start the review.

Checklist includes:

- User persona identified;
- Use case identified;
- Heuristics defined;
- Test prototype, Web site, application, or low-fidelity prototype;
- Task list confirmed;
- Notes grid or template to record findings;
- Data analysis plan;
- Final report.

# Field Studies Review Checklist

Spend time planning ahead. Make sure you identify the user persona and use case before you go into the field. Even if you are working to confirm current personas or discover new ones, you should start by sketching out your assumptions. Who do you, or the stakeholders think are the user personas.

Checklist includes:

- User persona identified;
- Use case identified;
- Research question identified;
- Identify tool the participant will use (mobile device, etc.);
- Interview questions identified;
- Camera to record interview;
- Data analysis plan;
- Final report plan, how will you pull together your data to present to your client?

# Moderator's Guide

The moderator's guide provides consistency for interviewing and testing with users.

The moderator's guide should include:

- Research goals: what is the focus of the test and what questions do you hope to answer?
- Script:
  - Introduction, explaining the purpose of the test to the participant as well as what they can expect and how long the session will last. This also includes an explanation of the informed consent usually signed by the user
  - Preliminary questions
  - Task and scenario descriptions
  - Key notes or observations, what to be looking for
  - Post-task questions
  - Rating scales (System Usability Scale Questionnaire)
  - Thank participant summary

# Sample Usability Report

Sample
Consulting Company

## Project Goal

- What is the project trying to achieve?
- How will you define success?

## Executive Summary

- Describe the project in high level details. What is being tested, what methodology and why it was chosen
- How many participants, how many personas
- Context of study (where it takes place, what kind of object is being tested?)

## Methodology of Work

- Describe the methodology in enough detail so the stakeholder who is not a UX professional will understand
- Why this methodology was chosen
- What this methodology will seek to find

## Data and Results

- List findings
- What did the analysis show? What are the results?
- Recommendations based on these findings

Conclusions

Suggestions for Further Inquiry

- Tie it back to strategy, what is the next logical UX step for the project
- Back up your recommendations with corresponding user and business goals

Specific Data

Tables and charts are appropriate, showing details such as participant demographics, metrics, findings charges, etc.

- User workflow specification
- User Mental model and demographic description
- User interface screen wire frames (number of screens to be determined)
1. Usability prototype testing
    - Test protocol: goals, procedure, and script for usability test
    - User interview questions
        - Pre-test questionnaire
        - Post-test questionnaire
    - 8 Users perform specific tasks including following tour, changing stops on tour and completing tour.
    - Test report presentation, including recommendations for next iteration
2. Iterative heuristic evaluation work with technology development team
    - Expert review of new revision of design including recommendations
3. Innovative user interaction design as the product develops further, including but not limited to additional

# Roadmaps

Roadmaps create actionable steps to help the project reach its goals. Strategic models and diagrams help provide the big picture and set goals and the roadmaps are the tactics to use in reaching those goals (Figures 16.1 and 16.2).

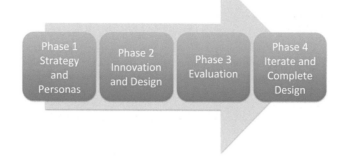

Figure 16.1 General roadmap.

Figure 16.2 Detailed roadmap.

# Glossary

**Agile** a highly iterative software development methodology, where cross-functional teams evolve requirements and functionality

**Artificial intelligence (AI)** an area of computer science that includes the study and development of software systems that provide intelligence for computing machines

**Cognitive walkthrough** a usability inspection method that is task specific, comparing a user interface against a list of tasks to evaluate their ease of use

**Design thinking** a mindset and a methodology for innovation by balancing open creative thinking with problem solving for specific situations

**End-to-end** a design principal for computing networks whereby application-specific functions reside in the end nodes, or with the end user

**Environmental scans** the study of competing products or systems

**Ergonomics** field of practice whose goal is to create products, systems, and services that optimize the well-being of the person using it

**Expert review** an evaluation done by a UX expert, using heuristics, personas and case studies

**Functional requirements** identify key functions and interactions with a product, system or service

**Heuristic review** a systematic usability inspection method that compares the user interface against an accepted set of usability principles

**Human factors** a multi-disciplinary field of practice whose goal is to design products, services and systems that are user-friendly, and comfortable for people to use

**Information architecture** the organization of information within a product, or system, including the design of system information. This includes navigational flows and menu structures

**Information design** the creation of an organizational system to store and retrieve information

**Intelligent user interface (IUI)** user interface design that incorporates artificial intelligence. This creates a user interface that has intelligence and thus provides a successful user experience

**Lean UX** a set of principles that are used to focus on the experience not the deliverables

**Mental model** the view, image or construct a person has about a scenario, process or environment

**NLP** Natural Language Processing can be seen as a subset of human-computer interaction. NLP is a field of computer science, focused with interactions between a human and a computer

**Object-oriented design (OOD)** the planning of a system of interacting software objects

**Qualitative studies** exploratory research that collects data about underlying motivations and challenges and can help provide insights and new ideas. These studies are formative and based on observations

**Quantitative studies** focuses on collecting numerical data that are analyzed through mathematical based methods. These studies are also defined as summative

**Scrum** the term originates from the sport of rugby and is used to describe a specific agile methodology. This particular approach defines roles such scrum master and product owner and has many events designed to encourage team communication

**Smartphone** a digital phone that has capabilities to access and interact with applications and websites on the internet

**Software bugs** the origination of this term dates back to computer software that was input via punch cards. The software program would produce errors if bugs got into punch cards and filled the punched holes. Although software has evolved past punch cards, the terms are still used for the errors produced in a software system

**Sprint** a single development iteration, typically between two to four weeks in length, that includes production work and scrum events. A given release will contain a certain number of these subsequently occurring iterations

**System usability scale (SUS)** a tool for measuring the usability of a system and consisting of a 10 item questionnaire, with a 5 point rating scale for each question

**Usability** the degree to which a product or system can be used easily; how easy it is to use; the measure of how useful an object or product or technology is to the person using it

**Usability metrics** specific measurements to determine how usable a product, system or service is

**Usability test** a UX methodology to evaluate how usable a product or system is

**User experience (UX)** the experience of the person, using the object, product or technology; the totality of a person's interactions with a product, system or service

**User requirements** a set of specifications that define what the user expects the product, system or software to do

**WIMP** Window, Icon, Mouse, Pointing Device

# Index

Note: Page numbers followed by *b* indicates boxes, *f* indicates figures, and *ge* indicates glossary terms.

**C**

Cambridge Trust, 60f, 63–64
Cardiac Catheterization, 180
Cardiac workstation
  feedbacks, 186–187
  moderator's guide
    environment, 183
    informative study, 187
    RAT, 181
    site visit members, 182
    site visit process, 182–183
    user feedback, 180–181
    user profile data, 183
    users, 185–186
    working environment, 184–185
    workstation, 183–184
Center for Medicare and Medicaid Services
    (CMS), 80–81, 188–189
  competitive analysis, 84
  environmental scan, 87
  evolution of, 89–90
  field studies, 84–85
  focus groups, 85
  goal settings, 88–89, 88–91f
  NHC, 82–83, 90–92
  online survey, 86
  persona development, 84–85
  primary goals, 81
  prototype, 83
  quality improvement, 81
  quality ratings, 82
  social media, 87–92
  success, 90
  usability test, 83, 85–86
  use case, 84–85
  web analytics, 87
Checklists
  data specification, 330
  expert review, 326
  field studies review, 327
  moderator's guide, 328–330
  suggestions, 330
  usability report, 329b
  usability test, 325
Cognitive science, 28
Cognitive walkthrough, 333ge
Community Emergency Response Team (CERT),
    137–138

disaster survivors, 141–143
Microsoft-Word-based reports,
    143–144
participants and recruitment,
    139–140
research program, 138
script development, 140
session setup, 140–141, 142f
valuable experience, 144
Compugraphic company, 166b, 169
Contextual inquiry, 179
Cross Channel e-Service design
  design concepts, 212–214
  in-depth user research, 208–212
  localization, 207–208
  X Thinking approach, 207

**D**

Data analysis, 135
Design thinking, UX, 32f, 333ge
  accessibility/disabilities, 28
  Accessible Rich Internet Applications,
    37–39, 38f
  Apple Inc, 39
  ARIA, 36, 37f
  capturing images, 34–35
  case study, 22b
  cognitive science, 28
  competitive analysis, 46–47
  creativity, 29
  definition, 20
  demographics, 27
  development team, 21–22
  goals, 27
  graphical layer, 42
  GUI, 42–44
  human factors, 28
  human memory, 28
  human perception, 28
  IA (*see* Information architecture (IA))
  innovation, 29–30
  iterate, 30–39
  Letizia, 37–39
  macro system, 20–21
  micro interactions, 20–21
  participatory design, 44–45
  personas, 47–57, 50b, 56f
  physical and graphical layer, 42

User experience touch points (UXTs), 9
User requirements, 335*ge*

**V**
Voter Verified Paper Audit Trail (VVPAT), 264
Voting Technology Project (VTP), 263

**W**
Web analytics (WA)
    customer methods, 242–243
    Medicare and Medicaid services, 236–243
    NHC web site, 237*b*
    what, 235
    when, 235–236
    where, 236

who, 235
why, 236–243
Williams, Scott, 312*b*
Window icons, menu, pointing device (WIMP)
    system, 94–96, 335*ge*
Wireframes, 45, 46*f*, 300
World Usability Day (WUD)
    accidental usability, 219
    attitude affects, 219
    charter, 217–218*f*
    events, 216
World War II (WWII), 13

**X**
XEROX Alto, 94